POLITICS
AND
PERFORMANCE
IN
CONTEMPORARY
NORTHERN
IRELAND

Edited by

JOHN P. HARRINGTON AND
ELIZABETH J. MITCHELL

UNIVERSITY OF MASSACHUSESTTS PRESS / AMHERST

Published in cooperation with the
American Conference for Irish Studies

Printed in the United States of America
LC 98-32257
ISBN 1-55849-196-1 (cloth); 197-X (pbk.)

Designed by Dennis Anderson
Set in Sabon
Printed and bound by BookCrafters, Inc.

Library of Congress Cataloging-in-Publication Data
Harrington, John P.
    Politics and performance in Contemporary Northern Ireland / edited
by John P. Harrington and Elizabeth J. Mitchell.
        p.   cm.
    Includes bibliographical references and index.
    ISBN 1-55849-196-1 (cloth : alk. paper). —
ISBN 1-55849-197-X (pbk. : alk. paper)
        1. Political plays, English — Northern Ireland — History and
criticism.   2. Theater — Political aspects — Northern Ireland —
History — 20th century.   3. Politics and literature — Northern
Ireland — History — 20th century.   4. English drama — Irish authors —
History and criticism.   5. Northern Ireland — Politics and
government.   I. Mitchell, Elizabeth, 1943–   .   II. Title.
PR8789.H38   1999
941.60824 — dc21   98-32257
                                                            CIP

British Library Cataloguing in Publication
data are available.

Contents

JOHN P. HARRINGTON AND ELIZABETH J. MITCHELL

Introduction

YOUNGSTERS IN NORTHERN IRELAND who exaggerate a hurt are apt to be urged by their parents to "Stop that playactin'!" The improper behavior of an acquaintance, especially one who has passed beyond earshot, may be demeaned in everyday conversation by the demand: "Did you see thon performance?" Despite a local wariness of contrived behavior, Northern Ireland's charged atmosphere of sectarian division encourages a considerable amount of dramatic political performance within, and about, its borders. Social and dramatic actors, in and out of the theater, give performances scripted to alter or confirm their particular definition of political reality. Paramilitary violence of the last thirty years has inflicted devastating casualties. In many instances, however, even that violence has been part of larger symbolic performances designed to preserve and consolidate contested political beliefs. As the essays in this volume show, in Northern Ireland the symbolic struggle continues both within and beyond the confines of the theater. This, the second collection of essays from the American Conference for Irish Studies, brings together contributors from many disciplines, and from Northern Ireland, the United States, Canada, and England, to study the junctures of politics and performance in contemporary Northern Ireland.

Symbolic struggle is especially important during the current period of fragile cease-fires and governmental agreements in Northern Ireland. With the cessation of paramilitary action, more attention now focuses on symbolic performances. Handshakes and photographs with heads of state have additional symbolic power when political violence recedes. Government activity is not all symbolic, and other phenomena of critical importance—such as economic development—need to be considered in a comprehensive analysis of social and political life; nevertheless symbolic performance is a form of social action that has had special resonance in Northern Ireland. As Marilynn Richtarik notes in the first essay in this collection, at the end of the twentieth century, the

I

playwright Stewart Parker imagined Henry Joy McCracken, leader of the United Irishman at the end of the eighteenth century, addressing the public in these terms: "Citizens of Belfast — you rehearse all your chosen parts and you play them." The citizens of Northern Ireland do so today, and, as these essays show, perhaps more than ever.

Erving Goffman's classic sociological work *The Presentation of the Self in Everyday Life* describes ordinary, public social interaction as "front stage" behavior. We interact with others in social situations to create the impressions we want to project; in the process, we provide for those others the images of ourselves that permit routine social interaction. "Performance," in current scholarship, is a term of great conceptual breadth that links many different disciplines. The essays in this volume are not a comprehensive treatment of ideas about performance, or of social and political activity in Northern Ireland; rather, each essay illustrates one of the numerous complicated dynamics that validate modes of behavior and belief in a divided society. And all describe political interaction whose conscious intent is to engage, impress and persuade an audience.

These front stage dramatizations can be categorized by the kind of theater in which they are played. Four authors (Jennifer Cornell, Maureen S. G. Hawkins, Helen Lojek, and Marilynn Richtarik) write about performances that are intended primarily for live theater or the television studio. The other five describe dramatic struggles played out in pubs and drinking clubs of Protestant Ulster (Bill Rolston), local district councils (William Hazleton), political party organizations (James White McAuley), the police force (Roger Mac Ginty), and even in the memories of young people who have learned their social roles in a context of contested political scripts (Mícheál Roe et al.).

Identity and ideology are central to several papers. Roe (and his research team of Kim Hodges, William Pegg, and Rebecca Trimm), along with Bill Rolston, ask how ethnic groups act to preserve, reproduce, or invent their past. Both authors enter the private sphere where sectarianism and fear of "the other" is perpetuated. To this end, Rolston analyzes and interprets loyalist songs while Roe draws on data from surveys and field research among young Catholics and Protestants. When ethnic identity is threatened, Roe tells us, group continuity and cohesion become increasingly valued, and commemorative rituals are used to bolster identity and emphasize distinctiveness. When ethnic distinctiveness is valued, the shared intercommunal characteristics that make cross-community forgiveness possible are diminished. Thus, such forgiveness becomes difficult for young people recently socialized in their own particular sectarian identity. Rolston's analysis of loyalist songs alerts us to the process through which loyalist lyrics (and the tunes that carry them) both articulate and interpellate loyalist ideology. Performed in intimate, secure loyalist clubs, loyalist songs interpret past and contemporary history for their audiences. Roe's words precisely describe Rolston's conclusion: that songs "become context and content for what will be jointly recalled and commemorated in the future." These two works show us how ethnic identity, sectarianism, and fear of the other survive in the synapses of individual memory and in community of family, peer group, and drinking club. Together they give us a better understanding of the selection process of ethnic memory: what is remembered and how.

Like Rolston, James White McAuley explores reactionary loyalism in a community whose economic and political dominance is threatened. But the two scholars emphasize somewhat different political responses from within the same community. In Rolston's analysis, loyalists voice their fears and frustrations in offensive sectarian songs. While McAuley agrees that much loyalist ideology remains sectarian and reactionary in nature, he describes a more progressive political response in the "new loyalist" movement. As he maps the fault lines between new and traditional loyalism, he reminds us that loyalism is no longer a monolithic entity. New loyalism originated in the paramilitary groups and, like more traditional Paisleyite loyalism, is based in the Protestant working class. It is still firmly committed to the union with Britain, but new loyalist leaders in the peace talks have demonstrated their willingness and ability to do business with nationalists and republicans. The future of this new loyalist departure, McAuley concludes, remains uncertain.

The "Good Friday agreement," engineered in April 1998, by Senator George Mitchell and the other participants of the peace talks, is a complex political arrangement that took months of negotiation and courageous leadership to accomplish. Those familiar with Northern Ireland know that "the way forward" is uncertain, and this skepticism is a realistic assessment of what the process can achieve and how soon. Those who act to move Northern Ireland along the road to "normality" must be aware of the depth and difficulty of changes that will be needed to enable the two communities to live together in mutual support. Roger Mac Ginty's study of policing in Northern Ireland provides an example of just such a challenge. Unionists and Protestants act to preserve the current organization of the Royal Ulster Constabulary, while nationalists and republicans insist that the force (with fewer than 10 percent Catholics on its payroll) must be reorganized to meet the needs and assuage the fears of the Catholic community. While Mac Ginty is reluctant to extrapolate his conclusions to other midlevel institutions that need to be reworked in the post-settlement phase of peacemaking, his analysis provides one example of conflicting goals in joint endeavors and contested areas.

Northern Ireland has been compared to other divided societies that in recent years have struggled to design conflict settlements as a first step on the road to peace. The South African experiment, while not without its problems, appears at this time to be more successful than the Israeli/Palestinian arrangement. Among the multiple reasons for its relative success is that former partisan leaders in South Africa have taken responsibility for leading their peoples toward political accommodation. Israeli and Palestinian leaders in contrast have failed in this regard. William Hazleton writes that any settlement in Northern Ireland will meet with only limited success unless future leaders develop "the skills, desires, and motivations" to promote and achieve intercommunal accommodation. Throughout the years of direct rule from London, local government in Northern Ireland languished without role or responsibility. Hazleton argues that the gradual expansion of authority and responsibility in local government can advance the peace process by encouraging unionist and nationalist councillors to act locally in the common interest of their respective communities. This experience, he believes, could develop much-needed leadership skills among locally elected representatives and help reduce the "democratic deficit" from which Northern Ireland has suffered in the last quarter-century. Such a development at the local level might complement current negotiations that are being propelled, in large part, by international interests.

Marilynn Richtarik's work also proposes a multidimensional model of local and international factors by placing a playwright's experience of Protestant Belfast in a cosmopolitan context. Drawing on Stewart Parker's plays, personal notes, letters, and the memories of his peers,

Richtarik delineates the intersecting fault lines of national and sectarian identity, tribal history, and education that tended to isolate Parker from every community on both sides of the Atlantic. Many of the people of the Irish diaspora are familiar with similar estrangement, but Richtarik highlights one particularly evocative memory that is shared by all Northern Irish residents and expatriates who are old enough to remember. The week in August 1969, when "the Battle of the Bogside" in Derry and "sectarian disturbances in Belfast" erupted, forever changed the political and social structure of Northern Ireland. Parker and his wife, Kate, may have been alone on the *Queen Elizabeth II* when they heard about the outbreak of political violence, but they belonged to a community of exiles who were horrified by the physical and emotional damage of faction fighting and saddened by injustice in Northern Ireland. The voice of these Protestant exiles who, like Parker, came of age with the expansion of higher education in postwar Northern Ireland has been largely missing in recent narratives of Irish history.

Helen Lojek directly addresses the topic of women in Northern Ireland by examining the unemployed women writers and actors who, from 1983 until 1995, worked to create the Charabanc Theatre Company. They played unique roles, on and off the Charabanc stage, and offer inspiration to others who must break through class, gender, and financial barriers that, too often render invisible their political and artistic endeavors. Lojek's comparison of Charabanc with the Field Day Theatre Company outlines the salient differences in experience, fame, and network that favored the well-connected, male Field Day company over the less known, and consequently underfunded, company formed outside established theater circles in England and Ireland. Lojek writes of the Charabanc plays, "They do not belong to one of Northern Ireland's divided communities more than another, despite the Protestantism of the company members. They offer no pat solutions. . . . Multiplicity and lack of dogma are, in fact, their politics."

Maureen S. G. Hawkins also cites feminist alternatives to patriarchal structures inside and beyond the professional theater. Like Richtarik, Hawkins explores the cosmopolitan dimensions of conflict in Northern Ireland, particularly how the local conflict controls receptions of performing arts in other venues. In her study of the performance history of works by Brenton and Rudkin, Hawkins describes the involvement of playwrights from different political identities. She, too, finds new significance in the Field Day project when viewed from the present perspective. Its acclaimed inaugural production of Brian Friel's play *Translations* in 1980 introduced audiences to the concepts of endogamein (within the tribe) and exogamein (outside the tribe). Like Hawkins, several contributors to this collection have found that, after successive and progressive exposures of division and separation, what once seemed successfully intertribal no longer does. Rising criteria for successful conflict resolution testify to some degree of progress in the past decades; they also, however, suggest the daunting challenges of the next few decades.

The final essay in this volume is in many ways a summary of the whole. Jennifer C Cornell examines television drama's theatrical presentation for a large audience. Several contributors to this collection describe changing representations and images in the midst of conflict, and Cornell reinforces this conception of a dynamic history in her description of mass-media's portrayal of parties to violence in Northern Ireland. Cornell finds that the mass media, clearly not a vehicle for reform, largely reflect rather than shape changes in governmental agendas. In conclusion, Cornell scripts for us the responsible roles that we as individuals, and especially as artists and commentators, should play in the peace process.

This volume deals with the reflexivity of political life in Northern Ireland. It shows how individuals have been shaped by the historical context of the Troubles, and even more so how social agents use their performances, in the theater and on the stage of everyday political life, to define identities, to reinforce ideologies, and to build institutional support. As we go to press, Northern Ireland once again stands on the brink. It is the brink of a better future, but one that is uncertain and problematic. The drama of the conflict is being transformed, and the peace process revises familiar elements of symbolic conflict. Politics and performance in action illustrate both the potential and the perils of the future.

Living in Interesting Times
Stewart Parker's Northern Star

In his 1984 play *Northern Star*, Stewart Parker performs the delicate feat of delivering a Protestant critique of Irish republicanism that is not a unionist one. Through a dramatic analysis of the 1798 rebellion, Parker exposes the contradictions in modern republican thinking about Ireland and challenges audience members to reject the roles that history has assigned to them. Parker was one of a number of Northern writers — including Seamus Deane, Seamus Heaney, Derek Mahon, James Simmons, and John Montague, to name a few — who lived abroad on the eve or during the early days of the Troubles, and this experience partly conditioned his reactions to that crisis. Parker thought about *Northern Star* for more than fifteen years before he actually wrote it, beginning when he was away from Ireland, so this most Irish of his plays has long and surprisingly cosmopolitan roots.

Parker was born in East Belfast in 1941 and grew up in the city during its last period of relative peace. Looking back later in life, he saw this background as an ideal preparation for a playwright. "Growing up in Belfast as a working-class Protestant," he said, "I had access to all sorts but did not feel a part of any of them. You're led to believe you're British, yet the English don't recognise you as such. On the other hand, you're Irish because you're born in Ireland, but the people in the Free State don't recognise you as such. The working class element adds another dimension, because you are alienated from the Unionist establishment. You feel conversant with all of those things, but not obliged to any of them" (Purcell 1987). After attending Queen's University, Parker taught for a time in the United States, where he took a keen interest in the fevered American politics of the late 1960s. He returned to Belfast in August 1969, arriving home the same week that the British Army was sent in to restore order in the city, and remained in Belfast for nine years before moving to Edinburgh and then London, where he died of cancer in 1988.

In the fall of 1967, when he was teaching at Cornell University, Parker decided to write a play about Henry Joy McCracken. He was drawn to the egalitarian, nonsectarian vision of the United Irishmen and particularly intrigued by McCracken, as any liberal Northern Protestant would be by one of the most radical leaders of the United Irishmen who also happened to be a Belfast Presbyterian.[1] Although the action of the play he wished to write would center on Ireland, Parker originally intended it to be a more general exploration of issues of political commitment. As he explained in his proposal to the BBC in 1970 for a ninety-minute radio play on the subject, "my concerns in this play extend beyond the Irish situation. In fact I conceived the play while living in America and engaging in the struggle against the Vietnam war and for Black liberation."[2]

Despite stirrings of political activism in the Northern Ireland of the mid-1960s,[3] the United States in 1967 seemed a much more likely setting for social and political revolution. As Parker researched and worked on the play sporadically throughout 1967–69, his host country was convulsed by events that included ghetto riots, the assassinations of Martin Luther King and Bobby Kennedy, the disruption of the 1968 Democratic convention in Chicago, campus unrest, and escalating protests against American involvement in Vietnam. Three experiences in this period captured Parker's imagination most particularly.

In the first of these encounters with the turmoil that was sweeping the country, Parker played the role of an observer. On 17 May 1968, nine antiwar protesters had marched into the office of the Selective Service System in the middle-class suburb of Catonsville, Maryland, filled two large wastebaskets with purloined draft records, carried the receptacles out to the parking lot, and set fire to them with homemade napalm. All of the demonstrators were practicing Catholics; two were priests. Philip and Daniel Berrigan — who would often joke about their Irish heritage when asked how they came to be such "troublemakers" — had focused in their respective ministries on issues of poverty and racial discrimination. Both had come to feel, however, that no progress could be made on domestic social issues unless and until the United States withdrew from Vietnam. Both had also become more and more frustrated with the scant effect that lectures, meetings with Congressmen, teach-ins, and marches seemed to be having on U.S. foreign policy. Gradually they turned to more militant methods. Philip Berrigan had already been tried and convicted for an earlier act of theatrical protest, in which he and three others (the "Baltimore Four") had destroyed draft records by pouring blood over them. He was due to be sentenced for this offense on 27 May — hence the timing of the raid on Catonsville (Curtis 1974).

The trial of the "Catonsville Nine" was held in a Baltimore Federal court, 5–9 October 1968. Parker followed it avidly, fascinated by the spectacle of compassionate, reform-minded individuals driven by their spiritual and social convictions to extreme, extralegal acts. The trial held special interest for people in Ithaca because at the time of the incident Daniel Berrigan was one of the heads of Cornell's United Religious Work program, a post he had assumed in the fall of 1967 (the same term that Parker began teaching there). University officials announced that there would be no penalties for students who missed classes to travel to Baltimore for the trial, and hundreds did (Berrigan 1987). The defendants were found guilty on three counts: destruction of U.S. property, destruction of Selective Service records, and interference with the Selective Service Act of 1967 (Berrigan 1970). In the month between the trial and the sentencing Daniel Berrigan returned to Cornell, and, on 24 October 1968, he and the defense counsel, Harrup Freeman (also a Cornell professor), spoke at a meeting on the trial. Parker attended and was profoundly moved, reflecting a few days later in his journal, "how can anybody fail to support what they did, the seriousness of their conviction? How can people dismiss them as 'martyrs'? Or why has that word suddenly taken on a pejorative ring? They *are* martyrs. Martyrs can be proud, wrong-headed. Martyrs are paradoxical, even inexplicable. Berrigan is in some ways a dangerous martyr, maybe a self-deluding one. But there is one inexorable truth about martyrs — that they suffer on behalf of the rest of humanity."

Perhaps as a result of his sympathy for the Catonsville Nine, Parker stepped up his personal involvement in the antiwar effort the following winter. Near the New York–Pennsylvania border, about a three-and-a-half-hour drive from Ithaca, was the Allenwood Prison Camp, a minimum-security facility connected with the Lewisburg Federal Penitentiary. Here a number of draft resisters had been incarcerated. Several Cornell professors resolved to demonstrate their support by holding classes in the prison, aimed at the political prisoners but open to any who were interested (Hertz 1994). Parker and his English Department friend Neil Hertz taught a creative writing class there every two weeks from February until July 1969. Rather to their surprise, the "ordinary" prisoners attended in greater numbers than the draft resisters. Moreover, since many of these were poor and black, the experience constituted, for Parker, a crash course in American race relations. He was struck by the "passionate political commitment" of the black prisoners, writing later, "no matter how the classes started out, they nearly always resolved into a noisy, volatile debate about Black oppression" (Parker 1970c). In 1973, Parker would apply his prison teaching experience to Northern Ireland when he taught a literature, drama, and creative writing class in the Long Kesh Internment Camp, where his brightest student was a young man named Gerry Adams. Parker told his friend Sam Fannin that Adams could win any intellectual argument on the justification of violence for political ends in Ireland. Despite Parker's respect for his student's views on the subject, he was not shaken from his own opinion that the use of force in politics was inevitably self-defeating (Fannin 1997; Fairleigh 1994).

Another public political event to engage Parker's attention during his time in the United States was the occupation of Cornell's Willard Straight Hall by armed black students on 19 April 1969, a protest against perceived racism at Cornell and, specifically, the reprimands meted out to three black students for their participation the previous December in disturbances accompanying students' demands for an Afro-American Studies program. His experiences in the prison had primed him for something like this. Indeed, the prison and campus worlds collided in literal fashion in the person of a black protégé from the creative writing class, Frank Smalls, who had been released from Allenwood a few weeks earlier and had moved to Ithaca at the urging of Parker and Hertz with the intention of pursuing higher education at Cornell. He arrived in town the day of the takeover and promptly joined the students, becoming their minister of defense (Hertz 1994). The students were persuaded to leave the building after a day and a half, but the crisis continued for several days as Cornell faculty and administrators revisited the question of reprimands. When a meeting of the whole faculty voted on 21 April to retain the reprimands, a more left-leaning group called Concerned Faculty sprang into action. Parker spent more than twenty-seven hours straight on 22–23 April at meetings of the Concerned Faculty, Arts College Faculty, Students for a

Democratic Society (SDS), and the whole faculty, which eventually rescinded its earlier decision and nullified the reprimands. Almost twenty years later, Parker would recall some of the incidents of that eventful week in his last play *Pentecost*, set during the Ulster Workers' Council strike of 1974, in which one character compares the state of emergency in Belfast with campus unrest at an unnamed American university: "it's not as if I'm unfamiliar with tense situations. Six years ago, I was standing in a human chain encircling a building. It was in America . . . a university. Black students had seized the building and smuggled in guns, the police were lined up in their hundreds, ready to storm it. Me and a fewscore of other white liberals had put our bodies in between, holding hands with each other, armed blacks behind us and armed cops in front . . . it was scary as hell, but there was playacting involved too, a big American psychodrama, the college president and the blacks' leader were up on a stage together at the end, hugging each other, I don't quite see that happening here" (Parker 1989, 184–85).

In between all of these demanding distractions, not to mention his teaching job, Parker was reading about the United Irishmen and thinking about his play. The United leader he was most drawn to was Henry Joy McCracken, and from the earliest mentions of the play in his journals and notes he referred to it as the "McCracken play" or "HJM." Certainly McCracken is an attractive figure. As Roy Foster writes, "In the well-stocked pantheon of Irish history, Henry Joy McCracken is nearly everyone's hero. Historians of all persuasions have a secret partiality for him; when he went to trial for treason, many refused to testify against him (or were prepared to perjure themselves in his favour); and after his execution in 1798 hundreds of respectable people filed past his bier, convicted rebel though he was" (1996, n.p.). McCracken is given pride of place, for example, in a nineteenth-century collection of *Ulster Biographies Relating Chiefly to the Rebellion of 1798* (which Parker read in January 1969). The author of this slim volume was a unionist who clearly deplored McCracken's conversion to republicanism but nevertheless proclaimed that "Henry Joy McCracken exceeded almost every other leader of the United Irishmen in forgetfulness of self and in attachment to his country. He was the great bond of union that held together the North and the South. He freely gave his life in a vain effort to save his country from oppression" (Latimer 1897, 20). In modern parlance, McCracken was the one left holding the bag when several high-ranking rebel military commanders were arrested or resigned on the eve of the rising in the North. With few men and little support, he performed creditably on the field of battle until, ironically, his reinforcements were routed by an enemy retreat, causing his own troops to flee in panic. A few weeks later, McCracken was captured and subsequently tried and executed. As early as the summer of 1968, Parker had noted in his journal that the last image of the play would be "Henry Joy on the scaffold, in darkness and lambeg drums."

McCracken's appeal for Stewart Parker was complex and multivalent. He was a model of disinterested leadership, who cared more about the work that needed to be done than about holding office or power in the organization of United Irishmen. He stuck by the cause when most of the others had deserted it, never losing sight of the ultimate goal. His personal warmth and good humor were such that even soldiers assigned to guard him as a prisoner were tempted on more than one occasion to let him escape. He was a practical joker and gifted mimic (a detail Parker cherished). He was apparently without sectarian prejudice. Finally, and perhaps most important to Parker, despite his middle-class background he genuinely understood and sympathized with the problems of ordinary working people. In his last, despairing letter to his sister Mary Ann, McCracken wrote, "You will no doubt hear a great number of stories respecting the situation of this country, its present unfortunate state is entirely owing to *treachery*, the rich always betray the poor" (McNeill 1988, 177). "When all our leaders deserted us," remembered Jemmy Hope, one of the few working-class men in the inner circle of the rebellion, "Henry Joy McCracken stood alone faithful to the last" (McNeill 1988, 173).

Parker may also have projected onto McCracken some of his feelings about his own political involvement in the late 1960s. Friends from Cornell remember Parker as being passionately interested in, yet critically detached from, the issues of the time. With a foreigner's diffidence, he did not present himself as a leader, but stayed on the margins of the action (Hertz 1994; R. Parker 1994). By June 1969, he had formulated in his journal a description of his play's theme: "HJMcC a man of compassion and altruism in a company of ideologues: Tone the Republican, Hope the Socialist, the Orange Monarchists, the Dublin Oligarchs, the Belfast Capitalists. He has no dogma, only the thrust of an imaginative and understanding character. But he cannot find a way to work outside the struggle for power between the dogmas, and he is drawn in and destroyed."

Parker and his wife Kate returned to Ireland on the *Queen Elizabeth II* in August 1969, but their enjoyment of what Parker termed in his journal "Days and nights of the best food drink dancing and interior design imaginable" was marred by the news from Northern Ireland relayed to the ship as it proceeded toward its destination. This was the week of the Battle of the Bogside in Derry and sectarian disturbances in Belfast so severe that the British government acceded to the request of the Northern Irish government to send in troops to act as a buffer between the two sides. As the first, confused reports of all of this reached him, Parker reflected in his journal: "Shadows of gunmen in the streets of Belfast, 8 people shot dead and many more wounded[,] 4,000 homeless, streets of houses and shops and factories burnt out, terror and vicious hatred rampant, refugee centres in the South, hospitals just over the border. The whole brutal historical nightmare of 1641 and 1798 and 1916 lurching through the streets again and across the breezy countryside. Approaching it with a deep sense of dread." Sam Fannin, who met Parker off the boat in Cork and drove him to Belfast, writes, "One can't understate the impact this [trip] had for him. Compared to the relative calm and normality when he left, we literally drove back into a war. Belfast—totally changed, streets full of soldiers, guns, barricades, burnt-out buildings, a terrible air of violence, like a great storm. . . . This really affected Stewart deeply" (Fannin 1997).

Upon his return to Belfast, Parker visited family, friends, and the new barricades, and life gradually settled down to what then passed for normal. During his first year back in Ireland, Parker earned a living mainly through research and writing for the BBC's Schools programs. He followed political developments, attending People's Democracy meetings at Queen's University and canvassing for the Northern Ireland Labour Party before the Westminster general election of June 1970. In company with most other Northern intellectuals, he was also interrogating his own past, his family's past, and the history of the province in an attempt to make sense of the political upheaval taking place around him. In conjunction with this, he managed to find time for projects that united his political and artistic interests.

Within weeks of his arrival in Belfast, Parker and Fannin were looking for an Irish language class to join. An early attempt to enroll in one

that was supposed to be meeting at the Rupert Stanley College in East
Belfast was aborted by a loyalist mob that threatened to use their car in
the barricade it was building across the end of the street. They ended
up, in October, in a class offered by Queen's Extramural Department.
Parker's interest in the language grew in large part out of his academic
study of Yeats's plays and a growing fascination with Irish mythology,
but he readily acknowledged political motivation as well. As he wrote a
few months later,

> I cannot sink my identity in Dublin, nor in New York or Toronto, or
> London or Glasgow either, for it is skulking somewhere in the fierce,
> drab, absurd streets of Belfast which was once Beal Feirste, and that's
> why I'm learning Irish.
>
> The taig gazes over his shoulder at the Dail while the prod turns his
> face towards Buckingham P., but they both know secretly that their
> corporate soul is out there somewhere in No Man's Land. Until it is
> located and defined, talk of the reunification of Ireland is empty. Not
> until the North can put words to its sense of selfhood will the island
> become united again, whether the Border goes or stays. The effort will be
> harder for the prod, there are so many things for him to learn (like Irish),
> but it will be subtler for the taig, since what he has to find out is al-
> together less easily described (Parker 1970a).

The same week that he started attending Irish classes at Queen's,
Parker approached the executor of Sam Thompson's estate, Brian Gar-
rett, about the possibility of editing Thompson's plays for publication.
Thompson had been a hero of Parker's for ten years. The son of a
lamplighter, Thompson had worked in the shipyard and as a painter for
the Belfast Corporation for twenty-five years before being "discovered"
by Sam Hanna Bell, a BBC Talks producer who frequented the same
pub. Bell encouraged him to put his stories of working-class life on
paper, and over the next few years Thompson wrote several radio features and a full-length stage play, *Over the Bridge*, about sectarianism
in the shipyard. This was to be produced by Belfast's Group Theatre,
but the directors of the company, fearful that the play might provoke
controversy, canceled the production. Most of the Group company
resigned in protest, and the play was eventually mounted in an independent production in 1960 (Devlin 1985). It was a stunning success,
bringing people into the theater who would never have dreamed of
attending before, including an uncle of Parker's who worked in the

shipyard and took the teenage playwright to one of the performances (Thompson 1994).

As Parker put it, Thompson "saw right from the start that poverty and sectarian violence were root and branch of the one ugly tree" (Parker 1970b, 9). His devotion to his art was matched by his commitment to trades unionism. In 1964, after *Over the Bridge* and his second play, *The Evangelist*, had made him a public figure, he ran for the Westminster Parliament on the ticket of the Northern Ireland Labour Party, and it was in the offices of the NILP that he suffered a fatal heart attack in February 1965. In Parker's view, Thompson's tragically early death was a "grievous loss," not only to Irish drama, but to a Northern Ireland standing on the brink of social dissolution: "He has never been needed more than in the dark days since his death. The painful missing factor in the whole Ulster equation is a sane and compassionate leader for the Protestant working class. There is no knowing how Sam Thompson would have fared in this perhaps impossible position, but he remains the nearest thing to such a man that we have yet seen" (Parker 1970b, 14).

Parker's original desire was to get all of Sam Thompson's plays into print, but he was unable to find a publisher willing to take the four, or even the three that had been produced. Eventually he succeeded in convincing Gill and Macmillan in Dublin to publish *Over the Bridge* in an attractive edition with photographs of the shipyard and a heartfelt introduction by Parker himself. This was launched in December 1970 (Rosenfield 1970). Parker also committed time over the second half of 1970 to the cataloguing of Thompson's manuscripts, papers, and correspondence for the Belfast Central Library.

In another attempt to engage intellectually with the developing political crisis, Parker undertook to conduct some of his Northern Protestant soul-searching in public, in the pages of the *Irish Times*, which had invited young writers to submit sample articles. The first piece accepted, in January 1970, was "Buntus Belfast," about his efforts to learn Irish. Over the next several months Parker had three more articles published. "An Ulster Volunteer" was a portrait of Parker's maternal grandfather, who had signed the Ulster Covenant, been a member of the original Ulster Volunteer Force (founded in 1913 to oppose Home Rule), and fought in the First World War. It began, "Nearly every day now in the North, the plea goes out to 'forget the past.' Such advice is both impracticable and pernicious. On the one hand, you can't forget a nightmare while you are still dreaming it. On the other, it is survival through comprehension that is healthy, not survival through amnesia. Besides, the past is not a dead letter. The past is explosive cargo in everybody's family dresser. Your grandfather is the past" (Parker 1970e). The third and fourth articles were about teaching at Allenwood and about Sam Thompson, respectively. Of *Over the Bridge* he wrote, "Plays of this calibre do not 'express' despair or hatred, they involve you in attitudes to those emotions. They conquer by defining them" (Parker 1970d).

This must have been what Parker wanted his McCracken play to do. He had recently returned to it, after long neglect. In February 1970 he had decided to offer the idea to the BBC for a radio play, in the hopes that writing that script would help him find his way into the subject. With the encouragement of Broadcasting House in Belfast he prepared a synopsis of the piece, tentatively entitled *Hurra! My Boys, For Freedom*, and a sample scene. These and his early notes for the play indicate that at this time Parker was especially interested in the process by which moderate impulses toward reform, when thwarted, will turn themselves into more radical channels, as he had observed in the antiwar and civil rights movements in the United States and was watching happen in Northern Ireland. He also maintained a focus on the question of how individuals position themselves in relation to ideologies. His Henry Joy McCracken was "only on the fringes" of United Irish politicking, as he explained in his BBC proposal:

> Politics bore him and perplex him. He is on record as being against French intervention. There is no knowing his private attitude to revolution, but my interpretation is that he was driven into taking the republican oath out of a sense of desperation at the futility of peaceful and legal methods. He pressed on with his work amongst the peasantry, leaving the intrigue and the limelight to the others. His great friend now was the Co. Antrim weaver, Jemmy Hope, a flinty indefatigable man, with a cutting wit and an unbending proto-socialism.

In comparison with *Northern Star* this early incarnation of the play would have paid much more attention to the prehistory of the United Irishmen: the efforts of the reform-minded to elect to the Dublin parliament Robert Stewart, Junior (later metamorphosed into Lord Castlereagh, bane of the United men); the formation of the Northern Whig Club, a liberal attempt to head off more thoroughgoing social questioning; the closing by the authorities of a Sunday school that McCracken and Samuel Neilson had been conducting for workmen. Beyond this, it is difficult to speak with any authority about the shape the play might have taken, because it was never written. By that time, purely regional BBC drama had been phased out, so programs had to be sold to the whole network before they could be produced in Northern Ireland (Hawthorne 1995; Mason 1995). "London" rejected Parker's proposal without explanation (Pine 1970), and the "McCracken play" receded into the back of his mind for a dozen years or so.

In 1981, Leon Rubin took over as artistic director of Belfast's Lyric Theatre. This change in management afforded Parker, whose relations with that company had long been strained, the opportunity to make a fresh start with it. In November 1982, the Lyric mounted a production of Parker's "Irish-Caribbean musical," *Kingdom Come*. Shortly after this, Parker wrote to Rubin and asked him to commission the Mc-Cracken play. After describing the play in outline, Parker explained that, in focusing on McCracken: "I am primarily concerned with his human predicament, but then also with a critical moment in the course of Irish history, a moment which can encapsulate the quandaries and contradictions which continue to confound us. For obvious reasons I would very much like this play to open in Belfast, and I hope you will consider commissioning it for the Lyric."[4]

The Board of Management of the Lyric, under the leadership of Rubin and Secretary of the Board Ciaran McKeown, did commission the play, but Rubin's tenure proved to be a short one. By the time Parker had finished the script in January 1984, Patrick Sandford was artistic director of the theatre. Nevertheless, the production of *Northern Star*[5] went ahead in November 1984. Remarkably, *Northern Star* was the only one of Parker's plays ever to have its first presentation in Belfast, and he took advantage of the commission from the Lyric to speak directly to Northern Protestants, the people among whom he had grown up. As Brian Friel was to do a few years later in *Making History*, Parker used the format of a history play to deconstruct habits of mind that sustain violence. The first stage direction informs us that the play is set in "Ireland, the continuous past." As Terence Brown has noted, this static conception of history characterizes both communities in the North, with each side cherishing certain totemic dates and images full of symbolic contemporary significance (Brown 1987). In response to

the remark that "they forget nothing in this country, not ever," Mc-
Cracken replies bitterly, "It's far worse than that. They misremember
everything" (Parker 1989, 64). Stephen Dedalus referred to history as
"a nightmare from which I am trying to awake." Parker implies that it
will remain one until people finally learn something from it.

Northern Star was the first in what Parker later termed a "triptych"
of plays about Ireland: three works set in the eighteenth, nineteenth,
and twentieth centuries respectively. Each centers on an event or personality quintessential of an era and simultaneously relevant today.
The rebellion of 1798 is popularly regarded as one in a long chain of
revolutionary rehearsals for an independent Republic of Ireland. The
United Irishmen are an inspiration to the Provisional IRA, who see in
their ancestors' resort to arms some justification for their own. The
United men are also venerated by more liberal republicans, however,
who embrace their goal of "a cordial union among *all the people of
Ireland*," regardless of religious persuasion (Bardon 1992, 220).

In Parker's opinion, though, the idealistic leaders of the United Irish
movement in the North, mainly Presbyterians of the professional and
mercantile classes living in the only region in Ireland where they constituted a majority of the population, never fully comprehended the
depth of sectarian animosity in the rest of the country. In response to
official persecution by the government of the day, the reformers-turned-
revolutionaries augmented their numbers by enrolling into their membership tens of thousands of Catholic Defenders. Forging links between
the two organizations was one of McCracken's most notable achieve-
ments, but one that Parker regarded with ambivalence. Kevin Whelan,
who has written extensively on 1798, describes the somewhat incompatible worldviews and aims of the two groups:

> While the United Irishmen rode the cusp of an Enlightenment wave,
> and saw themselves as moving purposefully and inexorably forward with
> the momentum of inevitable historical progress, the Defenders, the other
> great movement of the late eighteenth century, had no desire to repudiate
> history but rather to re-immerse themselves in it. They wished to use their
> shared history to create an imagined community with a common identity.
> Their claims to authenticity derived from their self-perception as the
> aboriginal inhabitants of the island. Time's arrow for them was not un-
> complicated, untroubled or progressive; they wished to flex time, to bend

it back to a pre-plantation, pre-lapsarian idyll, to suture the earlier lesions inflicted on the Irish body politic. Their potent sense of dispossession expressed itself in hopes of reversing the land settlement, overturning the church establishment and avenging their seventeenth-century setbacks (Whelan 1993, 273).

To Parker, the rising of 1798 looked like two separate rebellions. In the North, it was an abortive assault on government troops by the rump of United Irishmen left after a massive government crackdown in 1797. In the South, particularly County Wexford, it was a much more significant bloodbath that included the massacre of large numbers of Protestants. "So much for the great revolution of United Irishmen," the defeated McCracken remarks; "It comes out looking like just another Catholic riot" (Parker 1989, 59). Events in Wexford cooled the ardor of liberal Protestants for Catholic emancipation and contributed to a reaction against the idea of an Irish nation that could contain all the separate strands of Irish society. The rising as a whole solidified the British government's resolve to do away with the Irish Parliament completely through the Act of Union of 1800, which absorbed Ireland into the United Kingdom.

Parker, a modern-day Protestant sympathetic to the United Irishmen's original aims, believed that they had made two fatal mistakes. The first was resorting to arms; the second was allowing themselves to believe that an essentially sectarian force could be harnessed to achieve enlightened objectives. *Northern Star* holds out a double-edged message for Northern Protestants. To unionists, Parker says: you have a republican heritage, which you usually choose to deny. You, the Protestants of Northern Ireland, invented Irish republicanism. To those Protestants who may be well aware of and even pride themselves upon this heritage, he suggests that the United Irishmen were responsible not only for the ideal of republicanism, but also for its tradition of violence. In the anguished words of the disillusioned McCracken, "all we've done . . . is to reinforce the locks, cram the cells fuller than ever of mangled bodies crawling round in their own shite and lunacy, and the cycle just goes on, playing out the same demented comedy of terrors from generation to generation, trapped in the same malignant legend, condemned to re-endure it as if the Anti-Christ who dreamed it up was driven astray in the wits by it and the entire pattern of depravity just goes spinning on out of control, on and on, round and round, till the day the world itself is burst asunder, that's the handsome birthright that we're handing on" (Parker 1989, 65).

Perhaps Parker's most fundamental reconception of the play when he returned to it in the 1980s was to set all of the action in the aftermath of the rising. After the Battle of Antrim, McCracken was at large for a month, hiding in the hills. He was arrested on 7 July 1798, and the action of *Northern Star* takes place during one of his last nights as a free man.[6] This enables the character of McCracken in the play to look back on all of his actions with the benefit of hindsight. Part of the historical McCracken's legend is that he intended to make a speech from the gallows, but, as an eyewitness recounted, "Hoarse orders were given by the officers, the troops moved about, the people murmured, a horrible confusion ensued, and in a minute or so the manly, handsome figure on which the impression of nobility was stamped, was dangling at a rope's end" (Fitzhenry 1936, 148). In *Northern Star* Parker imagines what McCracken would have said to the crowd had he been allowed to speak. In the theater, the citizens of Belfast addressed by McCracken merge into the present-day citizens of Belfast in the audience, and one question that preoccupies him is the use that future generations will make of his legacy. In Parker's view, a man of McCracken's generous spirit could not have failed to see that this legacy might be malevolent, and his McCracken vigorously rejects the role of martyr for Irish freedom: "A whore's pox then on the future! And I forgive it nothing, for there's nothing it will learn from those of us who swung for it, no peace to be got from it, for those of us who want nothing more now than to finish, a cat's flux on whatever holy picture they may fashion of me!" (Parker 1989, 73).

Because the United Irishmen were playing to posterity, Parker's play is filled with theatrical figures of speech, with McCracken as an actor rehearsing for his "positively last appearance" (Parker 1989, 18). From his first notes on the play it is apparent that Parker was anxious to avoid some of the pitfalls of historical drama by incorporating non-naturalistic elements. It seems likely that he intended to juxtapose scenes from the 1790s with modern commentary, and one page of early notes lists characters such as tourists, a curator, a fashion photographer, an American lecturer, and a folk singer. Another early idea was to write the historical passages in verse. The device Parker finally settled on owes a great deal to his favorite writer, James Joyce. The bulk of the script consists of seven flashback scenes of the events leading up to the rising; each, in keeping with the theatrical metaphor, represents one of the ages of man: "They have their exits and their entrances and one man in his time plays many parts, his acts being seven ages" (16). The United Irish movement lasted seven years, and each scene also details one stage in the rebels' progress from innocence through idealism, cleverness, dialectic, heroism, and compromise, to shame. In the "Oxen of the Sun" episode of *Ulysses*, the subject of which is childbirth, Joyce recapitulates the history of the English language to illustrate "embryonic development." Parker, in this play about the "birth" of a nation, modifies Joyce's device to reinforce the theatrical parallel. Each of the seven scenes is written in the style of a different Irish playwright, from Sheridan to Boucicault to Beckett.

To Parker, this strategy seemed to help solve the problem of presenting the multilayered nature of Irish experience. In a note written for the play's program he explained the logic behind his approach: "So how to write an Ulster history play? — since our past refuses to express itself as a linear, orderly narrative, in a convincing tone of voice? Tune into any given moment from it, and the wavelength soon grows crowded with a babble of voices from all the other moments, up to and including the present one. I have tried to accommodate this obstinate, crucial fact of life by eschewing any single style, and attempting instead a wide range of theatrical ventriloquism" (Parker 1984). In this way, too, as Parker remarked in an interview the year after *Northern Star*'s premiere, he was able to "write a play set in 1798 which was speaking directly to people today. If I'd written it in a purely 18th century style it would have seemed remote and artificial. If I'd written it in a completely colloquial idiom of today it would have seemed unhistorical: people dressed up in fancy clothes talking as if they should be in jeans and T-shirts" (Carty 1985).

Although Parker imitates playwrights more or less in the order in which their own plays were written, the manner of expression chosen for each scene is remarkably appropriate to the matter being presented. For example, the Age of Compromise, "of finally taking sides," portrays McCracken being sworn in as a member of the Defenders by a pair of sharps modeled on Sean O'Casey's Joxer and the Paycock. The dialect they speak comments playfully on unionist fears of "Dublin" while at the same time making the serious point that McCracken is sacrificing ends to means.

> *Gorman*: Once we're fully riz, there'll not be an Orange cur left in the county with a skinful of life-blood to his name.
>
> *McFadden*: Oh the French are on the say, They'll be here without delay, And the Orange will decay, Says the Shan Van Vocht.
>
> *McCracken*: No. It must be understood that there is no vendetta against the Orange Society. It's true that many lodges have been formed into companies of yeomen by their landlords. They will be sent against us, just as the Catholic militia are, but all those men are the gulls of history. Our quarrel is not with the puppets, our quarrel is with the puppet-masters who pull the strings. The English landed and mercantile interests. That's the power and the only power which we unite to oppose.
>
> [*Pause*]
>
> *Gorman*: Wasn't I after employing the very self-same form of words as yourself, Mr McCracken, only minutes before your arrival here? Croaker, sez I, if you're after the fellows that's done us the detrimental damage in this country, you need cast your net no further than the English maritime investments.   (Parker 1989, 62)

Parker's careful matching of style to subject is evident in the other flashback scenes as well. A passage about cultural renewal (the Age of Cleverness) is written in the epigrammatic mode of Wilde; a political debate between McCracken and the British officer who attempts to arrest him (the Age of Dialectic) is haunted by the ghost of Shaw; the Age of Idealism, in which "the noble and fearless young McCracken" is shown trying to "unit[e] the rabble in a common love for his shining youthful ardour," is cast as a popular melodrama after the manner of Boucicault.

This "theatrical ventriloquism" serves political as well as aesthetic ends. In *Northern Star* Parker, a Protestant writer from a unionist background, deliberately positions himself within an Irish literary tradition. By imitating great Irish writers in turn he indicates that he sees himself as their inheritor. Moreover, the Irish authors he invokes, like the republican revolutionaries the play is about, are overwhelmingly Protestant. In lines for McCracken, Parker voices the defensiveness of liberal Protestants who consider themselves to be Irish but feel that identification to be subtly denied them: "Look at me. My great-grandfather Joy was a French Huguenot, my great-grandfather Mc-

Cracken was a Scottish Covenanter, persecuted, the pair of them, driven here from the shores of home, their home but not my home, because I'm Henry Joy McCracken and here to stay, a natural son of Belfast, as Irish a bastard as all the other incomers, blown into this port by the storm of history, Gaelic or Danish or Anglo-Norman, without distinction, it makes no odds, every mother's son of us children of nature on this sodden glorious patch of earth, unpossessed of deed or inheritance, without distinction" (Parker 1989, 17).

Parker's McCracken argues that the truly radical contribution of the United Irishmen was a new answer to the question "What did it mean to be Irish?": "When you distilled it right down to the raw spirit? It meant to be dispossessed, to live on ground that isn't ours, Protestant, Catholic, Dissenter, the whole motley crew of us" (16). What in the 1790s was an uncommonly generous attitude toward Catholics looks in the 1990s like a plea for a reciprocal generosity. An exchange between McCracken and Hope near the end of the play makes this point explicitly:

> Hope: One thing's for sure, though, Harry. Without the Protestants of the North, there'll never be a nation. Not without them as a part of it.
> McCracken: Not without them at the heart of it, Jimmy. Our own people. (57)

As Fintan O'Toole astutely observes, the form of *Northern Star* reminds us that "the events of 1798 are still being, literally, played out": "An extraordinary tension is created by the way the styles of writing and performance move forward in time from the 18th century to the 20th. In terms of content, we are looking back on Henry Joy's tragic dilemmas. In terms of style, they are rushing forward to meet us" (1996). The play's visual imagery similarly reinforces parallels between the past and present. McCracken is hiding in a burnt-out house, a common sight in the Northern Ireland of the 1970s. The soldiers who burst in to search it at the end of act 1 have blackened faces, like their contemporary counterparts in the British Army. The prison scene, in which McCracken and his fellow inmates huddle wrapped in blankets and are ordered to "muck out" their cell by a sadistic guard, is reminiscent of the dirty protest and hunger strikes in the Maze Prison. These echoes climax in the brutal interrogation scene that takes place behind McCracken as he faces forward to deliver the last of the literary pastiches, a bleak Beckettian monologue, straight to the audience. A lambeg drum is beaten as the signal for a blackout, after which a bright white light comes up slowly, directly overhead, to reveal the three actors who had been McCracken's cell mates in the previous scene "*standing facing the back wall, leaning on their fingertips, arms akimbo, against the wall, feet splayed out, with hoods over their heads.*" As McCracken's speech ends, the prisoners howl as they are subjected to deafening white noise, and "*An* INTERROGATOR *bursts in carrying a baton. He pulls the first hooded prisoner away from the wall, throws him to the ground, and pinions him across the throat with the baton*" — demanding to know "Who commanded the rebels in Down?" (Parker 1989, 72–73).

The flashback scenes are interspersed with dialogue in Parker's own voice between McCracken and his lover Mary Bodle, sister Mary Ann, and Jemmy Hope.[7] In early plans for the play, a scene with Mary Bodle would have been just one of a long list of scenes. In the final version, her point of view is the principal challenge to McCracken's. Mary urges him to escape to America, where they can live in safety with their child. When he hesitates, she argues that his honor may be misplaced, that what he regards as a noble intention to face the punishment for his actions is really a form of selfishness. Hers is a woman's critique of the heroic death wish: "The love of your family isn't enough. My love isn't enough. You want the love of the whole future world and heaven besides. All right, go ahead, let them love you to death, let them paint you in forty shades of green on some godforsaken gable-end!" (Parker 1989, 54). When Mary demands to know why he allowed himself to turn to the gun, McCracken feebly replies that it was the logic of events, not a conscious decision. She retorts that there is always the chance to say no, but McCracken insists that it is not so easy as that:

> *McCracken*: Saying no is a final exit. You act out your small parts in a huge drama, Mary, but it's not of your own creation. You're acting all along in the dark, no matter how clear it seems at the time. You only have one choice. Either retire from the stage altogether. Or play out all your allotted roles until the curtain falls.
> *Mary*: Aye, that's right. On a stage full of corpses.   (53)

Another character who grew in importance as Parker continued to think about the play was Jemmy Hope. In the Lyric production, upon which Parker worked closely with the director, Peter Farago, Hope is the only character besides Mary and McCracken not to be double-cast. He is "banging on about his labouring classes" from the beginning of the play, even (anachronistically) before he would actually have been a member of the United Irishmen. In 1969 Parker had regarded Hope's proto-socialism as just one of the many dogmas McCracken had tried and failed to avoid. By the time he came to write *Northern Star*, however, he saw it as the only reasonable chance for the future, and Hope himself as "The steadfast light, the real Northern Star" (Parker 1989, 58).[8] In a crucial conversation with Hope, "a ghost from the future times," McCracken confesses that he failed to recognize the material basis of the conflict until it was far too late: "all the time the brute fact staring us in the face, only we never looked. A field, with two men fighting over it. Cain and Abel. The bitterest fight in the history of man on this earth. We were city boys. What did we know about two men fighting over a field?" (57). The aptly-named Hope offers the consolation that the conflict might not be intractable if every man were equally rewarded for his labor, but McCracken wearily dismisses this optimism: "Forget it, Jimmy. They won't listen. Have you ever known them to listen?" (57).

One senses that Stewart Parker shared both Hope's ultimate faith in the common man and McCracken's disillusionment about when the inhabitants of Belfast would come to their senses. After all, he had lived in the city through the grim years of the 1970s, a time in Ireland that bore more than a superficial resemblance to the 1790s. Parker, too, had seen an idealistic crusade for civil rights degenerate into a sectarian standoff. He had seen a socialist analysis of Northern Ireland's problems, as promulgated by groups such as People's Democracy and the Northern Ireland Labour Party, drown in Yeats's "blood-dimmed tide." And his life, too, had been consumed by the matter of Ireland. In a last, long speech for McCracken, Parker gives vent to his own obsession with Belfast:

> Why would one place break your heart, more than another? A place the like of that? Brain-damaged and dangerous, continuously violating itself, a place of perpetual breakdown, incompatible voices, screeching obscenely away through the smoky dark wet. Burnt out and still burning. Nerve-damaged, pitiable. Frightening. As maddening and tiresome as any other pain-obsessed cripple . . . we can't love it for what it is, only for what it might have been, if we'd got it right, if we'd made it whole. If. It's

a ghost town now and always will be, angry and implacable ghosts. Me condemned to be one of their number. We never made a nation. Our brainchild. Stillborn. Our own fault. We botched the birth. So what if the English do bequeath us to one another some day? What then? When there's nobody else to blame except ourselves? (Parker 1989, 75).

No resolution is possible, for the baleful cycle of history is not yet through with Belfast. Midway through the play McCracken had declaimed, "Citizens of Belfast—you rehearse all of your chosen parts and you play them with the utmost zeal—except that maybe they're really playing you. Think about it" (34). The end of *Northern Star* throws the questions it has raised back at the audience, as the play ends where it began: "Citizens of Belfast . . ." (76). The lights fade to black, as the pounding of a lambeg drum overwhelms McCracken's last words.

Notes

1. This identification with the United Irishmen is something of an Ulster Protestant literary tradition. Edna Longley delineates this theme in the writings of Sam Hanna Bell and John Hewitt (Longley 1986, 54–55). More recent examples can be found in the work of Tom Paulin.

2. I thank Stewart Parker's executor, Lesley Bruce, for allowing me to examine Parker's journals, notes, and manuscripts.

3. The Northern Ireland Civil Rights Association (NICRA) was founded in February 1967, to call for "one man, one vote," an end to electoral gerrymandering, fair employment legislation, an end to discrimination in public housing, repeal of the Special Powers Act, and the disbanding of the B Specials.

4. This quotation comes from an undated draft of the letter to Rubin preserved among Parker's papers. I have not been able to see the letter that was actually sent, but have no reason to believe that it would be substantially different.

5. Parker took the title of his play from the United Irishmen's newspaper, the *Northern Star*.

6. In some of his notes for *Northern Star* Parker specifies that the play is set on the night of 6 July 1798. In the final version, however, the date is left vague, probably in order to accommodate the visit from McCracken's sister Mary Ann, which took place somewhat earlier.

7. A schema of the play among his notes divides its scenes into the "Confessional" and the "Rhetorical."

8. Lynne Parker, the playwright's niece, who directed *Northern Star* for Dublin's Rough Magic Theatre Company in 1996, suggests that Hope was associated in Parker's mind with Sam Thompson: a sensible leader for the

Protestant working class, what he had termed the "painful missing factor in the whole Ulster equation" (L. Parker 1997).

Literature Cited

Bardon, J. 1992. *A history of Ulster.* Belfast: Blackstaff.

Berrigan, D. 1970. *The trial of the Catonsville Nine.* Boston: Beacon.

———. 1987. *To dwell in peace: An autobiography.* San Francisco: Harper and Row.

Brown, T. 1987. History's nightmare: Stewart Parker's *Northern Star. Theatre Ireland* 13:40–41.

Carty, C. 1985. Northern star rising on the tide. *Sunday Tribune,* 29 September.

Curtis, R. 1974. *The Berrigan brothers: The story of Daniel and Philip Berrigan.* New York: Hawthorn.

Devlin, P. 1985. The *Over the Bridge* controversy. *Linen Hall Review* 2, no. 3:4–6.

Fairleigh, J. 1994. Interview by author. Belfast, 30 June.

Fannin, S. 1997. Letter to author, 5 October.

Fitzhenry, E. 1936. *Henry Joy McCracken.* Dublin: Talbot.

Foster, R. 1996. Program note for the Rough Magic production of *Northern Star.* Dublin, October.

Hawthorne, D. 1995. Interview by author. Derry, 22 February.

Hertz, N. 1994. Telephone conversation with the author, 5 February.

Latimer, W. T. 1897. *Ulster biographies relating chiefly to the Rebellion of 1798.* Belfast: James Cleeland and William Mullan.

Longley, E. 1986. Progressive bookmen: Politics and Northern Protestant writers since the 1930s. *Irish Review* 1:50–57.

Mason, R. 1995. Interview by author. London, 26 March.

McNeill, M. 1988. *The life and times of Mary Ann McCracken, 1770–1866: A Belfast panorama.* Belfast: Blackstaff. (Originally published 1960.)

O'Toole, F. 1996. Second opinion. *Irish Times,* 12 October.

Parker, L. 1997. Interview by author. Dublin, 18 July.

Parker, R. 1994. Interview by author. Ithaca, N.Y., 14 January.

Parker, S. 1970a. Buntus Belfast. *Irish Times* 28 January, 9.

———, ed. 1970b. Introduction to *Over the bridge* by Sam Thompson. Dublin: Gill and Macmillan.

———. 1970c. School for revolution. *Irish Times* 7 April, 11.

———. 1970d. The tribe and Thompson. *Irish Times* 18 June, 11.

———. 1970e. An Ulster volunteer. *Irish Times* 6 March, 11.

———. 1984. Program note for the Lyric production of *Northern Star.* Belfast, November.

———. 1989. *Three plays for Ireland.* Birmingham: Oberon.

Pine, R. 1970. Letter to Stewart Parker, 22 June.

Purcell, D. 1987. The illusionist. *Sunday Tribune*, 27 September.

Rosenfield, R. 1970. Sam Thompson's *Over the Bridge* in book form. *Irish Times*, 8 December, 10.

Thompson, M. 1994. Interview by author. Belfast, 30 June.

Whelan, K. 1993. *The United Irishmen, the Enlightenment and popular culture*. Edited by David Dickson, Dáire Keogh, and Kevin Whelan, 269–96. Dublin: Lilliput.

. . . .

Music and Politics in Ireland
The Case of Loyalism

Introduction: "The Ulster Girl"

In 1973, a loyalist male prisoner in Crumlin Road jail in Belfast, using only the initials J. McC., penned a song that was later published in the *Ulster Song Book*. The song was titled "The Ulster Girl," but no indication was given of the tune. Years later, a chorus was added, and the lyrics were set to the tune of a popular love ballad, "Sometimes When We Touch." In 1989 the song was recorded by a Belfast-based group called The Platoon on a CD titled *UVF Songs*. The lyrics are as follows:

> An Ulster girl in heart and soul, I love our dear old land,
> I honour those who in her cause lift voice or pen or hand.
> And may I die before I see this land we fought to save
> In rebel grasp and I at worst the mother of a slave.
>
> Through many a bloody time of woe old Ulster's heart has bled,
> But still she makes her enemy know her spirit has not fled.
> God bless the men who for her sake their love and freedom gave,
> God bless the mothers of these sons who nursed no cowardly slave.
>
> *Chorus:*
> The Ulster girl is me; I'll tell it honestly
> That I'd die to keep this land of ours still free.
> And if we lost our freedom, my heart would break in two,
> And if I couldn't stay here, I don't know what I'd do.
>
> God bless the men who make the stand in Ulster's patriot host.
> I'd give the youth all treasures grand who served his country most.
> And if he fell, I'd rather lie beside him in the grave
> Than wed a meek apologist and be the mother of a slave.

It is often easy to dismiss loyalist songs on the basis of the text alone. Many fall far short of what might be termed poetry; others are sectarian and chilling in their calls to eliminate Catholics. Yet it has to be said that, on the basis of lyrics alone, "The Ulster Girl" is not the worst of songs, even if somewhat archaic and melodramatic. Its sentiments of freedom and liberty are not unknown in political struggles in other societies where stirring songs and poems are written. But to begin to appreciate "The Ulster Girl" we must do more than read the lyrics. If you know the popular ballad whose tune it uses, sing the song; at least, imagine the words sung to the tune of a romantic ballad by a woman with a fine singing voice on a CD whose production is highly professional. Better still, imagine yourself as a loyalist in a crowded, smoky loyalist club with good friends and lots of drink as The Platoon sings this song. Only then can the power of the song be understood. The purpose of this article is to examine the effect of loyalist songs such as this. Why and how do they stir the heart of a loyalist?[1]

Politics and Music in Ireland: A Living Tradition

The relationship between music and politics is well established in Ireland. On the nationalist side, there are numerous ballads in English dating back to the United Irishmen rebellion of 1798; some, like "The Rising of the Moon," are still popular. In the 1840s, the Young Irelanders sought to form a unified nationalist consciousness; in doing so they engaged not merely in military rebellion, but also in a major cultural project. They adopted a tricolor that was eventually in 1937 to become the Irish national flag; their newspaper, *The Nation*, published poetry. As part of this project, Thomas Davis wrote stirring nationalist songs; despite their archaic language, some of these, such as "A Nation Once Again" and "The West's Awake," are still sung.[2]

On the unionist side, there is also an old tradition of political music. It is not confined to the tunes played by marching bands that have accompanied Orange Order parades from at least the middle of the nineteenth century, but also includes songs such as "Lilliburlero" (one of the oldest of Orange songs) and "Dolly's Brae" (which celebrates a skirmish between Orangemen and nationalists in 1849). Unlike the situation on the nationalist side, these songs were not the products of a nationalist "invention of tradition"[3] (Hobsbawm and Ranger 1983) designed and managed by middle-class intellectuals (most of whom, incidentally, were Protestant), but were anonymous ballads. Many of the old unionist songs have been forgotten, even by unionists. With a few notable exceptions, such as "Dolly's Brae" and "The Aghalee Heroes," the traditional Orange songs are no longer popular. The repertoire of unionist songs has been drastically narrowed, with the result that haunting ballads such as the unusual love song "The Orange Maid of Sligo" are no longer sung.

Nationalist songs, in the words of singer and broadcaster Tony McAuley, "concern themselves with endurance, defeat and with the possibility of one day winning. The big songs always have to do with losing. . . . But constantly throughout the song is the idea that the loser will one day become the winner."[4] Unionist songs on the other hand are about winning battles, real or imaginary, and about siege. Musician and broadcaster Bobbie Hanvey sums up the siege mentality thus: "Keep to your own clan, don't mix. . . . The Protestant songs are bordering on paranoia at times because this is the way they have seen themselves down the years, because they *have* been under siege."[5] Hanvey also concludes that very few nationalist songs have been anti-Protestant: "All republican songs have been aimed towards the British." This conclusion may be too definitive, implying as it does that Irish nationalism has been incapable of producing sectarian songs. It may merely be that the sectarian songs were the first to have been forgotten by nationalists. Even that would be significant, however, when comparison is made with traditional unionist songs. While it is clear that some of the more sectarian unionist songs have been forgotten over time, it is also a fact that some of the songs that have endured are indeed sectarian. "Dolly's Brae" is a case in point. It recounts the story of an Orange march on 12 July 1849 in County Down, a march to which some local nationalists objected:

> Just then two priests came up to us and to Mr. Spiers did say:
> "Come, turn your men the other road and never cross Dolly's Brae."
> "Begone, begone, you papish dogs, you've hardly time to pray
> Before we throw your carcases right over Dolly's Brae,
> Before we throw your carcases right over Dolly's Brae."

> And when we came to that great hill, they were ranked on every side,
> And offering up their papish prayers for help to stem the tide.
> And we loosed our guns upon them and we quickly won the day,
> And we knocked five hundred papishes right over Dolly's Brae,
> And we knocked five hundred papishes right over Dolly's Brae.

The tradition of political songs is still very much alive in Ireland. From the early 1970s on, both republicans and loyalists have produced songs that voice their aspirations, celebrate their heroes and victories, and justify their respective "armed struggles." Countless songbooks have been produced and have circulated widely. Numerous singing groups have performed the key songs of each political persuasion in drinking clubs to enthusiastic and participative audiences. At times their songs have been as popular as those heard on radio stations and have provided in effect an alternative hit parade. Finally, the singing groups have recorded vinyl records, tapes, and CDs, the quality of which has ranged from the embarrassing to the highly professional.

Songs and Conflict

The relationship between music and political conflict in the North of Ireland is underresearched. A notable exception was a conference sponsored by Cooperation North that considered the question of "ownership" of traditional music (McNamee 1991). It was clear that most participants took pains to distinguish between traditional music and political music, especially songs. One participant, Ciáran Mac Mathúna, for example, condemned those who "are making money, to put it crudely, with records over dead bodies" (77), while another participant, Cathal Goan, stated, that, as far as political music was concerned, "Most of it is rubbish; you wouldn't want to play it anyway! . . . If you get a couple of guitars in tune, you're lucky" (77). Musician Fintan Vallely was slightly less exclusivist, but was still concerned to distinguish between what he termed "the art side of music" and political music. The latter, he argued, had the right to exist: "but the sort of musicians that I know, generally speaking, rebel songs are not part of their repertoire; and the Protestant musicians who play jigs and reels and things, the Orange songs are not part of their repertoire" (98).

In his address to the conference, singer and collector Sean Corcoran seemed to sum up the general mood: "There is only one tradition musically speaking. . . . If an Antrim fiddler is playing 'Miss McLeod's Reel,' there is no way of telling if he is a Catholic or a Protestant: 'Miss McLeod's Reel' has absolutely no political position on the border, no position on contraception, on abortion, or anything at all like that. Music is simply music" (8).

Some other commentators have focused specifically on political songs, but only in order to emphasize the supposed contribution of such songs to the exacerbation of violence. Republican songs have been singled out; they are said to stir up old, archaic sentiments, to perpetuate tired old myths. It is said that young men have gone out to kill and to die simply so that they will be remembered in a ballad. For example, writing of the period of the Irish war of independence (1919–21), Whitfield (1990, 68) concludes: "The ballads performed an indispensable function for the freedom-fighters of Ireland and their supporters, giving them courage to continue, warming their hearts in bitter times and, above all, keeping their hopes alive. Without the ballads, there might not have been the same continuity of aspiration, the same steady stream of young idealists, the same unending attrition."

The conclusion that songs lead to conflict, rather than vice versa, is succinctly rejected by Kiberd (1991, 13): "The notion that the glorification of 1916 in poems or ballads leads to recruits for the IRA is insulting to the intelligence of the general public and of the IRA. What created the modern IRA was not any cultural force, but the bleak, sectarian realities of life in the corrupt statelet of Northern Ireland." The culturalist argument that sees songs as major contributors to the continuation of violence rests easily within a more general revisionist critique. Nationalists in general, and republicans in particular, are said to be victims of a mythmaking tendency that is not merely culturally and politically intolerant but also psychologically pathological. Supposedly guided by "theology" (Berman, Lalor, and Torode 1983) rather than political ideology and locked in a mythical view of time as cyclical rather than linear (Kearney 1984), republicans are prime targets for criticism; everything they represent stands opposed to the virtuous ideals of democracy, tolerance, pluralism, and modernism. Despite the value of an approach that seriously questions myths and conventions, the revisionist argument reveals its political bias by confining its critique to nationalism and republicanism.

Revisionism contains little critique of unionism and its myths; neither does it charge that loyalist music contributes to stirring up old hatreds or fanning current conflict. Needless to say, there is scope for such critique. As Bell (1990) has shown convincingly, members of "blood and thunder" or "kick the Pope" bands are often at the forefront of asserting the loyalist cause, and that can often mean being close to violence. Take the sectarian riots in Belfast in July 1932 as one random example. During these riots, the worst since the foundation of the state, an eighteen-year-old Protestant, Edward Withers, was shot dead. A loyalist band from Glasgow, the Billy Boys, came to his house to deliver a wreath; as they did so, they played loyalist tunes loudly. As a result, another riot began that left two people, both Protestant, dead. In an editorial, the *Glasgow Herald* commented: "Why do the authorities permit a party of people to march behind a band carrying a wreath to the home of a man who had been shot the night before? Of course, the wreath was a sincere tribute to the dead, but the manner of its delivery cannot be called anything but an ostentatious piece of provocation for the living" (Munck and Rolston 1987, 50). Nor is the relationship between loyalist bands and violence confined to the past; for example, in a period of heightened tension over loyalist marches, an Apprentice Boys march went ahead with nationalist approval in Derry in August 1997. However: "Shortly after 2 P.M. here today a group of bandsmen from one particular band broke away from the main parade as it was going around the Diamond. They went over to Butcher Street where they attacked a group of onlookers" (RUC [Royal Ulster Constabulary] statement, cited in *Irish News*, 11 August 1997). Members of the band concerned, Cloughfern Young Conquerors, were, in the words of a newspaper reporter, "using their flutes to simulate the action of gunmen towards nationalists, while shouting abuse about the 1993 Greysteel murders, the death of Belfast solicitor Pat Finucane and any other dead nationalist they could think of" (ibid).

It is significant that the only case of a prosecution under incitement to hatred legislation in Northern Ireland was that of hardline loyalist John McKeague in 1971 for publishing the *Loyalist Song Book*, and in particular, one song in it entitled "I Was Born Under the Union Jack" (a parody of the song "I Was Born Under a Wandering Star" from the film *Paint Your Wagon*):

> I was born under the Union Jack.
> I was born under the Union Jack.
> Falls was made for burning, taigs[6] are made to kill.
> You've never seen a road like the Shankill.
>
> I was born under the Union Jack.
> I was born under the Union Jack.

If taigs are made for killing, then blood is made to flow.
You've never seen a place like Sandy Row.

I was born under the Union Jack.
I was born under the Union Jack.
If guns were made for shooting, then skulls are made to crack.
You've never seen a better taig than with a bullet in his back.

The case against McKeague was unsuccessful.

Despite these instances, it is difficult to locate any attempt to accuse loyalist music and songs of having a major role in the continuation of political violence. As in the wider representations by the media, novels, and films, the venom — and less usually the romance — is reserved for republicans.

I am not proposing that the situation would be improved by repeating the culturalist error of seeing loyalist songs, like their republican counterparts, as the source of conflict. But even that would be an acknowledgment of the existence of loyalist songs, an acknowledgment that is often missing in academic accounts of "the Troubles." A number of key texts on unionism and loyalism (for example, Bruce 1992, 1994) do not consider loyalist songs at all. Even highly informative texts that focus on issues of ideology and culture (such as Ruane and Todd 1996; Jarman 1997) and are in other ways incisive do not focus on loyalist songs. There are anecdotal accounts in Beattie (1992) and Belfrage (1987) of the loyalist clubs where songs are sung; Belfrage in particular is scathing, if brief, in her rejection of the lyrics of loyalist songs. Nelson (1984, 63) has a passing reference where she notes the contribution of loyalist songs to extolling the "heroic, martial aspects of loyalist ideology." Bell (1990), as was noted earlier, has produced a fundamental analysis of the role of marching bands in loyalism, but he does not consider songs. This leaves very few texts that do consider loyalist songs. McAuley (1994, 98) notes how the lyrics of some such songs have changed over the course of the Troubles, from asserting a British identity originally to articulating an Ulster identity at a later stage. Finlayson (1996, 97–99) repeats this argument, even to the extent of quoting the same lyrics as McAuley. Bryson and McCartney (1994) do consider anthems, along with other potentially divisive symbols, but have little to say about popular songs. Bell (1976) devotes more space to loyalist songs than all the other authors put together, and convincingly demonstrates the extent to which the songs reveal key elements of loyalist ideology. However, there is no analysis of the songs themselves; rather, the lyrics are used merely as a source of quotations, like a political pamphlet or a newspaper report, to back up the author's argument.

Denselow (1989) and McCann (1989, 1995) have considered republican songs, the former in a sympathetic journalistic account, the latter in a more substantial analysis that looks at the mythlike accounts of the exploits of heroes. It would be tempting simply to lift such an analysis and apply it as a template to loyalist songs on the grounds that, despite the radically opposed political ideologies involved, similar functions are performed by the songs. Such an approach would fit well with Davis's (1994) review of republican and loyalist propaganda, which he sees as mirror images. Certainly, at a superficial level there is much similarity: the uniforms of marching bands, the instruments used, even, as Belfrage (1987, 158) notes, the ambience of the clubs where the songs are sung.

But such abstraction does not do justice to the ways in which loyalism and republicanism are different, and consequently to the manner in which the songs of each tradition differently contribute to the perpetuation of their respective ideologies. This is not to deny that there is much scope to the concept of "relentless reciprocity" (O'Dowd, 1990), where neither the colonized or the colonizer can exist without reference to the existence of the other. But such interconnectedness has to be seen within the structural context of colonialism and inequality. In the Irish context, colonialism led to the dominance of unionism, the suppression of nationalism, and an inequality of power at the economic, political, and cultural levels that exists in the North to this day. Ruane and Todd (1996, 210) sum up the unequal relationship between unionists (Protestants) and nationalists (Catholics): "As the winners in successive struggles, Protestants have more to celebrate; as the culturally dominant community, they have greater freedom to construct, sustain and validate their chosen identity; as the community which formed Northern Ireland in its own image, they have the material symbols of their past and present throughout the public sphere. As the losers, Catholics have more to come to terms with; they must do so from a position of continuing cultural inequality which precludes the distance necessary to accept the past; they have few public memorials which symbolise and objectify their past and present, and those they propose (for example, bilingual Irish/English signs) are opposed by unionists as offensive." It is within that structural context that the role of loyalist songs will be considered now.

Loyalist Songs: What's in a Tune?

What is loyalist about loyalist music? Irish dance and folk music is immediately distinguishable globally, thanks to such commercial successes as *Riverdance*. But political taboos can prevent loyalist music adding its own political lyrics to Irish dance and folk tunes. The problem is that there is, for loyalists, no single style into which their music can fit easily. Scottish dance music might seem a likely candidate, given the assertion of many loyalists that they are Ulster-Scots, but neither that genre nor indeed the option of adding new lyrics to old loyalist favorites is often chosen. Consequently, loyalist songs come in a range of styles: from folk, through country and western, to pop, and what is termed in the United States "adult-oriented rock."

It could be argued that such hybridity is a healthy sign, revealing loyalism's postmodernist credentials or its multiculturalist ideals. However, there would be great difficulty in sustaining such an argument. Instead, the range of styles in loyalist tunes is in fact symptomatic of a more general problem within loyalism: that of defining identity. As a result, there is often great incongruity in loyalist songs. For example, one song, "Don't Feel Bad," is a tribute to a loyalist killer, Joe Bratty, himself shot dead by the IRA shortly before they called their 1994 ceasefire. The tune is a jaunty, upbeat, country-style number, completely at odds with the chilling lyrics, which are all about murdering nationalists:

> Now listen people while I tell a story
> About a hero that was bold and true.
> His friends knew and respected him, Joe Bratty,
> A man loved and admired by all he knew.
>
> Now seven times they tried to kill our hero
> Before that fateful Sunday when he died.
> But we know Joe took so many with him
> And we were proud to have him on our side.

Chorus:
And now he's gone; don't you feel bad,
He was the best commander you ever had.
His cry was: "There's a taig; take him out
With all the strength that you have;
Kill that rebel scum; don't you feel bad."

Another example is that of a CD entitled "Undefeated Ulster," a self-styled "tribute to the Protestant People of Ulster who have withstood the murderous onslaught [*sic*] of Roman Catholic Terrorism for over 25 years in this present phase of the troubles." Of relatively recent vintage, it is manufactured by 4 Batt Music Ltd.; the name of the performing group, however, is not acknowledged. Songs such as "Orange Wings" (to the tune of "Green Beret") and "Quis Separabit" (the motto of the UDA [Ulster Defence Association] to the tune of the folk song "Black Velvet Band"), mix with country-and-western–style numbers and a song called "The Losing of the Green," to the tune of the traditional loyalist song "The Sash my Father Wore." In the midst of these, some instrumental numbers acquire a most bizarre treatment; they are overdubbed with sounds of exploding bombs, automatic-weapon fire, and people screaming. The CD begins with a woman screaming: "Any of you pricks move, I'll execute every motherfuckin' last one of you" — this seems to be taken from the soundtrack of some Hollywood movie. At the end, after a supposedly moving instrumental tribute to "Fallen Comrades," there is a version of the "Loony Tunes" closing melody, followed by a soundtrack of someone vomiting violently and then flushing a toilet. The same woman's voice as at the beginning then states: "If Jesus Christ were here tonight he would not dare to drop another bomb," after which the CD fades out to the sound of bombs. Irish folk music has prided itself recently in its ability to fuse with other forms: the Chieftains playing with Chinese musicians, Donal Lunny with African musicians, the U.S. groups Black 47 and Seanachie mixing folk, reggae, and rap. "Undefeated Ulster" displays no such ingenuity.[7]

The incongruity is evidenced in another important way: the practice of borrowing existing tunes from other sources. This practice is common in the folk tradition where it is not seen as stealing; rather, the belief is that a good tune is a good tune and should not be wasted on

Table 1. Some Popular Song Sources for Loyalist Tunes

Loyalist Tune	Popular Song
All Kinds of Everything	All Kinds of Everything
Battle of Belfast	Battle of New Orleans
Bloody Sunday	Beautiful Sunday
Chase Them Home	Take Me Home, Country Roads
Fallen Hero	The Wind Beneath My Wings
Goodbye My Loyal Friend	Seasons in the Sun
I'd Like to Teach the World to Sing	I'd Like to Teach the World to Sing
The Imprisoned Volunteers	A Scottish Soldier
I Was Born under the Union Jack	I Was Born under a Wandering Star
Lest We Forget	Abraham, Martin and John
My Old Man's an Orangeman	My Old Man's a Dustman
No Pope of Rome	Home on the Range
The Prisoner	There but for Fortune
Proud to be a Prod	The Beverly Hillbillies
Silent Too Long	The Wind Beneath My Wings
The Times They are a Changing	The Times They are a Changing
An Ulster Anthem	Amazing Grace
The Ulster Girl	Sometimes when We Touch
Watching the Heroes	Billy, Don't be a Hero

only one song. Loyalists "raid" far and wide for tunes, taking in contemporary ballads and republican songs, as Tables 1 and 2 show.

How does a loyalist song work if its tune has been borrowed from popular or republican culture? Is a good tune simply a good tune? Walter Benjamin (1977, 219–255) argued that a work of art has an aura that is not reproducible. It is possible, he contended, in an age of mechanical reproduction to reproduce endlessly a masterpiece, such as the Mona Lisa. However, what cannot be transferred to the poster or print is the aura of the original painting. Given the spectacular advances in "mechanical reproduction" since Benjamin wrote this, it is possible to call into question the validity of his conclusion. To take an example from popular rather than "high" culture, the tune of a romantic ballad has the potential of being partially transferable. Together the lyrics, tune, production, and overall sound of the song can create an aura that is more than merely the meaning of the lyrics or the topic

Table 2. Some Republican Sources for Loyalist Tunes

Loyalist Tune	Republican Song
Billy McFadzean	James Connolly
Come All Ye Young Protestants	The Patriot Game
A Loyal Heart	Roddy McCorley
Lindsay Mooney	Banna Strand
The Loyal Protestant	Off to Dublin in the Green
The Orangemen in Crossmaglen	Crossmaglen
Red Hand Brigade	Belfast Brigade
There'll Always be an Ulster	The Wearing of the Green
The Ulster Story	Take it Down from the Mast, Irish Traitors
Ulster Won't Die	The Patriot Game

considered in the song. That aura can be transferred to another song that has different lyrics. In the case of "The Ulster Girl," considered at the beginning of this article, the way in which the original song has worked on an audience to create feelings of romance and tenderness means that the tune can be detached from its original lyric and can begin to work subliminally to create similar feelings, even before the new lyrics are heard or understood. The aura of the song precedes it. To use Barthes's (1968, 89–94) distinction, the tune as a sign works not merely at a "denotational" level, but also at a "connotational" one. It conjures up feelings and emotions that are instantly retrievable by the audience when being presented on later occasions with the sign. This is not to say that the words of a song are unimportant; it *is* to argue that the effect of the song derives from more than just the words.

This transferability is evident in other elements of popular culture. For example, the actor Alan Rickman played a superb "bad guy" in the film *Die Hard*. Whether by intention or not, when director Neil Jordan cast Rickman as Eamon de Valera in the film *Michael Collins*, the aura that Rickman had from the previous film was carried over to the new film; the audience already "knew" that Rickman was sinister, cold, and manipulative and could begin to see de Valera in exactly the same light.

But there are limits to the transferability of auras, especially in relation to tunes. For example, a republican tune comes carrying the stigma of its origins and is not so easily absorbed into a loyalist song. The situation is similar to the limits of transferability of other republican and nationalist symbols. A case in point is the image of Cuchulain. The legend of Cuchulain, the mythical warrior of Ulster who fought against the army of Connacht, was an important one in the Gaelic revival of the last century. In 1936 a bronze image of the dying Cuchulain by the sculptor Oliver Sheppard was placed in the General Post Office in Dublin, the headquarters of the rebels who staged the 1916 Rising (see Breathnach-Lynch 1997). Sheppard's image was thus inextricably linked to the nationalist and republican cause. In the 1970s two UDA leaders, John McMichael and Andy Tyrie, embraced the historical writings of Ian Adamson (1974). In a splendid attempt at the "invention of a tradition," Adamson argued that Irish nationalists were wrong to see the legend of the great Ulster warrior Cuchulain as a nationalist story. Cuchulain, he argued, was a Cruithin or Pict, and had defended Ulster against the ancestors of Irish nationalism, the Celts. To all intents and purposes, Cuchulain was the first loyalist. Imaginative as this may have been, it had limited popularity in loyalist ranks. There may be a wall mural with the Sheppard image on the Newtownards Road in East Belfast and another on a UDA wing in the Maze Prison near Lisburn, but as one lower-ranking UDA man stated to McAuley (1994, 95), "That's John (McMichael) and Andy's (Tyrie) baby and I don't take much to do with it."[8] The limits of transferability of auras are most obvious in the case of republican tunes. The tune of a romantic ballad can transfer; because of its connotations, however, a republican tune finds the migration less easy.

Tunes are important because songs are much more than merely words. At its best a good song combines both tune and lyrics for effect. But sometimes a good tune can even manage to carry weak lyrics; in the right circumstances, lyrics can be the least important component of a song. At the same time, political songs are concerned with delivering a message; thus, the words must be effective. In the case of loyalist songs, where the tunes are often not instantly recognizable as loyalist, there can be a much greater burden on the lyrics to carry the loyalist message.

Why Do Loyalist Songs Have Words?

Frith (1988) asks the question: why do songs have words? He begins by rejecting "reflection theory," the notion that there is a "direct relationship between a lyric and the social or emotional condition it describes"

(112). On that basis, pop music has been dismissed for its supposed banality from the time of the Frankfurt School because theorists such as Adorno viewed words as the totality of the song; when the words apparently said little, the song was worth little in the eyes of the mass culture theorists. But, says Frith, the beauty of, for example, a good blues song is not in its documentary value, but in its ability to be heard as poetry. Songs are not just spoken words, but are "the sign of a voice" (120); "Songs are not just any old speech act—by putting words to music, songwriters give them a new sort of resonance and power" (121). Songs can speak to the heart; they can express and entice feeling; they can make everyday speech into poetry.

Taking on board Althusser's concept, Frith argues that the power of songs is in "interpellation"; they hail people. Despite the denial of subjectivity inherent in following such an argument through to its logical conclusion, Frith's conclusion is nonetheless insightful. It is not, he argues, so much a case of subjects creating ideology through songs, but of songs creating subjects. As Frith (1988, 123) puts it, "Pop love songs do not 'reflect' emotions, then, but give people the romantic terms in which to articulate and so experience their emotions."

By extension, it can be argued that political songs give people the words to express feelings they could not so easily express otherwise. This effect can be brought about by the complete lyrics of a song, or even by one phrase or word. And this powerful meaning can work independently of the intentions of the song's authors and the noneffectiveness of the words for other listeners. Thus, a ballad such as "The Fields of Athenry," sung by nationalist folk groups and transformed into a loyalist song ("The Fields of Ballynafeigh"), can be regarded as merely a pleasant, tuneful, sing-along song about a distant historical event, the transportation of a felon from Ireland in the seventeenth century. But to the mother whose husband is serving time in prison for a political offense, even one line in the song—"And you must raise our child in dignity"—can become a source of identification and emotional strength. Similarly, key words such as "freedom" and "slavery" (as occur in "The Ulster Girl") become powerful signifiers to people in the midst of political conflict.

Moreover, political songs can have this effect on people not merely as individuals. Songs can confirm group identity, creating and reinforcing a sense of community in the face of apparently overwhelming odds.

They do so through their words, their tunes, their performance, and the venues in which they are heard. No matter how banal they seem to the outsider, they represent the community articulating and celebrating itself.

Articulating Loyalism

It is easy to conclude that loyalism has little to say, that as Bennett argues loyalist culture has little to offer: "To remain is to be enclosed in a world where 'culture' is restricted to little more than flute bands, Orange marches and the chanting of sectarian slogans at football matches" (R. Bennett, "An Irish answer," *Guardian Weekend*, 16 July 1994, 55). In reply, Aughey (1995, 13) berates the tendency of "cultural nationalists" like Bennett to confuse what is "distinctive" and what is "representative" of loyalist culture: "What is distinctive of political Protestantism — its Orange marches, its flute bands, its lodge banners, its sectarian songs — is taken to be the sum of all cultural life in that community. . . . What might be representative of that community — cultural life which bears a great resemblance to what goes on elsewhere in the British Isles from brass bands to jazz groups to amateur dramatics to choral societies to creative writing classes — is invisible to a cultural nationalist because it is not exclusively Irish."

But this retort fails to acknowledge that it is precisely because it is distinctive that loyalist ideology and culture deserves to be analyzed. To contrast sectarian songs with jazz bands is to make no comparison of any worth because it avoids focusing on the specific importance of sectarianism — sung, spoken, or lived — within this society. Now, the least that can be said of the specificity of loyalism is that it is remarkably inarticulate about its fears and aspirations; elsewhere, Aughey himself (1989, 1) agrees: "the way in which unionists have presented their own case, or failed to do so, has in no small measure contributed to their sense of isolation and ineffectiveness." In contrast, as many commentators have noted, nationalism is highly articulate. The question is how deep this dissimilarity goes. Is it merely at the level of rhetoric or opportunity, or is it more fundamental? Brown (1985, 5) concludes that the problems of unionism in this respect are deep-rooted. Focusing on a comparison of nationalist and unionist approaches to history, he argues that the unionist historical imagination is "starkly simple in outline and depressingly lacking in emotional range and complexity." The explanation is that, as the losers in the process of colonization, nationalists needed history for inspiration and sustenance. On the unionist side, however, "history has had to perform fewer functions and is necessarily simpler" (Brown 1985, 8).

An alternative approach to the same question is to consider the extent to which unionism constitutes a nationalist ideology. As O'Dowd (1991, 154) points out, many authors have concluded that the problem of unionism has been the failure to develop as a nationalist ideology. This has had profound effects on unionist intellectual and cultural life. "Its intellectuals . . . had no language to revive and no sustained critique of foreign oppression . . . it neither romanticised its peasantry nor linked its local folklore to a national cultural ideal" (O'Dowd 1991, 160). Bell (1990, 20) makes the same point, referring to two key intellectuals (one of whom was a northern Protestant) in the Gaelic revival of the late nineteenth century: "We'll find no Hyde or Pearse on the streets of Portadown." In fact, because of its position within the colonial relationship between Britain and Ireland, unionism was unable to align itself convincingly not merely with nationalism but with any of the major political ideologies of the late nineteenth and twentieth centuries: liberal democracy, socialism, feminism, even fascism. This was compounded with partition and the formation of the northern unionist state. Ruane and Todd (1996, 181) argue convincingly that when the Northern Ireland state was formed, it was difficult to distinguish a distinct Ulster identity. The main task of unionist politicians was to distance themselves from the Irish tradition and thus form a specific Ulster identity. This project was eventually successful: "Over time, the Protestant sense of the island and of being part of an island-wide culture diminished"; instead, the two "main cultural foci of the new state" became Protestantism and Britishness.

Aughey (1989, 16) rejects conclusions such as these, arguing that nationalism in Ireland is a construct of Irish nationalists who have then used their invention as a gauge to reveal the supposed inadequacies of unionism. In short, unionism is only inadequate when measured by the exclusivist criteria of Irish nationalism. Consequently, Aughey's avowed purpose is to show that unionism is "defensible in terms that are rational and coherent" (1989, 1). But this retort misses the substance of the fundamental point raised by the commentators he opposes; all ideologies create myths, but those created by unionism are narrower than those of nationalism; all ideology is a form of "invention of tradition," but the tradition created by unionism is much more simplistic than that created by nationalism; all history operates on the basis of selecting from the past, but the selection made by unionism is much more restricted than that made by nationalism. And finally, because of the structural confinement necessarily experienced by unionism and its intellectuals, there has been an inevitable skewing of loyalist culture in particular toward "the popular and visual rather than literary or intellectual," as O'Dowd (1991, 165) puts it. From a different starting point and for entirely different reasons, Aughey (1989, 1) concurs that often "unionist politics has been reduced to its most paranoid and emotional elements." Nowhere is this more obvious than in relation to loyalist songs.

The Message of Loyalist Songs

The extent and value of ideological simplicity within unionism cannot be underestimated: "The one-dimensional nature of unionist political ideology contrasted . . . with the complex differentiation of the unionist community along class and religious lines. The thrust of popular loyalism . . . was to keep that ideology simple and pure. Within the unionist community it had peculiarly democratic connotations — it could be formulated by any ordinary unionist as eloquently and as effectively as any political expert" (O'Dowd 1991, 167). One important way in which many ordinary unionists manage to articulate their ideology eloquently is through song. To paraphrase Frith from earlier, loyalist songs give people the terms in which to articulate and so experience their emotions. The fact that these terms are often simple does not in itself distance the articulation from that of those who might be termed a political elite. There is a close match between the popular expressions of ideology in loyalist songs and the representation of loyalist ideology by political experts.

Siege Mentality

For many political commentators, the most notable aspect of loyalist ideology is the sense of siege. The ideological effect of feeling constantly under threat takes various forms. The perceived relentlessness of the threat leads to a notion of timelessness, as summarized by MacDonagh (1983, 15): "Their historical self-vision is of endless repetition of repelled assaults, without hope of absolute finality or fundamental change in their relationship to their surrounding and surrounded neighbours." Many songs articulate this siege mentality very clearly. Some present what can only be referred to as a litany of suffering experienced during the last quarter-century by the unionist community; an example is the chorus of "Chase Them Home" (sung to the tune of John Denver's "Take me Home, Country Roads"):

> Burned our homes, blocked our roads in the place where I belong.
> Trouble-torn, cities roaring; chase them home, country roads.

Nor, according to the songs, is there anything new in these experiences; unionists have been under siege since time immemorial:

> All down through the ages, they tried in vain
> To take over Ulster — they'll try it again.
> But we'll never falter to fight for the cause
> That gave us our freedom, religion and laws.
> . . . For we'll cut you down and you'll fall like rain;
> We've done it before and we'll do it again.
>
> ("Come All Ye Young Protestants,"
> sung to the tune of Dominic Behan's "The Patriot Game")

In fact, the problem for unionism is that the siege is both historic and current:

> Many times they tried to take our land,
> Their attempts have been in vain.
> For as in the past, we'll fight to the last,
> Till our bodies' blood does drain.
>
> ("A Loyal Protestant," sung to the
> tune of the republican song, "Off to Dublin in the Green")

The same point is made in another song ("A Loyalist Prisoner's Call", sung to the tune of the traditional loyalist song "The Blackman's Dream"):

> Arise! No longer must our flag be trampled in the dust.
> The enemy's at hand again and fight them now we must.

The flag we hold so dear to us, defend it to the last,
Just like our fathers did before in days not long gone past.

The simple use of the one word "again" in the second line says it all: the battle is timeless. As the song "Ulster's My Home" puts it, the current conflict is simply "Another bloody chapter in an endless civil war."

The feeling of isolation experienced not only by loyalists, but also by "settlers" universally, leads to an emphasis on self-reliance, as O'Dowd (1990, 41–42) argues: "As the 'natives' revolt, loyalists refurbish their most durable myth, that of the besieged garrison. It is threatened on several fronts by the besiegers without, Irish Catholic Nationalists and their sympathizers across the world, by fifth columnists who would compromise with the enemy, and by the inconstancy of a motherland with a history of putting its own interests before those of its most patriotic citizens abroad. From this entrapment, the Ulster Protestant has built a myth of self-reliance." In this situation, the loyalist must be eternally vigilant, because: "One cannot trust one's enemy, one does not know one's friend" ("The Ballad of Tommy Herron," sung to the tune of "The Boston Burglar"). For the writer of "The Magnificent Seven" (also sung to the tune of "The Boston Burglar"), in the case of loyalist prisoners betrayed by a former colleague, a "supergrass," the situation is even worse: "One cannot trust one's enemy, one cannot trust one's friend." Loyalists are alone, with no one to depend on but themselves.

Traitors apart, loyalism clings to an ideal of unity; despite differences of class, and denomination, all unionists are under siege. The ultimate consequence of the siege mentality is what Brown (1985) refers to as "the historical myth" of "the whole Protestant community." Or, as one song ("Upside Down," sung to the tune of "John Brown's Body") puts it:

> But we're a happy, happy nation.
> We're a happy, happy nation.
> We're a happy, happy nation.
> God bless the RUC.

Liberty, Protestantism and Britishness

Beyond the sense of shared victimhood, actual or potential, loyalism sees itself as being an upholder of liberty. For some this liberty is defined in religious terms, for others it is more secular. Bruce (1994) contends that evangelical Protestantism is at the core of unionism. Aughey (1989) disagrees, preferring to emphasize the importance of secular liberalism in unionist thought. Whichever is the dominant force with any particular group of unionists at any particular time, there is no denying that unionist definitions of liberty rest on the two elements of Protestantism and Britishness. For loyalists, these two elements are inseparable, even if, to their annoyance, that connection is no longer firmly espoused by either the British or more secular unionists: "The loyalist lays claim to be the true protector of 'freedom, the Protestant religion and laws' — the 'core values' of British civilization — which he keeps alive in Ireland. In his mixture of love and resentment of Britain, he reminds its leaders he fought for British civilization not only throughout the course of Irish history, but in the cataclysmic circumstances of two world wars. He is still called to fight and die for his heritage in a way Britons are seldom called on to do" (O'Dowd 1990, 40).

The fight may be, in the words of "The Red Hand Soldier" (sung to the tune of the Irish folk song "Mursheen Durkan"), "To strike a blow for freedom and a land to call our own," but this could equally justify republican struggle in Ireland. What is loyalism specifically fighting for? "There'll Always be an Ulster" (sung to the tune of the republican song from 1798, "The Wearing of the Green") makes the case clearly:

> There'll always be an Ulster, an Ulster that is free,
> As long as there are Protestants to stand for liberty.
> The union jack will flutter across our native land
> To show the whole wide world around for truth and faith we stand.
>
> *Chorus:*
> There'll always be an Ulster, an Ulster that is true,
> As long as we united stand to keep our liberty.
>
> There'll always be an Ulster, a watch tower it will be,
> To fly the flag of liberty for all the world to see.
> The Crown will give us courage, the Bible give us faith.
> For God and past has been our stay, and bless our Ulster race.

The religious references make it quite clear: "freedom" equals "liberty" as defined in the Protestant tradition: the Bible, and the word of God. By definition this rules out Catholicism; freedom is for Protestants:

Now here's to good King William, for all the deeds he's done,
For saving us at Derry and making us his sons.
He gave us all our freedom, to him we must give praise.
It's great to be a Protestant and high our banners wave.

("My Old Man's an Orangeman," sung to the tune of Lonnie Donegan's
hit of the early 1960s, "My Old Man's a Dustman")

The struggle is "To shake off the shackles of popery / And fight for the freedom we love" ("To the Memory of Bro. David Linton"). Because popery is the antithesis of liberty, God is undoubtedly on the side of loyalism. He is called upon frequently and with assurance to back the loyalist cause:

And when I see the King, it reminds me once again that
there is but one king, God Almighty, and of the motto
given to us by the Ulster Volunteer Force: In God our
Trust.

("Deck of Cards," spoken, with "The Lord Is My Shepherd" playing
in background; based on the U.S. country hit, "The Deck of Cards")

The juxtaposition of religion and calls to violence is worthy of any jihad: "So, Lord, show me the message / And I'll show the republicans" ("Sons of Ulster," sung to the tune of "This World Is Not My Own").

Loyalists are quick to point out that their defense of liberty has cost them dearly. The prime example is World War I, and in particular the Battle of the Somme in July 1916 when thousands of former members of the UVF (Ulster Volunteer Force) incorporated in the British army as the 36th Ulster Division, were annihilated. Songs such as "Billy McFadzean," sung to the tune of the republican song "James Connolly," commemorate the sacrifice made by loyalists in order to stay British. Less historically sustainable is the claim that in World War II loyalists played a key role in stopping the advance of Nazi Germany in Northern Ireland:

Now the Germans came over in the year forty-one
And they tried to destroy us by bomb and by gun.
But history could have told them of others who tried
And how our sons defended Ulster, how they fought and they died.

("A Wee Spot in Europe," sung to the tune of the ballad
"Lovely Derry on the Banks of the Foyle")

Accurate or not, the song clearly underlines a key element in loyalist ideology: the sacrifices made by loyalists on behalf of Britain. Surely, then, Britain can be relied on to aid Ulster in its hour of need, just as Ulster aided Britain. A song from early in the Troubles ("Hell of a State," sung to the tune of Percy French's "The Mountains of Mourne") states just this:

> We trust this trouble will come to an end
> And Britain continues our cause to defend.
> We know we can trust them, they did it before
> And here's to King William, in good days of yore.

But such innocence was quickly dispelled in loyalist thinking by experiences such as the Sunningdale Agreement of 1973 and the Anglo-Irish Agreement of 1985.

> From under the table they dreamed up this plan,
> To sell our wee Ulster to a dark foreign land.
> It was Maggie Thatcher who knifed me and you
> And that's what she thinks of the red, white and blue.
>
> ("There are my Comrades," sung to the
> tune of the ballad "These are my Mountains")

Another song, "Proud to be a Prod" (to the theme tune of the U.S. television series *The Beverly Hillbillies*), also comments on the Anglo-Irish Agreement:

> He's proud to be an Ulsterman, proud to be a Prod,
> Proud to have his home in dear old Ulster's sod.
> So Maggie and your cronies, we all hate your guts,
> And you can stick your darned agreement where the monkey sticks his nuts.

Clayton (1996, 233) argues that for the "settler," "the most important task is to keep the enemy at bay — whether the 'enemy' is the Catholic population, the Republic of Ireland, or those 'passing friends,' the fickle alien British." For loyalists, the lesson of the Troubles is that trusting the British is a precarious pastime; ultimately, as one song ("A Volunteer's Song") hints, loyalists are on their own:

> O comrades, this Ulster's a terrible sight,
> Where our heroes are hounded by day and by night,
> Where some are imprisoned and some are shot down
> By fenians and traitors and thugs of the Crown.

Armed Struggle

Faced with such odds, loyalists argue, they have no choice but to rely on violence: "Violence in settler societies, on the part of both settlers and 'natives,' is normal. Colonies were won and maintained by violence and the threat of violence. 'Native rebellion,' however, is painted as arising out of the primitive nature of the people rather than out of legitimate complaints. Settler violence, on the other hand, is often part of the structure of coercive domination, carried out by legally-constituted authorities, and is characterised merely as the upholding of 'law and order' which is necessary in any civilised society"[9] (Clayton 1996, 159). Often the threat of rebellion requires actions beyond the merely constitutional. But even then, as the songs argue, violence against those who threaten one's way of life is legitimate; now, as in the past, it is no more or less than self-defense:

> Whenever I was just a child upon my mother's knee,
> She told me I must always fight to keep my liberty.
> Her words in memory still come back right to this very day
> For freedom now is threatened by the rebel IRA.
>
> ("The Rise of the UDA," sung to the
> tune of the ballad "The Homes of Donegal")

There are many ways to defend oneself, including the ingenious "defending by attacking" referred to in "Shankill Will Be Shankill" (sung to the tune of "John Brown's Body"). This song refers to a real battle, when loyalists burned nationalist homes on the Falls Road in August 1969. Another song ("Ardoyne") refers to the same period:

> So, listen all you fenians, you rebels to the core,
> The next time you start trouble, Ardoyne will be no more.

So the songs are filled with stirring tales of countless battles, whether real — such as August 1969 — or fantastic, as in the claim of one song ("Bloody Sunday," sung to the tune of the popular song "Beautiful Sunday") that loyalists were involved in the massacre of civil rights marchers on Derry's Bloody Sunday, 30 January 1972.

> Taigs to army said, "It was you."
> Didn't know that I was there too.
> Hey, hey, hey it's a beautiful day.

Who is the enemy in this armed struggle? The IRA, rebels; as is already apparent, however, this easily comes to mean any "taig," "fenian," Catholic, nationalist:

> We have bombs, we have guns, we have fenians on the run,
> And the ones that we killed were all bastards, every one.
>
> ("Goodbye My Loyal Friend," sung to the
> tune of the popular ballad "Seasons in the Sun")

Catholics become fair game because they are all, in the title of one song by a group known as the Billy Boys, "double-crossing fenians." "Taigs are made to kill," in the words of the song quoted earlier ("I Was Born under the Union Jack") because they are "scum" and "animals." "Kill that rebel scum; don't you feel bad" is part of the chorus of "Don't Feel Bad" (quoted earlier); another track on the same tape, *In Memory of Joe Bratty,* urges: "There's no place that rebel scum can go; / When you pull that trigger, think of Joe" ("Fallen Hero," sung to the tune of Bette Midler's "The Wind Beneath My Wings"). In short, the "Enemies of Ulster" (to quote the title of one song) are not even human:

> They shoot and kill, then run away and crawl back to their den.
> These monsters are not human, they're not even men.
> But their time will come for, mark my words, they'll pay the price some day,
> For they will be cut down like the mad dogs they are by the men of the UDA.

Conclusion

It would appear that in many ways loyalist songs have developed little from the days of "Dolly's Brae"; their most common themes are still fear of attack, tales of battles won, and, most frighteningly of all, sectarian viciousness. In one sense that is probably not surprising. As a stark, easily intelligible statement of loyalist fears and isolation, they articulate the wider condition of loyalism. It would be remarkable if the songs were somehow less strident than the wider ideology from which they derive. There are those, such as Porter (1996), who argue convincingly that what unionism needs is an alternative vision. His belief is that this will come neither from the "cultural unionism" of loyalists or the more "liberal unionism" of the professional classes, but from a new strain which he calls "civic unionism." The case for a new vision is put equally convincingly by Brown (1985, 20): "A people who have known resistance as well as dissent, rebellion, dispute, religious enthusiasm in the midst of rural and urban deprivation, have an interesting story to tell of themselves — one of essential homelessness, dependency, anxiety, obdurate fantasising, sacrifices in the name of liberty, villainous political opportunism, moments of idealistic aspiration. And in the telling of it, they may come to realise at least where they are most at home and with whom they share that home." As yet, there are no loyalist songs that articulate that vision.

Notes

With thanks for help and encouragement to Louis Edmondson, Neil Jarman, May McCann, Paula McManus, and Mike Tomlinson, as well as the staff of the political collection in the Linenhall Library, Belfast.

1. Unionists are those who seek to preserve the political links between Northern Ireland and Britain; simply put, loyalists are the most militant unionists. As such they have been involved in military action throughout the last thirty years. As Sutton (1994, 201–2) points out, loyalists were responsible for 911 (or 28 percent) of the 3,285 deaths in the Northern Ireland conflict between 1969 and 1993. Of these, 713 (or 78 percent) were cases of sectarian murder, that is, "deliberate killing of Catholic civilians." Loyalist songs, it is argued here, provide a window into the mentality of loyalism. They do not necessarily reveal the subtleties of loyalist ideology wherein some groups perceive themselves as being on the political left, while others are more right-wing. Moreover, although loyalism shares a number of ideological components with unionism in general, this is not to say that every unionist would agree with the sentiments expressed in loyalist songs.

2. For a brief but comprehensive history of nationalist songs from the early seventeenth to the late nineteenth century, see McCann (1995, 54–62). The continuing popularity of songs from 1798 is evidenced in the production of a recent CD, "Who Fears to Speak," featuring singers, such as Liam Clancy, backed by the Irish Philharmonic Orchestra. Amazingly, the CD is produced by RTE, the state broadcasting organization, which assiduously suppressed the broadcast of these and other republican songs between 1971 and 1994. The final irony is that RTE is unwilling to broadcast tracks from its own CD because of their republican content!

3. " 'Invented tradition' is taken to mean a set of practices, normally governed by overtly or tacitly accepted rules and of a ritual or symbolic nature, that seek to inculcate certain values and norms of behaviour by repetition, which automatically implies continuity with the past" (Hobsbawm and Ranger 1983, 1).

4. "Party Tunes and Rebel Yells," part 1 of The Food of Love and Hate, BBC Radio Ulster, 26 February 1995.

5. "Party Tunes and Rebel Yells," part 1 of *The Food of Love and Hate*, BBC Radio Ulster, 26 February 1995.

6. "Taig," like "fenian," is a slang word for "Catholic."

7. In similar vein are the somewhat bizarre attempts of loyalist muralists to raid popular culture for images. Thus, for no apparent political reason, a mural in Ballymoney depicts Bart Simpson standing on the neck of a rat that has the head of Gerry Adams (see Rolston 1995, 18).

8. Aughey (1989, 28) is curt in his rejection of the Cruithin myth, dismissing it as "parochial self-indulgence. This is what nationalism is all about, but it need not absorb the energies of unionism."

9. This "lawful coercion," as O'Dowd (1990, 44) argues, rests ultimately on a belief in "the demerits of the 'natives.'" In the Irish case, the "settlers'" view of the "natives" as being lesser beings owes its origins in part to the metropolitan distinction between "civilization" and "barbarism," a distinction wittily observed by Deane (1983, 12) in his portrait of the "typical barbarian": "First he is Irish; next Catholic. . . . He is from an area of dirt and desolation, not to be equalled in Western Europe, a blot on the fair face of the United Kingdom. He drinks a lot for, since the Fenians, it has been a standard piece of English lore that all Irish guerrilla groups meet in pubs when they are not blowing them up. Sometimes, they manage to do both. Finally, and worst of all, he is sometimes a she."

Works Cited

Adamson, I. 1974. *The Cruithin: A history of the Ulster land and people.* Belfast: Pretani.

Aughey, A. 1989. *Under siege: Ulster Unionism and the Anglo-Irish Agreement.* Belfast: Blackstaff.

——. 1995. *Irish Kulturkampf.* Belfast: Ulster Young Unionist Council.

Barthes, R. 1968. *Elements of semiology.* New York: Hill and Wang.

Beattie, G. 1992. *We are the people: Journeys through the heart of Protestant Ulster.* London: Heinemann.

Belfrage, S. 1987. *The crack: A Belfast year.* London: André Deutsch.

Bell, D. 1990. *Acts of union: Youth culture and sectarianism in Northern Ireland.* London: Macmillan.

Bell, G. 1976. *The Protestants of Ulster.* London: Pluto.

Benjamin, W. 1977. *Illuminations.* London: Fontana.

Berman, D., S. Lalor, and B. Torode. 1983. The theology of the IRA. *Studies* 72 (Summer):137–44.

Breathnach-Lynch, S. 1997. The Easter Rising 1916: Constructing a canon in art and artifacts. *History Ireland* (Spring):37–42.

Brown, T. 1985. *The whole Protestant community: The making of a historical myth.* Derry: Field Day.

Bruce, S. 1992. *The red hand: Protestant paramilitaries in Northern Ireland.* Oxford: Oxford University Press.

———. 1994. *The edge of the union: The Ulster loyalist political vision.* Oxford: Oxford University Press.

Bryson, L., and C. McCartney. 1994. *Clashing symbols? A report on the use of flags, anthems and other national symbols in Northern Ireland.* Belfast: Institute of Irish Studies.

Clayton, P. 1996. *Enemies and passing friends: Settler ideologies in twentieth-century Ulster.* London: Pluto.

Davis, R. 1994. *Mirror hate: The convergent ideology of Northern Ireland paramilitaries, 1966–1992.* Aldershot: Dartmouth Publishing.

Deane, S. 1983. *Civilians and barbarians.* Derry: Field Day.

Denselow, R. 1989. *When the music's over: The story of political pop.* London: Faber and Faber.

Finlayson, A. 1996. Nationalism as ideological interpellation: The case of Ulster loyalism. *Ethnic and Racial Studies* 19:88–111.

Frith, S. 1988. *Music for pleasure.* Brighton: Polity.

Hobsbawm, E., and T. Ranger, eds. 1983. *The invention of tradition.* Cambridge: Cambridge University Press.

Jarman, N. 1997. *Material conflicts: Parades and visual displays in Northern Ireland.* Oxford: Berg.

Kearney, R. 1984. *Myth and motherland.* Derry: Field Day.

Kiberd, D. 1991. The elephant of revolutionary forgetfulness. In *Revising the Rising,* edited by M. Ní Dhonnchadha and T. Dorgan, 1–20. Derry: Field Day.

MacDonagh, O. 1983. *States of mind.* London: Allen and Unwin.

McAuley, J. 1994. *The politics of identity: A loyalist community in Belfast.* Aldershot: Avebury.

McCann, M. 1989. Making history? Songs of "the Troubles." In *Musique, Histoire, Democratie,* 1:193–208. Paris: Editions de la Maison des Sciences de l'Homme.

———. 1995. Music and politics in Ireland: The specificity of the folk revival in Belfast. *British Journal of Ethnomusicology* 4:51–75.

McNamee, P. ed. 1991. *Traditional music: Whose music?* Belfast: Institute of Irish Studies.

Munck, R., and B. Rolston. 1987. *Belfast in the thirties: An oral history.* Belfast: Blackstaff.

Nelson, S. 1984. *Ulster's uncertain defenders: Loyalists and the Northern Ireland conflict.* Belfast: Appletree.

O'Dowd, L. 1990. Introduction. In *The coloniser and the colonized* by A. Memmi, 29–66. London: Earthscan.

———. 1991. Intellectuals and political culture: a unionist-nationalist comparison. In *Culture and Politics in Northern Ireland,* edited by E. Hughes, 151–73. Milton Keynes: Open University Press.

Porter, N. 1996. *Rethinking unionism: An alternative vision of Northern Ireland.* Belfast: Blackstaff.

Rolston, B. 1995. *Drawing support 2: Murals of war and peace.* Belfast: Beyond the Pale.

Ruane, J., and R. Todd. 1996. *The dynamics of conflict in Northern Ireland: Power, conflict and emancipation.* Cambridge: Cambridge University Press.

Sutton, M. 1994. *Bear in mind these dead: An index of deaths from the conflict in Ireland, 1969–1993.* Belfast: Beyond the Pale.

Whitfield, É. 1990. Another martyr for Old Ireland: The balladry of revolution. In *Revolution? Ireland, 1917–1923,* edited by D. Fitzpatrick, 60–68. Dublin: Trinity History Workshop.

Songbooks

Lilliburlero. 1988. Craigavon: Ulster Society.

Loyalist song book. N.d. Scotland: n.p.

The loyalist song book. N.d. Belfast: Ulster Defence Association.

The Orange Cross book of songs, poems and verse. 1972. Belfast: Orange Cross.

The orange lark. 1987. Craigavon: Ulster Society.

Orange loyalist songs. 1970. Belfast: Shankill Defence Association.

Orange loyalist songs. 1971. Belfast: Shankill Defence Association.

Orange loyalist songs. 1972. Belfast: Shankill Defence Association.

Orange songs and ballads. 1976. London: Toman Music.

That's Ulster. N.d.: n.p.

The UDA Detainee Song Book. 1974. Belfast: Ulster Defence Association.

Still "No Surrender"?
New Loyalism and the Peace Process in Ireland

I think nationality is based a lot on emotion and is based a lot on a person's natural identity and affinity. People can change, but the reality is that the vast majority of people in Northern Ireland were born British, see themselves as British, have a British heritage, have grandparents who died at the Somme so they could remain British. They are, therefore, extremely loyal to their interpretation of what Britain is and what it means to them.

— Ian Paisley Jr., DUP (*Observer,* 11 December 1997)

The fight is for the Union!

— Ian Paisley Sr., DUP (*Belfast Telegraph,* 1 December 1997)

Consternation, induced by the perceived treachery and duplicity of the British government, underlies much of the negative reaction of Ulster loyalism to contemporary events in Ireland. Many loyalists firmly believe that the British administration has neatly fallen in step with a "peace process" that is inspired and motivated by an amalgam of political forces, including the Irish government, the Irish-American lobby, the Social and Democratic and Labour Party (SDLP) and, of course, the Irish republican movement. Two political parties, the Democratic Unionist Party (DUP) and the United Kingdom Unionist Party (UKUP), have made it clear that they will not sign on to any negotiation or political process that includes republicans. Indeed, at the time of writing, neither DUP nor UKUP have been directly involved in the peace process. While the largest unionist political group, the Ulster Unionist Party (UUP), engaged in multiparty talks that included Sinn Fein and led to the recent peace agreement, there remains much internal dissension concerning this decision to support the peace process. Within the larger unionist community, it is those political groups representing the loyalist paramilitary organizations, the Progressive Unionist Party

(PUP) and the Ulster Democratic Party (UDP), that have most consistently been prepared to promote unionist involvement in a negotiated settlement.

So how can we best understand these Ulster loyalists? To begin, it is important to understand the construction of loyalist identities as part of a fluid process. Part of this identity has been manifest, at times, in political violence. Such violence, however, is only one expression of widespread social divisions in Northern Ireland. Others include high levels of physical and social segregation that result, through a process of collective remembering, in the communal construction of self-generating values, myths and political norms (Middleton and Edwards, 1990). This process of social construction is noteworthy for strength and historical consistency. Remembered victories and scenes of resistance have been enacted and reenacted in Protestant working-class districts of Northern Ireland for more than fifty years. A recent observation illustrates this well: "The symbolism of . . . Protestant victory remains deeply rooted today as Protestants see themselves under threat from a British government prepared to do business with the Irish Republic under the aegis of the Anglo-Irish Agreement and the developing 'Peace Process.' There's a huge slogan painted on the walls of the Protestant Fountain estate, within Derry's ancient city walls that says, '1998 — Londonderry Still Under Siege' " (Taylor 1989, 118).

In contrast to what we have seen in the past, one of the most important outcomes of the contemporary peace process has been the emergence within larger unionism of a coherent political voice opposing, or at the very least seeking to reformulate, some of unionism's key tenets. A new set of voices, openly profane, liberal, and sometimes class-aware, has been strongly heard from within loyalism. Is it possible then to talk of progressive political mutations and the development of a "new loyalism" within the unionist community? If so, how does this new loyalist ideology differ from traditional loyalism?

This essay addresses some of these questions by considering the major perspectives of loyalist representatives. It reviews the development of the Progressive Unionist Party and the Ulster Democratic Party, the two major political organizations that represent "new loyalism," and highlights important differences between these new political groups and other major representatives of loyalism, particularly Ian Paisley's Democratic Unionist Party. It further considers some of the resulting conflicts and tensions within unionism and loyalism, particularly in relation to the peace process and the search for political settlement. Through this analysis, the essay identifies the differing voices that currently compete in the structuration of loyalism as a social movement.

The Politics of Loyalism

To begin, it is necessary to outline and examine some of the differing options that are currently presented to Ulster loyalists. The genesis and development of those parties most closely associated with loyalist paramilitary groups, PUP and UDP, can be directly compared with DUP, the political group that has dominated Ulster loyalism for over two decades.

The origins of PUP can be traced back to 1977 and an attempt at politicization by sections of the Ulster Volunteer Force (UVF). This resulted in a group, initially based in Belfast's Shankill area and known as the Independent Unionist Group, that in 1979 became the PUP (Flackes 1980). From the beginning, PUP sought to locate politics directly in the working class, which the group claimed had been underrepresented and misrepresented by traditional unionist leadership. Indeed, the contemporary period has often revealed overt antagonism between PUP and the unionist politicians of UUP and DUP. As Cusack and McDonald (1997) have demonstrated, PUP leaders regarded the failure of the unionist establishment to formulate an effective campaign against the 1985 Anglo-Irish Agreement as a watershed in unionist politics. As they put it, "UVF and PUP already harboured a mistrust about parties like the DUP ever since the failure of the 1977 Ulster Workers Strike. Now those suspicions were transformed into deep hostility and mistrust" (Cusack and McDonald, 254).

Since then, PUP has set about formulating policies distinct from mainstream unionism. It is possible to characterize some of the central features of contemporary PUP thinking as reflecting overt concern for Protestant working-class issues. For example, PUP describes itself as a party for the common people, and projects itself as "pre-Blairite British Labour" in orientation. Its views also include a belief in the sharing of responsibility between unionists and nationalists in any future governance of Northern Ireland. Indeed, PUP has sought a compromise with Irish nationalists on the grounds that they are "a sizable minority and 'fellow citizens'" (PUP, Support the Progressive Unionists, *Election Communication,* Forum Election 1996, 1). Therefore, PUP has argued, the representatives of Irish nationalism must have an executive role in the formulation of any legislature and has actively promoted a bill of rights for Northern Ireland (PUP, Support the Progressive Unionists, *Election Communication,* Forum Election 1996).

Furthermore, recent PUP literature has promoted core ideas such as commonality, equality, and plurality among all of Northern Ireland's citizens (Progressive Unionist Party, *Manifesto for the Forum Election* 1996). Hence, the party claims that it is antisectarian and that one of its main goals is to bring about an equitable Northern Irish society. The PUP has further described itself as an organization that seeks to represent and attract support from the working class, the nonworking class, and the underclass, and one that is based on membership open to any citizen of Northern Ireland regardless of creed or color (PUP, *Manifesto for the Forum Election* 1996).

The PUP, of course, strongly supports the continuance of the union with Great Britain, and claims that it is this constitutional arrangement that is best for all the people of Northern Ireland and for their future well-being. The party has stated, and shown in its support of the April 1998 British-Irish agreement, that it is prepared to cooperate voluntarily with the Irish Republic on matters of mutual concern. Leaders believe that there should be a break with earlier divisive practices that caused suffering among ordinary people from both communities: "It has been mostly working class people who have borne the brunt of the violence over the past twenty-five years and more and they are sick and tired of political saber rattling and mischievousness from whatever quarter. There can never, ever, be a return to the awful political and social abuses of the past and Stormont as we knew it is dead and gone, never to be resurrected. We would oppose as vehemently as anyone else a return to such a divisive and partisan system of government." (PUP, Support the Progressive Unionists, *Election Communication,* Forum Elections 1996, 1).

The other main political group, based like PUP in the paramilitary organizations, that has found wider support within the working class Protestant areas is the Ulster Democratic Party. The UDP's direct ancestry can also be traced to the mid-1970s and the development of a political movement within the Ulster Defence Association (UDA) (Mc-

Auley 1991a, 1991b, 1994a, 1995a, 1996b). The new political direction of UDA was first made transparent in the 1970s by the formation of the New Ulster Political Research Group (NUPRG) which strongly promoted, in their policy document *Beyond the Religious Divide* (1979), the idea of a negotiated "Independent Ulster." Throughout the 1970s and the 1980s, UDA continued to promote this notion along with the idea of a shared identity between Protestant and Catholic as the basis for conflict settlement in Northern Ireland. These concepts were reworked in light of the 1985 Anglo-Irish Agreement and republished as the *Commonsense* document (Ulster Political Research Group 1987). It was written largely by two paramilitary leaders, John McMichael and Harry Smallwood, and among its central proposals was the reestablishment of a devolved power-sharing government in Northern Ireland.

This position still constitutes the core of UDA's official political agenda, as expressed by UDP, although the party subsequently added a proposal for the establishment of a Council of the British Isles as a means of pursuing better relations and mutually beneficial cooperation across both islands. The consistency of UDP thinking in this respect is visible in its support for the British-Irish agreement that proposes (as strand 3 of the document) a British-Irish Council to be composed of representatives from Britain, Ireland, Scotland, Wales, and Northern Ireland and designed to "promote harmony" among the peoples of the British and Irish islands (http://solution.unite.net/customers/alliance/agreement). Another consistent discourse of UDP has been a criticism of established unionist leaders and their failure to represent working-class loyalism properly. In this context UDP has declared its major aim as giving voice to those who have been without proper representation for the past quarter-century. As UDP puts it, "our community has been plagued with political leaders who refuse to lead" (UDP, *Election communication*, Forum Election 1996, 1).

Such statements represent a barely disguised attack on the Democratic Unionist Party and the political effectiveness of the Reverend Ian Paisley. The DUP, which has always claimed to be the last line of defense for the Protestant working class against Ulster's enemies, has therefore seen the growing eminence of UDP, and especially PUP, as a direct challenge to this self-appointed status. Increasingly, this can be seen in the lexicon of DUP's response and the party's ever-increasing discourse of deceit and deception — terms that are applied by DUP to almost all other political groups involved in Northern Irish politics — both within and far beyond the boundaries of unionism. Such rhetoric highlights views that have been consistently apparent in DUP ideology throughout the party's existence. DUP supporters have continued to promote the view that the union is in danger of erosion, particularly in relation to the peace process and the developing relationship between the British and Irish governments.

Such a view was demonstrated in the DUP approach to the 1996 Forum election, when the party stood on an abstentionist ticket, claiming that the whole process was designed to negotiate away the very future of Ulster (Democratic Unionist Party 1996), and again in its denunciations of the British-Irish peace accord (http://www.dup.org. uk/index.htm). In the run-up to the Forum election, DUP in typical style offered an unbreakable covenant with the Ulster people, the purpose of which was to ensure that Northern Ireland's constitutional position was recognized without ambiguity. Elsewhere, DUP promoted the establishment of democratic and accountable structures of government for Ulster and demanded that IRA/Sinn Fein dismantle its terrorist machine, arguing that what was needed was the defeat of the terrorists, "not some accommodation with them" (Democratic Unionist Party 1996, 1). In the 1997 U.K. general election, which DUP claimed was the "most important election since the setting up of the Ulster state," the party argued that "a vote for the DUP . . . is a vote for consistent traditional Unionism that has no truck with Sinn Fein/IRA. It is a vote to keep Ulster firmly within the Union with proper democratic structures and no interference from Dublin" (*New Protestant Telegraph* 1997, 1).

Underpinning this representation is the clearly articulated belief that the union is being weakened. Any move toward negotiated settlement has constantly been referred to as the first step on a shortening road to a united Ireland. Such discourse incites anxiety and alarm across all factions of the larger unionist community. What is more, DUP consistently seeks to highlight a process that the party identifies as a congruous plan to degrade unionist culture as part of an agenda to move Northern Ireland out of the union. Hence, DUP leader Peter Robinson has outlined what he sees as some of the major results of the peace process. For him, unionists "are being spoon-fed 'Irishness.' They are weaned off their 'Britishness' to prepare them for their intended destination. Anything and everything British must be expunged from the Province's daily life. The National Anthem, the Union Jack, the Queen's portrait, Orange culture and unionist traditions have become targets for extinction and demonisation. Even the act of remembering our gallant dead of two world wars is subject to a nationalist veto. Unionist must be made to feel guilty—embarrassed to expound unionist principles. Wholesome unionist values taught and nurtured for generations are rendered sectarian, right-wing, old fashioned, extreme and backward" (DUP *Press Release*, no. 27, 1997, 1).

Such ideas are increasing in strength and influence within many sections of the unionist community. Despite new loyalism's considerable ideological innovations, many still subscribe to the familiar tenets of traditional unionist thinking. As the main publication of the Orange Order (The Loyal Orange Institution of Ireland) put it: "Unionists are not naive and they realise that due to the Anglo-Irish Agreement and the establishment of Maryfield, the people of this Province are being subjected to a daily diet of 'Irish' events and every effort is being made to try and make British Ulster people feel more Irish than British . . . it is irritating that so many people of influence seem to believe that if they keep on trying to remind Ulster people of their Irishness it will somehow dilute their pride in being British" (*Orange Standard*, December 1997, 1).

This thinking mirrors other views within the unionist community. There is even some evidence that these perspectives may be becoming widespread within mainstream unionism, absorbing those who have previously been hostile to the DUP analysis. The concern that the British government has allowed a foreign administration a key role in the political development of a part of the United Kingdom remains central for many loyalists who are resistant to the peace process. This concern can be seen clearly in the following statement from UDP: "What is being implicitly demanded, if not politically and economically reinforced by the British government is a compromise on our citizenship. The British government has for seventy five years qualified, and therefore delegitimised NI's membership of the UK. The IRA's bloody campaign of terrorism, not least those carried out in England, along with various international pressures have forced successive governments to give Dublin an increasing role in NI affairs" (UDP *Press Release*, no. 19, November 1996, 1).

There remain tangible tensions within loyalism. The politics of PUP and UDP, and the antithesis of DUP, have become primary in a struggle to redefine loyalism and unionism. At its most fundamental level, loyalism has always rested on its sense of cultural separateness and political distinctiveness, expressed through the social identity of Britishness (Bew, Gibbon, and Patterson 1995; Coulter 1994, 1997; English and Walker 1996; Gilligan and Tonge 1997; Hall 1994, 1995; McAuley 1994a, 1995b, 1996a, 1996b. 1997a, 1997b; Porter 1996; Ruane and Todd 1996; Shirlow and McGovern 1997; Todd 1987, 1994). In the contemporary period the fluidity of political and cultural expression of Britishness has been demonstrated. One result has been the contrary visions of unionism forwarded by different political groups. Yet another result has been a degree of internal reflection far from commonplace in the history of unionism. Within working-class districts a combination of political forces, originating among ex-paramilitary prisoners, local councillors, community activists, and members of UDP and PUP, has demonstrated a challenge to the hegemonic position of DUP. The broad contours of much of the discourse, although always unionist at its core, have been self-critical and pluralistic. It was expressed well by those in the Shankill Think Tank (1995) who have argued that intercommunity dialogue provides the most realistic basis from which to develop a solution to the conflict.

Partly in response to this community feeling, the loyalist parties of the UDP and PUP have sought to stretch the distance between themselves and the more established representatives of unionism. PUP in the 1996 Forum election claimed, for example, that the "real issues" were missing from political debate. The party strongly restated its commitment to Northern Ireland's position within the United Kingdom but defended the right of any group to seek constitutional change by democratic, legitimate, and peaceful means. Elsewhere, the Progressive Unionists promoted a new constitution and a Bill of Rights for Northern Ireland that would contain safeguards and mechanisms for the protection of individuals, associations, and minorities (PUP, Support the Progressive Unionists, *Election Communication,* Forum Election 1996).

The period of the peace process has continued to reveal friction between the representatives of the paramilitaries and established unionist politicians. Many within the paramilitary organizations have continued to blame established unionist leaders for their involvement in the conflict. Hence, at the UDP annual conference in March 1997, a statement from prisoners of UDA and UFF (Ulster Freedom Fighters) directly condemned the role played by unionist politicians when it said the "so-called recognised Unionist parties are now learning that the Protestant people have woken up to the phony politics that have been preached by our outdated politicians" (*Irish Times*, 24 March 1997).

Importantly for the future development of loyalist politics, UDP and PUP have increasingly argued that DUP is tactically limited and at best misguided in the strategies the party uses. The political representatives of the loyalist paramilitaries are thus in direct competition with the DUP for the allegiance of Protestant working-class loyalists. The ideological and pragmatic conflicts between the two groups have continued throughout the period of the peace process. Ian Paisley, for example, has referred to both PUP and UDP as dupes of government policy. Another leading DUP member, Sammy Wilson, has claimed that PUP is in the pocket of the Northern Ireland Office (*Belfast Telegraph*, 23 July 1997). The UDP leader Gary McMichael has, in turn, accused DUP of "failing in its duty" by absenting itself from the debate, while David Ervine of the PUP has argued that DUP deserted Northern Ireland during its time of greatest need (*Belfast Telegraph*, 23 July 1997). Indeed, the reality that Sinn Fein has been involved in the formal negotiating process, and the boycott of these talks by DUP and UKUP, has only brought the difference between loyalist political leaders into sharper relief. Both of these parties claim they are taking the best route towards defending Ulster's interests.

There are those who see themselves as Ulster's defenders in much more candid terms. Throughout most of the period of the peace process, the concerns of the main loyalist paramilitary groups have been voiced by the Combined Loyalist Military Command (CLMC), which was formed as an umbrella organization to represent the major loyalist paramilitary groups, including UVF, RHC (the Red Hand Commandos), and UFF. It did so from the declaration of the loyalist cease-fires in October 1994 until October 1997 when the UFF withdrew, seemingly because of internal tensions. Throughout that time, the loyalist paramilitaries, albeit sometimes reluctantly, fell in line with the politicized leadership of PUP and UDP.

Others beyond this umbrella organization, however, have consistently promoted loyalist armed resistance. Central among these has been the Loyalist Volunteer Force (LVF) which, since its formation in 1996, has drawn support from discontented loyalist paramilitaries, including the most sectarian elements of the main loyalist paramilitary organizations, the UDA and UVF. The willingness of this section of paramilitary loyalism to take violent action was brought into frightening reality in the wave of sectarian murders that followed the December 1997 killing of LVF leader Billy Wright by the Irish National Liberation Army (INLA).

Indeed, although both the UDA and UVF have claimed to maintain their formal ceasefire, there has been some movement toward violence by all the loyalist paramilitary groups (Cusack and McDonald 1997). This, in part, reflected discontent from within the loyalist paramilitary ranks about the direction of the peace process. UDA prison leaders have complained that the talks worked to a republican agenda that has resulted in considerable concessions to Sinn Fein and IRA. This has given rise to a further set of concerns within loyalism, most often expressed in terms of the demotion and dilution of unionist culture. Such concerns are expressed in the following statement from loyalist prisoners: "We are now in the fourth year of our loyalist ceasefire and we acknowledge that the Talks in their present form are working to a Republican agenda of appeasement and constant concession to Sinn Fein/IRA. We have witnessed Government concessions to the Republicans on all fronts, be it a reduction in security levels or the erosion of political and cultural identity. We ask, therefore, where is the parity of esteem for loyalism and its prisoners of the conflict?" (*Belfast Telegraph*, 23 December 1997, 1).

A UVF statement echoes these concerns: "We have once again witnessed on the part of the British Government a reluctance to accept Loyalism as having a legitimate culture. Time and time again Nationalist/Republicans have been appeased by the governing bodies who seem to believe that acts of nationalism stem from a wide cultural base, but anything Loyalist is simply sectarian" (*Combat Christmas Issue 1997*, 5). This interpretation has filtered through many layers of loyalism and takes an extreme form in the statement by LVF supporters that "for the last 4 years we, and other True Loyalists, have stated time and time again that there is nothing in the 'Peace Process' for Ulster Protestants, pointing out that the whole process is designed to weaken the political, social economic and cultural links between Northern Ireland and the rest of the United Kingdom. At the same time, the three governments (British, Irish and American) intend creating dynamic 'North/South' bodies with substantial powers which will ultimately be the foundation stones for All Ireland/United Ireland administration/government" (*Rank and File Issue* 22:1). The future political and paramilitary direction of unionism and loyalism will be determined in large part by the outcome of the struggle between those who accept, however reluctantly, the peace process as a basis for settlement and those who see it as a "sellout" that merits a military response.

A Changing Loyalism?

While the analysis above may suggest some political movement, the most important question is whether the views of the UDP and PUP mark a permanent rupture within loyalist ideology. Certainly the UDP and PUP have remained highly critical of traditional unionism and, more particularly, the political leadership of Ian Paisley. Furthermore, since UDP and PUP together attracted almost 10 percent of the combined unionist and loyalist vote in the 1996 Forum election, there is identifiable electoral support for their political position. It is, therefore, increasingly difficult to dismiss them, as several mainstream unionists have sought to, as merely representing the margins of loyalist politics. Meanwhile, both PUP and UDP continue to claim that it is they who best reflect the thinking of the broader working-class loyalist community.

There are indications that the new loyalist parties may be willing to undertake some reconstruction of loyalism, both by contesting the legitimacy of DUP and in seeking to formulate a new approach to politics in Northern Ireland. The UDP, for example, has argued that traditional unionism must adopt a broader vista and integrate more fully with politics in the rest of the United Kingdom: "Unionism must decide what it believes is the best way forward for the people of the UK in coming years. It must seriously consider throwing in its lot with those who would democratise the UK state, destroying the power of the Establishment to deny the people of Northern Ireland their rights" (UDP, *Election communication*, Forum Election, 1996, 1).

So, while there has clearly been social and political movement within loyalism, its extent needs to be carefully assessed. There are still those who are more than willing to reengage, both politically and militarily, with unionism's traditional agenda. Many loyalists still perceive their core political and social identity as being endangered. Indeed, even those who are otherwise positive toward the peace process have at times demonstrated this belief. UDP leader Gary McMichael, for example, recently highlighted the importance of such loyalist concerns in any future political development when he said that republicans "must learn that it is not the British government with whom peace must be negotiated, it is the other democratic representatives who disagree with Sinn Fein's analysis . . . it is people like me . . . with whom they must learn to share Northern Ireland, it is me and the rest of the population who will not accept the analysis and will not accept Irish unity" (*Irish Times*, 24 February 1997).

The major problem surrounding the Protestant working class, however, remains the ability of loyalist sectarian consciousness to structure people's lives. Members and supporters of PUP and UDP have not necessarily superseded sectarianism, but the peace process has brought into relief the nature of the relationships that exist between loyalist political representatives and the Protestant working class. The eventual direction and force of loyalist reaction to the peace process will be determined, in some degree, by the outcome of negotiations between these two groups. It is, therefore, important to identify and consider some of the ideological and political alternatives on offer to contemporary loyalism and unionism.

Without doubt some of the strongest arguments promoting a cultural pluralism — and possibly some form of political accommodation with Irish nationalism — are those that emerge from sections of paramilitary loyalism. Such groups draw directly on the values of traditional working-class communities. The response of many loyalists to the peace process can only be understood in the context of a disintegrating social world that has involved the removal of political responsibility, economic decline, deindustrialization, political disarticulation, and ideological fragmentation (Belfast Community Economic Conference 1995; Community Development in Protestant Areas 1991, 1993; Gallagher 1991; Lower Ravenhill Community Association 1991; Shirlow and McGovern 1997).

All of these processes have served to expose further incongruities in relationships between Protestant workers and their loyalty to the state. Until recently, any criticism offered by the Protestant working class of social, economic, or political issues was open to accusations of disloyalty from mainstream unionism. The PUP and DUP thus have provided focal points for increasingly coherent challenges to accepted unionist ideology; however, while the peace process has enabled the parties to open up debate within working-class communities, new loyalists have not weakened their commitment to the union. Their current position should be seen in the context of renegotiating the ideological terms that for them best express their identity. In the absence of overt violent conflict, and in the presence of changing social conditions, the expression of a more class-based politics has become possible. The fact that deliberation is taking place at all should not be underestimated. As McKittrick (1994) has pointed out, the years of Stormont control robbed the community of much political skill to the point where its leaders have come to regard even the idea of discussion as dangerous.

The traditional discourses that legitimize the union as a defense of political and cultural identity, and as security against internal and external threat, are broadly accepted by unionists and loyalists from all social groups. In loyalist and unionist ideologies, past experiences are understood through the construction of narratives that reshape the past in direct response to current perspectives, needs, and desires. This constructed memory seeks to match the past with the present. The peace process, by emphasizing many of the internal contradictions within unionism, has exposed different, often conflicting but sometimes overlapping interpretations, all of which seek to shape Ulster Protestants' relationship to the union.

Political developments within loyalist communities have attracted groups that, in the past, have been excluded from political debate. One such group is women from unionist and loyalist backgrounds. While they form a highly diverse category, most women share a common experience of exclusion from the public arena of politics. The Troubles and a particular interpretation of Christian ideology have both reinforced the subordinate position of women (Edgerton 1986; McAuley 1994a; McKiernan and McWilliams 1997; Morgan 1995; Northern Ireland Women's Coalition 1996; Sales 1997; Walker 1997). As Dunne (*everywoman* 1996, 14) puts it: "Northern Ireland's politics have always been dominated by men. . . . The male face in Northern Ireland is incredibly divisive, not just between the communities but within them."

There is, however, recent evidence that women from loyalist backgrounds have increasingly created the opportunity to discuss their own identity and social relations in a more meaningful way. This movement has occurred partly as a direct result of the relative absence of overt paramilitary violence, as was certainly the case in the period immediately following the first IRA cease-fire. There seems to be at least the potential for many more women to become engaged in politics, particularly at the community level. As Walker has indicated: "the (relative) silencing of the guns has opened up a massive amount of talking where many women and men came forward with ideas about how to rectify the political impasse" (Walker 1997, 3).

Furthermore, as Sales (1997) shows, there has been a rapid growth of campaign groups, based on issues of particular interest to women in Northern Ireland, that have made a difference at the local level. An indication of this dynamic in cross-community politics has been the formation of the Northern Ireland Women's Coalition (NIWC) that contested the 1996 Forum elections, finished within the top ten parties, and thus qualified for two seats at the peace talks. The NIWC stood on a manifesto of reconciliation, accommodation, and inclusion as "a non-sectarian, broad-based coalition of women of all political hues and religions" (Northern Ireland Women's Coalition 1996). However, there is still need for caution in estimating the progress of women in politics. While the "development of cross-community links has allowed some valuable work to be done . . . formal politics in Northern Ireland remains dominated by men" (Sales 1997, 202).

Contested Unionism

The processes of reconstruction have not been confined to the working-class Protestant community alone. An important aspect of contemporary unionism is the increasingly articulate voice of the unionist middle classes. One example of this process has been the growing prominence of the United Kingdom Unionist Party. Its leader, Robert McCartney, has articulated a view of the peace process as part of a broad-ranging conspiracy against unionists and the union itself, the main purpose of this process being to create a functionally united Ireland (*Irish Times*, 26 January 1998). Thus, the suspension of violence by the IRA was only part of a much grander plan, a necessary precondition for selling the peace process to unionists and convincing them of its merits. The

UKUP, therefore, projects the view that the British government has sought, from the outset of the peace process, to offer terms for a conditional surrender of the IRA. McCartney argues that peace on these conditions could have been obtained at any time over the past twenty-five years (*Belfast Telegraph*, 19 June 1995).

Taking this as a starting point, McCartney has made some important criticisms of unionism (*Belfast Newsletter*, 7 March 1995). Since the formation of the state of Northern Ireland, he argues, the Ulster Unionist Party has relied on paranoia about Northern Ireland's place within the United Kingdom. One manifestation of this constructed constitutional anxiety was extreme sectarian loyalism. McCartney challenges this tradition and argues that if the benefits of the union are to be made clear and the union is to be preserved, then unionism must move away from its sectarian past to present a moderate, nonsectarian ideology, dedicated to resisting forces that pressure unionists in a direction they do not want to go (*Irish Times*, 3 May 1996).

The U.K. Unionists believe that the best that unionism can expect from the peace process is some stay of execution. McCartney believes that, for the British government, the main objective of the process continues to be a resolution of the conflict between Sinn Fein/IRA and the British state. His perception is that the British government wishes to disengage from Northern Ireland: "This is not only fundamental Labour Party policy, it was thought necessary, in pragmatic terms, by the Conservatives in order to resolve the conflict with Sinn Fein and safeguard the City of London" (*Irish Times*, 26 January 1998, 1).

Hence, UKUP believes that the future well-being of all the people of Northern Ireland has become subordinate to the need to appease terrorism. The peace process has raised Irish nationalist expectations to unrealistic heights and thus deepened the resentment of unionists through "an increasing awareness that their culture, their education, their tradition, the future values of their children and the symbols of their British identity are being systematically eroded to meet the requirements of violent republicanism" (*Irish Times*, 8 December 1997). This, for the UKUP, is the grand strategy to which the British and Irish governments, the United States administration, and SDLP have all devoted enormous energy. It is the blueprint for a united Ireland that, if successful, will render ultimate consent to a transfer of de jure sovereignty inevitable.

The leadership of the UKUP further believes that the peace process is designed not only to separate Northern Ireland from the rest of the United Kingdom, but also to sedate unionist opposition by a gradual process of all-Ireland harmonization. A cessation of violence and the promise of social and economic benefit are essential to persuade unionists to accept the inevitable greening of their cultural and political identity. As the UKUP argues: "Both governments, for their separate reasons, want a time-phased evolving scheme in which unionist acquiescence is obtained to a gradual replacement of their British identity with an Irish one. The Joint Declaration and the Framework Document represent the medium for achieving this objective, and central to its success are all-Ireland institutions with a dynamic for expansion, coupled with an escalating harmonisation in all spheres of social, political, educational and economic activity" (*Irish Times*, 26 January 1998, 1).

DUP and UKUP thus have forged a common position on the purpose of the Joint Declaration, the Framework Documents, the multiparty talks, and the proposals contained in the April 1998 British-Irish agreement. One manifestation of this has been a series of provincewide "United Kingdom Rallies" designed to coordinate opposition to the peace process. For both the UKUP and DUP, the future of the union is compromised by any peace package that contains elements of the Framework proposals as the basis of a settlement. It is this shared understanding that, for both parties, explains and justifies their absence from negotiations.

Such broad concerns have been reflected in another recent unionist phenomenon: the promotion by a loose grouping of unionist academics, historians, and intellectuals of the link between Northern Ireland and Great Britain. For example, the Cardogan Group formed in 1991 to challenge, in their words, the received wisdom that a solution can be found only within a nationalist framework (Cardogan Group 1992, 1994, 1995, 1996). Other academics (Aughey 1994, 1995; Foster 1995; Nesbitt 1995; Porter 1996) and several leading Irish opinion writers and polemicists (for example, Ruth Dudley Edwards and Eoghan Harris) have mirrored this perspective. Central to their argument is the view that unionists themselves have been extremely poor ambassadors for their own cause.

A key task for this group is to counter a notion that they believe has become a "dogma" among Irish republicans: namely, that the union of Northern Ireland with Great Britain is merely a convenient and barterable political arrangement. For these unionists, this reading of political history is rooted in the understanding and policies of the major British political parties and the worldwide media. This reading they strongly reject. For them, the union is a fundamental expression of the "realities" of the Irish situation. These writers offer a differing understanding of the union as a superior arrangement that reflects the political, economic, social, and cultural values of unionism.

The "Crisis" for Loyalism

Ulster unionists and loyalists are thus fragmented in their interpretations of contemporary events. The vast majority seeks an end to violence and a "peaceful" future; all still believe that it is the union that best guarantees their well-being. There is, however, a growing feeling among unionists that their whole social and political world is in danger and notions of "crisis" and "unionist alienation" have come to the fore. The DUP, for example, has argued that the British government has forsaken Northern Ireland (*New Protestant Telegraph*, June 1995) and that the sole aim of IRA/Sinn Fein is, "to coerce Northern Ireland into the Republic . . . their feigned new peacemaker image . . . [is] simply a tactical ploy to extort bottomless concessions from the government" (*Irish News*, 26 January 1998, 5).

The need to respond to this perceived crisis is what currently structures loyalism. While in the past DUP best articulated the concerns of working-class loyalism, more recently DUP support has been far from universal in this segment of Northern Irish society. Some key groups within the Protestant working class have always looked elsewhere for political expression. One example is the paramilitary organizations; another, those who have found political expression at the level of community politics. Both have set about constructing a new vision for loyalist politics. As John White, a spokesperson for UDP puts it: "Loyalism today stands for political empowerment of the people. It stands for an end to deprivation in Protestant working-class areas. Loyalists look forward towards a future for Northern Ireland—a future in which society will be equitable and just. Today, Loyalism is the only credible alternative to the bankrupt political establishment—a positive, vibrant, innovative and courageous form of Unionism" (*New Ulster Defender,* 4 December 1997, 13).

These views have given rise to tensions that have been reflected in a series of statements made by Ian Paisley, in which he has been antagonistic to the leaders of both PUP and UDP, particularly for their willingness to enter debate with political opponents (*Belfast Telegraph,* 14 October 1994 and 18 October 1994). For the DUP leader any form of negotiation, whether with republicans, or with the British or Irish governments, represents weakness and surrender. Thus, Paisley has claimed that 1997 marked a year of capitulation and concessions to republicanism (*Irish News,* 26 January 1998). His claim is that the British government can no longer be trusted to secure Northern Ireland's future in the United Kingdom and that the present Labour government, as was true of the previous Major administration, seeks to deceive unionists into accepting something that will undermine their British identity and weaken their constitutional position within the United Kingdom. As Paisley himself put it: "The Blair government's plan to sacrifice Ulster's constitutional position on the altar of political expediency is part of a cowardly, underhand deal with the IRA to escape a mainland bombing campaign. To achieve this the issue of consent has been surreptitiously divested of any geographical or numerical definition, so that the government could connive to omit completely the issue of the union from the most recently concocted road map pointing to Dublin, namely the Heads of Agreement proposals, in which the detested, rejected and unworkable Framework Document returns to the stage adorned in a robe of unionist-friendly deception" (*Irish News,* 26 January 1998, 1).

The DUP has made it clear that any group willing to engage in the peace process merely demonstrates feebleness. For the DUP this is as true of UUP as it is of the paramilitary representatives. To understand this, we need to return to the basic DUP perspective on the peace process. As leading commentators Cusack and McDonald (1997, 325) observe, DUP from the outset "took a more apocalyptic view of the framework proposals. The party pasted posters across the province claiming that it was another 'piece in the process.' The graphic poster design, showing Northern Ireland being lifted out of the UK, demonstrated that the process was moving towards a united Ireland. In DUP eyes the Framework Document was the first reward to the IRA for ending its campaign." This position, often repeated, clearly implies that no one beyond DUP can be trusted to defend Northern Ireland's constitutional location.

Hence, DUP has continuously projected a specific notion of crisis and constitutional insecurity as integral to, and indivisible from, the peace process. Indeed, the current phase is understood by them as the final battle for Ulster. This rhetoric has been consistently put forth by DUP almost since its formation, but has become increasingly heard since the signing of the Anglo-Irish Agreement in 1985. DUP's response to the agreement was to take the lead in restating the most basic of traditional unionist principles. As this essay has made clear, there are several items on the current political agenda that, for DUP, are simply not open to arbitration. For the Democratic Unionists, any political negotiation must result in the confirmation of Northern Ireland's constitutional position within the United Kingdom. This affirmation should be underpinned by a return to local political control. What is important here is how central the DUP's arguments are likely to become within the overall unionist response to proposed constitutional changes.

The Democratic Unionists have also projected a specific notion of democracy common to much of their analysis: namely, that it is for the people of Northern Ireland alone to determine their political future. As DUP has put it, "we will not negotiate the Union, because the Union cannot be negotiated by the government of this country, because it is bound into the people" (*Belfast Telegraph,* 7 August 1997, 1). This specific definition of the democratic will of the people informs much of DUP politics. Thus, the party has (1) condemned the British government for refusing to hold a border poll to confirm the constitutional status quo and (2) accused the British government of treachery in promoting a process whereby a settlement is to be put to the electorate on both sides of the Irish border. This, according to DUP, merely represents a further step on the road to the attainment of the full republican agenda and unionist submission to Ulster's adversaries.

The likely direction of DUP was indicated by its leader, the Reverend Ian Paisley, at the DUP Annual Conference in late 1997 when he reiterated that Northern Ireland was facing its gravest crisis ever and that no unionist should be holding negotiations with the British government, or SDLP, let alone Sinn Fein (*Irish Times,* 1 December 1997). Paisley's leadership speech at the conference sought to identify and attack the enemies of Ulster, among them the Ulster Unionist Party. He drew direct continuity between remarks made by UUP leader David Trimble that the union was secure, and similar claims made by previous UUP leaders Terence O'Neill, Brian Faulkner, and James Molyneaux. All, according to Paisley, have claimed that the union was safe and all had been proven incorrect. Unlike the other unionists, only DUP under his leadership will not sell out the unionist "birthright." Paisley reiterated:

> I have no intention of surrendering. Have you? I have no intention of negotiating with the armed IRA/Sinn Fein. Have you? I have no intention of bowing to any occupant of Washington's White House. Have you? I have no intention of insulting the memory of Ulster's honoured dead. Have you? I have no intention of going back on my resolve to keep Ulster from Dublin rule. Have you? I have no intention of lowering the Union flag. Have you? I have no intention of stopping from singing the national anthem. Have you? That being so, I use the words of our founding father, Lord Carson, and I say to this government — You may betray us but you will never deliver us bound into the hands of our enemies. We will defend and retain our liberties and Almighty God will defend the right. God Save Ulster. (*Irish Times* 1 December 1997, 3)

Central to the DUP analysis of unionism is the self-image and political discourse of resistance to any incorporation of Ulster into an all-Irish state.

Such rhetoric again taps into broader unionist concerns. The increase in unionist alienation and fear has been noted by several observers in recent years. Summarizing research carried out in late 1993, Dunn and Morgan (1994) have outlined the consequences of Protestant alienation. For many Protestants, issues such as peace and the cessation of violence are rarely discussed as priorities: "no one was opposed to peace; . . . there was an anxiety and an almost paradoxical nervousness about the future changes that might have to accompany it. Even when some sort of accommodation within Northern Ireland between the communities was supported, there were two coexisting concerns: first a fear that the results would compromise, reduce or put in jeopardy the essential Britishness of Protestants; and second, a determination that such an accommodation would not be brought about by murder and violence. In other words, anything resembling a united Ireland was not an acceptable alternative to violence" (Dunn and Morgan 1994, 20–21).

For many Protestants, such consternation has compounded during the course of the peace process. Gary McMichael, the UDP leader, described the prevailing unionist mood when he observed "a growing feeling within unionism and loyalism that the government is valuing the concerns of nationalism above those of loyalism and unionism. Within the loyalist community there is a serious feeling of alienation — people are starting to question the value of this peace process" (*Irish Times*, 24 December 1997). Especially important in the political reaction to the peace process is the perceived strength of the Democratic Unionists' claim that it is only they who are able and willing to take the necessary action to defend the union.

Some Conclusions

Any understanding of the political life of unionists and loyalists must begin by focusing on how they construct their political identity. This involves relationships between individuals and their immediate community, and an understanding of how that community relates to the wider social and political world. This political understanding is usually expressed through folk knowledge, folk ideology, and commonsense understandings of the world. There are indications, particularly among some of the political organizations of Protestant working-class communities, of a much deeper questioning of some long-standing unionist political values. There is also some evidence from the same sources of a willingness to envisage, if not actively seek, an accommodation with Irish republicanism.

Loyalist group identities are maintained by communal memories of defeat and victory, and by the construction of an enemy who is always deceitful and double-dealing. This political-cultural memory of loyalism informs the ways in which individuals and groups secure their understanding of everyday life. Key factors in this, of course, are the ways in which constructed memories legitimize sectarianism and explain the power relations that characterize Northern Irish society. Physical and social conflict has tended to intensify that part of working-class culture that has placed the accent on division. It was the specific articulation of these views by the DUP that formed the basis of its support in the loyalist working class.

The emergence of PUP and UDP is, therefore, of no little conse-

quence. The continued growth of the parties reveals a clear political dynamic that represents a distinctive ideological position within
the larger unionist community. However, their new loyalism remains
firmly rooted in the experience of the Protestant working-class communities. Whether or not new loyalism can really imprint itself as a sustained break with the past is still to be determined. The contemporary
position of such loyalists indicates something that may, or may not,
develop into a permanent fissure and a redirection within the larger
unionist community. Many of the conflicts that have occurred within
loyalist politics in the period of the peace process need to be understood
in the context of rapidly changing conditions and experiences. For
some, it is the new discourse offered by the loyalist paramilitaries that
best explains these anomic experiences. The history of Ulster unionism,
however, suggests that any major political and ideological shifts will
not have an easy gestation.

Much of the explanation of current events offered by the UDP and
PUP competes directly with the dominant discourses within unionism.
It is important to realize that there is a strong counterconstruction to
this analysis that involves the idea of a final conflict for Ulster and the
belief that the peace process is something that is following a pan-
nationalist agenda. This interpretation, promulgated by the DUP, currently has resonance with many who may, or may not, be DUP members. The DUP discourse effectively imposes specific meaning on contemporary political events. The precarious character of the peace
process and the genuine fear felt by many unionists and loyalists means
that, if the DUP were to succeed in its political agenda, hopes of success
for the negotiated settlement may prove barren. It is also likely that any
political and ideological shifts will be partial and tentative. There is still
much internal discussion, debate, and deliberation to take place before
the birth of a larger "new unionism."

Works Cited

Aughey, A. 1994. Irish Kulturkampf. *Ulster Review* 15:11–16.
——. 1995. The end of history, the end of the Union. In Selling unionism:
    Home and away. Belfast: Ulster Young Unionist Council. Belfast Commu-
    nity Economic Conference. 1995. Conference proceedings. *Island Pam-
    phlets* 12. Newtownabbey: Island Publications.

Bew, P., P. Gibbon, and H. Patterson. 1995. *Northern Ireland, 1921–1966: Political forces and social classes*. London: Serif.

Cardogan Group. 1992. *Northern limits: The boundaries of the attainable in Northern Ireland politics*. Belfast: Cardogan Group.

———. 1994. *Blurred vision, joint authority and the Northern Ireland problem*. Belfast: Cardogan Group.

———. 1995. *Lost accord: The 1995 Frameworks and the search for a settlement in Northern Ireland*. Belfast: Cardogan Group.

———. 1996. *Square circles, round tables and the path to peace in Northern Ireland*. Belfast Cardogan Group.

Community Development in Protestant Areas. 1991. *A report on two seminars held during 1991*. Belfast: Community Relations Information Centre.

———. 1993. *Poverty amongst plenty: Surveys of Taughmonagh and Clarawood estates, 1992*. Belfast: Community Training and Research Services.

Coulter, C. 1994. Class, ethnicity and political identity in Northern Ireland. *Irish Journal of Sociology* 4:1–26.

———. 1997. The culture of contentment: The political beliefs and practice of the unionist middle classes. In *Who are the people? Unionism, Protestantism and loyalism in Northern Ireland*, edited by P. Shirlow and M. McGovern, 114–39. London: Pluto.

Cusack, J., and H. McDonald. 1997. *UVF*. Dublin: Poolbeg.

Democratic Unionist Party. 1996. Our covenant with the Ulster people. In *Manifesto for the Forum election*. Belfast: Democratic Unionist Party.

Dunn, S., and V. Morgan. 1994. *Protestant alienation in Northern Ireland: A preliminary survey*. Coleraine: Centre for the Study of Conflict, University of Ulster.

Edgerton, L. 1986. Public protest, domestic acquiescence: Women in Northern Ireland. In *Caught up in conflict*, edited by R. Ridd and H. Callaway, 61–79. London: Macmillan.

English, R., and G. Walker. 1996. *Unionism in modern Ireland*. Dublin: Gill and Macmillan.

Flackes, W. D. 1980. *Northern Ireland: A political directory*. London: Ariel Books.

Foster, J. W., ed. 1995. *The idea of the Union: Statements and critiques in support of the union of Great Britain and Northern Ireland*. Vancouver, Canada: Belcouver.

Gallagher, A. M. 1991. *The majority minority review 2: Employment, unemployment and religion in Northern Ireland*. Coleraine: Center for the Study of Conflict, University of Ulster.

Gilligan, C., and J. Tonge. eds. 1997. *Peace or war? Understanding the peace process in Ireland*. Aldershot, England: Ashgate.

Hall, M. 1994. *Ulster's Protestant working class: A community exploration*. Belfast: Island Publications.

———. 1995. *Beyond the fife and drum*. Belfast: Island Publications.

Lower Ravenhill Community Association. 1991. *The Lower Ravenhill: A community survey.* Belfast: Lower Ravenhill Community Association.

McAuley, J. W. 1991a. Cuchulainn and an RPG-7: The ideology and politics of the UDA. In *Culture and politics in Northern Ireland,* edited by E. Hughes, 44–68. Milton Keynes: Open University Press.

———. 1991b. The Protestant working class and the state in Northern Ireland since 1930: A problematic relationship. In *Ireland's Histories,* edited by S. Hutton and P. Stewart, 114–28. London: Routledge.

———. 1994a. *The politics of identity: A loyalist community in Belfast.* Aldershot, England: Avebury.

———. 1994b. Loyalists and their ceasefire. *Parliamentary Brief* 3 (October): 14–16.

———. 1995a. *Not a game of cowboys and Indians: The Ulster Defence Association in the 1990s.* In *Terrorism's laboratory: The case of Northern Ireland,* edited by A. O'Day, 137–58. Aldershot, England: Dartmouth.

———. 1995b. The changing face of new loyalism. *Parliamentary Brief* 1 (Spring):45–47.

———. 1996a. From loyal soldiers to political spokespersons: A political history of a loyalist paramilitary group in Northern Ireland. *Etudes Irelandaises* 21:165–82.

———. 1996b. (Re)constructing Ulster loyalism: Political responses to the peace process. *Irish Journal of Sociology* 6:127–53.

———. 1997a. Flying the one-winged bird: Ulster unionism and the peace process. In *Who are the people? Unionism, Protestantism and loyalism in Northern Ireland,* edited by P. Shirlow and M. McGovern, 158–75. London: Pluto.

———. 1997b. The Ulster loyalist political parties: Towards a new respectability. *Le processus de paix en Irlande du Nord, Etudes Irelandaises* 22:117–32.

McKiernan, J., and M. McWilliams. 1997. Women, religion and violence in the family. In *Women and Irish society: A sociological reader,* edited by A. Byrne and M. Leonard, 327–41. Belfast: Beyond the Pale Publications.

McKittrick, D. 1994. *Endgame: The search for peace in Northern Ireland.* Belfast: Blackstaff.

Middleton, D., and D. Edwards, eds. 1990. *Collective remembering.* London: Sage.

Morgan, V. 1995. Women and the conflict in Northern Ireland. In *Terrorism's laboratory: The case of Northern Ireland,* edited by A. O'Day, 59–74. Aldershot, England: Dartmouth.

Nesbitt, D. 1995. *Unionism restated: An analysis of the Ulster Unionist Party's "Statement of Aims."* Belfast: Ulster Unionist Information Institute.

New Ulster Political Research Group. 1979. *Beyond the religious divide.* Belfast: Ulster Defence Association.

Northern Ireland Women's Coalition. 1996. *Election communication.*

Porter, N. 1996. *Rethinking unionism: An alternative vision for Ireland.* Belfast: Blackstaff.

Ruane, J., and J. Todd. 1996. *The dynamics of conflict in Northern Ireland: Power conflict and emancipation.* Cambridge: Cambridge University Press.

Sales, R. 1997. *Women divided: Gender, religion and politics in Northern Ireland.* London: Routledge.

Shankill Think Tank. 1995. A new beginning. *Island Pamphlets* 13. Newtownabbey: Island Publications.

Shirlow P., and M. McGovern, eds. 1997. *Who are the people? Unionism, Protestantism and loyalism in Northern Ireland.* London: Pluto.

Taylor, P. 1989. *Families at war: Voices from the Troubles.* London: BBC Books.

Todd, J. 1987. Two traditions in unionist political culture. *Irish Political Studies* 2:1–26.

———. 1994. History and structure in loyalist ideology: The possibilities of ideological change. *Irish Journal of Sociology* 4:67–89.

Ulster Political Research Group. 1987. *Commonsense.* Belfast.

Walker, L. 1997. *Grandmothers and mentors: Women, politics and education in Northern Ireland.* Belfast: December Publications.

Playing Politics with Belfast's Charabanc Theatre Company

Charabanc Theatre Company operated in Belfast with distinction and with considerable popular success from 1983 to 1995. During much of that time the company's continued existence represented a triumph of will by the women who founded and nurtured it, and its story reveals important things about the politics of contemporary Northern Irish drama and about the way that drama is produced, researched, published, and critiqued.

In what used to be the company's office, stowed among theater directories and cans of coffee and typescripts and empty decanters was the "Charabanc Theatre Company Press Cuttings" scrapbook, a dog-eared jumble of memorabilia begun in 1983. Telegrams and notes wished the company well on its first production. Early press clippings referred to the founders as "girls," or as Martin Lynch's "bevy of beauties," and reporters often had difficulty spelling the company name. The title of their opening production — *Lay Up Your Ends* — was variously and intriguingly misreported as "Hang Up Your Ends" and "Lay Down Your Ends." News stories contained repeated assurances by both company members and reporters that *Lay Up Your Ends* was not a "feminist play." Press coverage would come a long way in the years that followed, but the vibrant disorder of the scrapbook that tells Charabanc's story continues to be an appropriate emblem of the company's strengths and of the challenges it poses for analysts.

The challenges for those of us who are fairly conventional academics emerge with particular clarity when Charabanc's history is juxtaposed to that of Field Day, a company with which it had a number of things in common. The value of this comparison was pointed out in 1993 by Maria R. DiCenzo, but the parallel histories are worth deeper analysis, particularly now that Charabanc (and, more ambiguously, Field Day) have ceased to produce plays.

In 1980 playwright Brian Friel and actor Stephen Rea, soon joined by four other prominent Northern Irishmen including Seamus Heaney and Seamus Deane, founded Field Day Company, based in Derry and determined to "contribute to the solution of the present crisis by producing analyses of the established opinions, myths and stereotypes which had become both a symptom and a cause of the current situation" (Field Day Theatre Company 1985, vii). A Field Day is, of course, a day of exciting or unusual events: a break from regular work or activity, an opportunity for reevaluation and reassessment. The term also has military echoes in its sense of a day for the official parading of troops. Beginning with Brian Friel's *Translations*, Field Day mounted annual theatrical productions that toured Ireland as part of the company's commitment to taking new plays to "audiences unused to going to the theatre" (Hadfield 1993, 47). Field Day also published a series of pamphlets on various Irish political and cultural issues and assembled the massive *Anthology of Irish Writing* that has been so widely criticized for underrepresenting the work of women.

In 1983 five unknown, unemployed women actors, unwilling to leave Northern Ireland to find work, decided to mount their own production. They formed Charabanc Theatre Company, based in Belfast, but it was only after the success of the first production that they contemplated continuing the company and began consciously to craft a focus and purpose (Methven 1994a). Originally the company committed itself to "presenting plays which reflect Northern Irish society" —new work that either grew from its own research or was commissioned. The company hoped "to contribute towards political, religious and social understanding in our society" (Statement of Policy 1983). In the early 1990s the company refined that statement of purpose to include a commitment to "putting women's experiences to the fore" (Charabanc Theatre Company n.d.). A charabanc is a benched wagon open to the air; such buses were commonly used early in the century for group excursions—times off from regular work or activities.[1] Beginning with the original collaboratively written *Lay Up Your Ends*, Charabanc mounted productions that toured Ireland and appeared in unconventional venues such as leisure centers and parish halls. Charabanc also toured internationally and in 1993 and in 1994 organized an International Workshop Festival.

Both Field Day and Charabanc, then, made clear assumptions about the power of drama and its connection with contemporary reality; both sought audiences beyond the urban middle class; and both offered food for thought to observers interested in the relationship between drama and culture in Ireland. The parallels are often so close that it is tempting to assume that Charabanc consciously modeled itself on the slightly earlier Field Day. Marie Jones, Eleanor Methven, and Carol Scanlan (three of the five founding members) and Martin Lynch (who collaborated on the first production), however, are unanimous in their recollections that in 1983 the group's knowledge of Field Day was limited and did not include a desire to imitate. Any parallels in rhetoric or approach, they feel, simply resulted from parallel efforts to confront a troubled society (Jones 1994a; Methven 1994a; Scanlan 1994; Lynch 1994).

Despite surface similarities, however, a variety of factors combined to ensure that Field Day would receive vastly more attention and support than Charabanc — for reasons that at bottom had little to do with the quality of work done by either company. The six directors of Field Day, for example, all had established academic or artistic reputations, or both. Brian Friel, Stephen Rea, Seamus Heaney, Tom Paulin, David Hammond, Seamus Deane and, later, Thomas Kilroy — those were names to reckon with, even in the early 1980s, and whatever they had done would have attracted attention. The company also attracted Arts Council funding right from the start, and although they toured to reach wider audiences they also regularly played at major dramatic venues. Denis Donoghue once described the first three Field Day pamphlets as having "in common, a rejection of the authority exercised from the centre" (1985, 113), and it is easy to see what he meant and to agree that Field Day was an important questioner of canonical versions of Irish history and literature. It is equally easy to argue that these six names are actually *part* of the authority exercised from the center, that they are themselves establishment figures — which is precisely why they would inevitably have garnered considerable attention.

On the other hand, while many students of Irish drama and culture would today recognize the names Marie Jones, Eleanor Methven, Carol Scanlan (Moore), Brenda Winter, and Maureen Macauley, in 1983 they were unknown and unemployed actors. There was nothing about the personnel of this new theater company that would inevitably draw attention. Furthermore, the drama they created and produced was outside the accepted norms of established theater — norms into which Field Day's work fit easily. And Charabanc (perhaps because it played the self-promotion game with less skill) was funded initially not by an Arts Council grant, but with Belfast City Council support and an agreement from the Department of Economic Development to meet 90 percent of the salaries because all of the actors were unemployed. The other 10 percent was donated by individual friends of the company.

From its founding Charabanc has almost always been identified as a women's company. Field Day, despite its obvious dominance by men, is just a theater company, and this terminology suggests it has a wider scope. Even in its early years, when Charabanc had two male board members and was insistent that it was *not* a feminist company — that it would, in fact, be happy to hire men actors if it could find unemployed ones who qualified for the available grant funds — the company was routinely identified as a women's company. Later the difference in labels is perhaps more understandable. After its first few productions Charabanc (which by this time regularly employed men actors) began to identify *itself* as a company that put women's experience to the fore, whereas Field Day seemed to identify a broader cultural focus. In fact, however, Field Day put men's experience to the fore just as clearly as Charabanc emphasized women's experience. Field Day just did this without mentioning the orientation.

Field Day, quite direct in its opposition to the traditional ruling groups in Northern Irish politics, was less self-aware of the extent to which it allied itself with the ruling gender group. This easy assumption of the traditional male perspective was directly related to Field Day's assumption of a fairly narrow definition of what it means to be political. Plays like Field Day's *Translations* (Brian Friel), *Double Cross* (Thomas Kilroy), and *Cure at Troy* (Seamus Heaney), foreground men's experience as clearly as Charabanc's *Lay Up Your Ends* and *Somewhere Over the Balcony* foreground women's experience, and both orientations are essentially political. The habitual assumption of a male perspective by writers, audiences, and critics, however, has meant that Field Day's foregrounding of men has not usually been identified as a choice just as clear as Charabanc's foregrounding of women. Rather, Field Day's perspective was unanalytically accepted as broader than that offered by a "women's theatre." Though she would no doubt argue the point somewhat differently, Edna Longley (1990) is right that we need to reexamine the extent to which Field Day, which she numbers among the long list of "Ancient Orders of Hibernian Male-Bonding" (16), has spoken "for Ireland" (12).

The established reputations of Field Day members also made it comparatively easier for them to risk failure, and indeed to fail. An unsuccessful Field Day effort seemed merely an aberration in the distinguished careers of its members, a low point from which they would quickly rise back into deserved prominence. Failure for Charabanc was greeted not as a low point of limited duration but as an indication of larger difficulties.

Field Day's productions all had credited authors, which meant the plays could be discussed in the context of previous work by the same men. Single authorship also meant the plays were attractive to publishers and that the company could argue for Arts Council support for commissioned work. Initially Charabanc was performing devised or collaborative work in which authorship was difficult to pinpoint. Such a situation traditionally makes critics and publishers and Arts Councils uneasy and meant that company members could secure funding only for production time — not for the substantial time invested in devising the works. Collaborative authorship also virtually eliminates plays from consideration for existing prizes, which have a clear bias for individually authored literary texts.

Single authorship by writers accustomed, as the men of Field Day were, to working with publishers also increases the likelihood of publication. All of Field Day's productions have been published. Only the Charabanc/Marie Jones play *The Hampster Wheel* is in print, although Claudia Harris (Brigham Young University), a longtime Charabanc board member, is preparing an edition of four early Charabanc plays. Marie Jones, the company's principal writer virtually from the beginning, has said that she is not certain the Charabanc scripts are polished enough to warrant publication, and thinks it unlikely she will ever make revisions (1994a). Her lack of interest in publishing the collaborative scripts contrasts with her practice since leaving the company. Jones now writes for Dubbeljoint, a theater company whose name echoes the Dublin-Belfast split and whose productions frequently open at the West Belfast Festival. Pam Brighton, who directed the original Charabanc production, is now Dubbeljoint's principal director. And Jones's plays *A Night in November* (1994) and *Women on the Verge of HRT* (1996) appeared in print shortly after production. Jones's sensitivity to the nuances of Belfast politics, language, and humor remains undimmed, but her publishing history changed when she began writing on her own, without collaboration. This is, of course, a chicken-egg problem. Jones's decision to seek publication, like her decision to work alone, undoubtedly coincided with her increasing confidence as a writer. But the link between solo authorship and publication is strong.

The better-funded, more theoretically oriented Field Day Company produced not just plays but public discussions of issues. Program notes for early productions were elaborate attempts to place the productions in the context of the cultural debate the company sought to encourage. The series of Field Day pamphlets that began in 1983 extended the theoretical context of the productions. Field Day began its existence with a pronouncement about its purpose, with a new play by an established and popular author, and with extensive verbiage to support both its artistic and its theoretical work. Charabanc began with an effort to create employment opportunities, with a collaboratively written play, with programs that focused on information rather than on cultural theory, and with no supporting publications.

For academics, the results were inevitable. We could read the text of *Translations,* see regional productions if we could not see the original, read the supporting Field Day publications, and write articles that would be attractive to journals because they were about work endorsed by Friel and Heaney and Deane, men whom journal editors already knew were significant. On the other hand, even academics who had heard of Charabanc would have been hard-pressed to analyze their work. There was no script to touch and reread; no theoretical pronouncement to tell us where to look for significance; no chance we could see the same play in more than one production.

Anthony Roche's perceptive 1994 study *Contemporary Irish Drama: From Beckett to McGuinness* illustrates a common result. Roche continues the male orientation of Irish critics: his first five chapters are devoted to six male playwrights, and there are no chapters focusing on women playwrights. "Waiting for Your Man" (the subtitle of the chapter on Beckett and Behan) could stand for the whole. Roche's final chapter, which focuses on Northern Irish drama and is subtitled "Imagining Alternatives," has more balance and includes useful considerations of Anne Devlin and Christina Reid. Roche describes the founding of Charabanc as "A major development in women's theater in Northern

Ireland" (1994, 241) and devotes just over a page to discussing the
company. He describes Field Day as important in the "Northern Irish
context" (*not* in men's theater in Northern Ireland), and he devotes
more than twenty pages to in-depth textual analysis of two Field Day
plays (1994, 242–65).

Christopher Murray's 1997 *20th Century Irish Drama* reveals how
the problem persists. He mentions Charabanc as a group for which
Martin Lynch wrote, praises their "remarkably vital" style, asserts the
company "deserves attention in its own right," and laments their fold-
ing as "premature" (1997, 195). He does all of this in a single paragraph and then moves on to fuller consideration of (largely male) playwrights with published works.

Clearly some factors that inhibited response to Charabanc's work
were and remain practical matters of accessibility. Clearly some resulted from the politics of journal publication. Equally clearly, some
emerged directly from standard academic training — training that values text over performance, training that values single authorship over
collaborative work, training that imparts a restrictive notion of what
constitutes appropriate forms and subjects for serious literature.

In part what Field Day managed was to bridge the gap between
theory and practice that frequently plagues dramatic analysis. The use
of accepted forms also meant that whatever challenges they issued to
received social and political opinion were not accompanied by challenges to the familiar, comfortable hierarchies of academic analysis.
They spiced up academia without otherwise changing its traditional
mix of ingredients. Charabanc, no doubt without fully intending to,
challenged all of academia's standard hierarchial propositions, and
these propositions are essentially political.

Because they operated outside the context of valued procedures,
forms, or approaches, Charabanc did not receive the benefit of the sort
of analytical debate that surrounded Field Day's work. While Charabanc was praised for the vigor of its work, for its rollicking humor, and
for attracting new audiences, full critical response never emerged. This
lack of debate was and is unfortunate: the function of criticism surely
includes enriching the creative capacities of new artists by helping to
articulate their aims, educating audience members about new productions, and providing a vocabulary for appropriate discussion.

Field Day and the directors who served it so well accomplished a great deal, but it was not considerations of quality alone that led to the vast attention focused on Field Day and the comparatively scant attention accorded Charabanc. Rather, the politics of theatrical production, the politics of critical and academic attention, gave most of the votes to Field Day (not to mention the simple truth that critical responses to work by both companies were written by people who knew the directors of Field Day but not the directors of Charabanc).

An added factor was Charabanc's Irishness. If women's theater is outside the male-dominated mainstream, Irish theater is likely to strike English critics in the same way; and Northern Irish theater strikes even analysts from the Republic as fringe. By the time they founded Field Day, Heaney and Deane and Friel had made names for themselves within the academic mainstream of "mainland" England. They were thus assumed to be significant by analysts to whom Charabanc continued to appear intriguing but marginal.

Northern Ireland is a province of Britain, a "Troubled" foster child known primarily for its drain on British lives and coffers. The English undervaluing of the Irish is evident in a story Charabanc founders often tell about one impetus for starting their company. An English director at Belfast's Lyric Theatre imported English actors to play Belfast women, even though the roles were small, thus implying that Northern actors, despite their authentic accents, were inferior (Methven 1994a; Scanlan 1994; DiCenzo 1993). When Marie Jones repeated this story in 1996 she added, perhaps influenced by recent analysis of Irish literature and history, the word *colonial* and thus indicated the political implications of the event: "we'd started to think, in that colonial way you found here: 'We're not even good enough to go on the stage' " (1996c).

Female and Irish, Charabanc seemed unlikely to offer much of interest to English analysts, particularly to those reluctant to cross the Irish Sea, and so response to the company was affected by yet another political reality. Lizbeth Goodman's informative 1993 study *Contemporary Feminist Theatres: To Each Her Own*, for example, sets a focus on British feminist theater since 1968, but mentions Charabanc only twice, both times as part of longer lists. Because Goodman distinguishes between "women's theatre" and "feminist theatre" (1993, 1), it may be tempting to assume that she omits Charabanc because they were initially reluctant to use the term feminist. But when Goodman *does* mention Charabanc she clearly regards them as part of her larger

subject group, and the real reason for omission of full discussion seems
to be that although she is an American she was conducting her research
in England, centered in establishment Cambridge, a location from
which Northern Irish theater no doubt seemed marginal indeed.

From the start, American academics (perhaps sensitized by their
own provincial status, perhaps intrigued by work emerging from a
region that was home to so many of their ancestors) were more interested in Charabanc than were the English analysts who lived in closer
proximity. In any event, Charabanc lacked a network and a PR machine as effective as Field Day's, or as Marie Jones's would become
when she left Charabanc. Further, the company's first productions did
not fit easily into prevailing notions of serious drama.

For one thing, *Lay Up Your Ends* (1983) resulted from cooperative
theatrical work unusual in Northern Ireland. Certainly there were alternative theater companies working elsewhere, and it is one sign of the
isolation of theater in Belfast and the relative naïveté of Charabanc's
founding members that they seem to have been unaware of such companies as England's Women's Theatre Group and Monstrous Regiment, which would have provided clear models for their own efforts —
even though English director Pam Brighton, who joined the rehearsal/
script development process midway, had worked both at the Royal
Court and with Monstrous Regiment (Brighton 1994).

The realities of the writing and production of *Lay Up Your Ends*
also resonate in the politics of its content. Based on the 1911 strike of
women mill workers in Belfast's linen industry, the play was researched
and workshopped by the five women who would act it. Because none
had writing experience, Charabanc's founders worked with established
playwright Martin Lynch, whose 1981 play *Dockers* dealt with labor
problems in the Belfast shipyards. The typescript of *Lay Up Your Ends*
lists both Lynch and the company as authors, and the threads of contribution are so tangled that it is impossible to sort them out precisely.

The typescript also specifies that the male characters are to be played
by women and that the "set should be minimal, e.g. 6 beer boxes." The
six beer boxes were variously used to establish settings ranging from
inside the mill to the steps of the Customs House to a park bench. The
actors changed costumes and roles in front of the audience and frequently spoke directly to the audience. Recorded mill noises were

woven into the production. The play is, then, quite deliberately anti-illusionist.

This is not cottage drama in which an interior set is lovingly re-created and audiences are encouraged to enter into the fiction that the actors have become the characters. Rather, audiences are encouraged to remember that actors play roles, and that gender is also a role that may be played. There is no fourth wall not just because one or more of the first three were missing in most venues, but because the script calls for the actors to violate the fourth wall tradition regularly and to engage the audience directly. The audience is, in fact, both more and less involved than in more typically illusionist drama. More, because they are asked to engage intellectually not just with the labor issues the play presents, but also with the mode of presentation. Less, because they are distanced in Brechtean alienation and not allowed to lose themselves in the illusion.

Lay Up Your Ends has a structure more reminiscent of low-culture music hall and pantomime than of high-culture realism, juxtaposing a series of quick scenes laced with songs and bawdy humor. This is ensemble work in which each actor takes multiple roles. The play, then, refuses in its very structure to preserve the traditional hierarchy of forms, refuses to preserve clear distinctions between high and low culture. Caren Kaplan (1992) has described such subversive forms as "out-law genres," and David Lloyd has pointed out how unsettling both colonizers and nationalists find popular culture's "indifference to cultural hierarchies" (1993, 94–96).

The vested, often unconscious, interest of academic and theater analysts in preserving cultural hierarchies makes them equally uneasy with hybridized forms. Accessible works cannot be serious; popular culture, not needing explanation, is devalued.

Charabanc's indifference to hierarchies might have mattered less if the company's founders had had a more theoretical bent: if they had provided critics with issues to raise, if they had supplied academics with explanations of the politics of their style, if they had contextualized their work. They did not and probably could not.

Lay Up Your Ends, like most pre-1990 Charabanc plays, abandons other hierarchies as well, replacing an individual protagonist with a communal protagonist. The focus shifts from identification with a single character to understanding of what shapes several characters at a particular moment in time. The standard closure of marriage/death/ victory/defeat gives way to an almost anti-closure in which the ending seems a beginning as well. Though the strike gives *Lay Up Your Ends* a dominant narrative, it would be difficult to argue that anything traditionally dramatic ever happens, and subsequent Charabanc plays such as *Somewhere Over the Balcony, Gold in the Streets,* and *The Girls in the Big Picture* do not even have dominant narrative lines.

Difficulties facing the linen mill workers in *Lay Up Your Ends* parallel those that faced the actors who portrayed them. For both, patriarchal work environments and a generally patriarchal society exacerbated economic problems. The mill workers are already out on strike before it occurs to them to create a list of demands to provide theoretical backing for their actions, just as Charabanc was created out of immediate felt needs and only later formulated a theoretical basis. The company's decisions about minimal props and cross-gender casting were also driven initially by necessity, not by theory. Accustomed to action that proceeds from theory, analysts often regard action that precedes theory as unthinking and less significant. Ultimately, of course, the plays and the company made choices that had broad implications whether or not they originated in theory. Neither the strike nor the company could succeed without cooperative effort, and for both that effort took place without hierarchy.

Audiences, then, watched *Lay Up Your Ends* with a kind of double vision, simultaneously seeing workers build a cooperative strike and actors build a cooperative, ensemble company. In both instances, the women's actions constituted a denial of dependence on traditional power hierarchies and an assertion of their own power, independence, and capacity to make choices. Program notes by Ian McElhinney, a company director and later Marie Jones's husband, pointed out the parallels. A similar duality operates in the 1985 Charabanc play *Now You're Talking,* in which women at a Northern Ireland reconciliation center first oust their male group leader and then discuss why they did so and begin to forge their own nonhierarchial group. The rejected male-dominated hierarchy is again associated with issues of sexual domination and manipulation, and both plays implicitly equate public and private instances of domination. The heady, essentially political excitement that Charabanc's founders felt was recalled years later by

Martin Lynch (1994), who described the electric excitement of the first collaborative script development as unlike anything he had experienced "except in a political rally." That excitement carried over into performance.

The American premiere of *Lay Up Your Ends,* in April 1997, directed by Charlotte Headrick at Oregon State University, indicates that these broader political issues continue to be important ones in the play and that it is Charabanc's early work that continues to excite actors and audiences. Headrick worked to ground her production in the characters and guesses that it was "less agit-prop" than the original (which she did not see). Her largely young and inexperienced cast's enthusiasm for creating work of a sort they had never seen or been part of before, however, suggests they sensed broad implications for theater and women. Headrick's production also illustrates the difficulty of re-creating Charabanc plays without authoritative texts: she relied on personal connections with Charabanc company members and a typescript replete with errors and omissions. To re-create the play's music she depended on help from Methven and Scanlan, on guesswork, and on original music (Headrick 1997). Claudia Harris (1997), the only person to have seen both the original production and the Oregon State production, observed that each had its own intelligence. Charabanc's production was more irreverent, harder, faster; the Oregon State production, with the perspective of time and distance, was respectful and aware of the importance of the original Charabanc work. The theoretical underpinnings that received so little attention in the early days are beginning to be supplied.

If company organization and dramatic forms in Charabanc's early work raise interesting political issues, so does the content of *Lay Up Your Ends.* Some aspects are political in the common, left-wing, socialist sense of the word. Employers exploit workers, who express their feelings in songs of the sort typical of disadvantaged groups. The workers' strike is broken, but the women have learned solidarity and go back in singing — blunting some of the most onerous employer restrictions by acting together. The union is formed and the seeds of future success seem planted. This is fairly typical agit-prop material.

Lay Up Your Ends is low-key, undogmatic, unpreachy agit-prop, however, and in this it anticipates subsequent Charabanc plays, which are unlikely to endorse particular solutions. Rather, the plays parallel the structure of the best of what is often described as "women's talk":

speakers seeking to understand and connect while recognizing and respecting differences. Perhaps it is the awareness of multiple perspectives and delight in their creative clash that typically kept Charabanc
plays from being regarded as political. It's hard to hoist a flag over
them. They do not belong to one of Northern Ireland's divided communities more than another, despite the Protestantism of the company
members. They offer no pat solutions or even conclusions. Multiplicity
and lack of dogma *are,* in fact, their politics.

Critics who equate intellectual rigor with linear persuasion moving
toward particular solutions are unlikely to value plays that proceed by
resistance and negotiation (not by confrontation) toward greater understanding (not toward imagined or imposed solutions). The play's
content, then, presented difficulties parallel to those arising from
the company's failure to meet the expectations of critics who equate
dramatic excellence with articulated theory. Audiences, however, responded to the play's valuing of a little piece of Belfast history that does
not involve famous names. Again, parallels with the company's own
situation are clear: Charabanc asked to be valued not because their
names were famous or their theory convincingly articulated, but because their work was good. Again, it was the conjunction of the play's
content and the company's realities that gave the production particular
edge and vitality and that makes it difficult even now to isolate company history, playscript, production, or audience response.

Lay Up Your Ends raises other, less obvious political issues. Male
characters are stereotypical and were played in very broad strokes.
Their flatness seems to have derived from the company's research, during which former women mill workers talked animatedly about their
work experience but showed little interest in discussing their husbands
(Methven 1994b; Jones 1994a). Nevertheless, the stereotypes suggest a
political position. Allowed to make their livings in an upright position,
women in this play reveal the same interests and attitudes as working
men. Men were not part of the workplace camaraderie and existed
outside the world of the strike. They thus faded to stereotypes just as
women often fade to stereotypes in plays about war or men's strikes. It
is also true that all of the characters in this play are relatively flat. The
emphasis is not on psychologically subtle characters — another viola-
tion of traditional expectations of "serious" drama.

Sexual power is also an issue. The same women who resent the sexual power exercised by the male hierarchy delight in tormenting the one male under their control, a young cleaning boy. In a historic ritual also described by Betty Messenger (1975) and Gerry Conlon (1990), they make coarse sexual gestures and seek to remove the boy's trousers and grease his genitals. The issue is power, not gender, and the play presents no idealized female world in which things are better when women are in charge.

The more general focus of early Charabanc plays also has political implications. In 1985 Fintan O'Toole observed that "For the last hundred years, Irish culture and in particular Irish writing has been marked by [the] dominance of the rural over the urban." This was, O'Toole points out, "a political image of the countryside" (1991, 654). Furthermore, "the classic location for Irish urban writing has been the tenement building . . . essentially an urban version of the rural setting." What is excluded, O'Toole points out, is the world of streets and the world of work (656). This description fits drama from the Republic considerably better than it fits drama from Northern Ireland, but it does not fit Charabanc's work at all.[2] Such early plays as *Lay Up Your Ends; Oul' Delf and False Teeth; Weddins, Weeins and Wakes;* and *Somewhere Over the Balcony* have urban settings and, in various ways, focus on work and the streets. Charabanc foregrounded women's experience *and* work and street experience. Theirs was not an Ireland of rural peasant interiors.

In the six plays Charabanc produced in five years the company walked a fine line. The stories were not their own, but carefully researched both in libraries and, more extensively, through personal interviews. In creating them the company gave voice to elements of the Belfast community that had been relatively voiceless in the past: mill workers, market vendors, residents of the Divis flats. In giving these women voice, the company in many ways empowered them.

On the other hand, writing the lives of these other women, to whom Charabanc must have seemed the essence of the establishment, was also in some ways an act of power and control. The vitality of Charabanc's productions depended directly on a kind of plundering of the energies of these other communities. Company members contributed to the writing, but so did the women on whose lives the plays were based. The stories of the collaborators (a word with at least two edges) became part of the narrative. Charabanc largely avoided undue exploitation of these other communities, but there was invariably a risk that, seeking to avoid the power of traditional theater, Charabanc might exercise power over those even less part of the establishment.

Following their heady, productive, draining first five years, Charabanc, in which Jones, Methven, and Scanlan emerged early as the principal members, took a six-month break. Methven and Scanlan appeared in films and on stage. Jones had a baby. When they came back together, a shift in orientation was clear. Lacking time and energy to do their own writing and wanting in any case to branch out, Charabanc produced a play that they had not devised: Darrah Cloud's *The Stick Wife*, which concerns civil rights in Alabama in the 1960s. Although they would subsequently produce more of their own work, with Jones continuing as the primary writer, the company's more established status faced it with challenging questions. Changes in authorship, venue, and funding shifted their relationship with the very middle-class hierarchies they had sought to challenge.

Marie Jones left the company in 1990, in a split that was both personal and professional and about which company members still speak only sparingly and with obvious pain. Without a writer, Charabanc struggled. Audiences that had flocked to humorous, low-budget, relatively plotless portrayals of Belfast life did not appear for plays like Cloud's *The Stick Wife* or Lorca's *Blood Wedding* — plays that the company could produce only because its funding, most of it now Arts Council funding, was more secure. One reason may have been that such productions did not resonate with the connections between characters and actors that had marked the early collaborative work. In any case, the company's struggle to find a new direction appeared to many, including Martin Lynch (1994), to be a *loss* of direction. Ironically, Charabanc now seemed to be abandoning the niche it had carved for itself, and critical response was not helpful.

Speaking of wider social issues than drama, John Wilson Foster has suggested that the "failure of Irish society is the failure of criticism" and has pleaded for critical "reflection and self-examination in Ulster" (1991, 215). On the far narrower issue of seeking to understand the new direction, educate audiences, or help the company refine and articulate its changes, critics responded with simplistic regret that the new work was not what they had come to expect. There was now a persistent judgment that the company's early work was its best and most vigorous — a judgment reflected in Claudia Harris's decision to publish only early plays that resulted from collaborative, nonhierarchial work.

1993's anniversary celebration was designed to reinvigorate Charabanc and reclaim its audience. Irish director/writer Peter Sheridan, an experienced producer of collaborative work and one with whom the company had worked before, adapted Corneille's *The Illusionist* specifically for the celebration. Although Methven took over a role late in the production, during most of the preproduction time she was occupied with a role at the Lyric Theatre, leaving Scanlan the only long-time company member able to participate actively in script development and rehearsal. The adaptation should have been a natural for Charabanc. Issues of theatrical illusion and gender role-playing that had appeared in *Lay Up Your Ends* were also important in *The Illusionist*. The production mixed songs and rollicking humor with serious consideration of issues, and it was adapted for unusual venues. The production was, instead, a disaster that neither author, actors, nor audience understood. The problem may simply have been critical mass. There were just not enough company members left for the collaborative process to work, or to keep the script from heading in an abstract, intellectual direction unlikely to fit the company's style or appeal to its typical audience. Hiring an author to develop parts for actors who are cast after the script is complete is radically different than developing parts for a core group of actors who have worked regularly together — the procedure at which Charabanc had proved most adept.

Early Charabanc work had proceeded without hierarchy; now there were artistic directors who hired writers and auditioned actors. Instead of having group discussions in a living room, company members met in an office or in the adjoining conference room. Having secured funding they needed a business manager to keep records — and to solicit more funding. Success created a need for more specialization among company members and for a more organized structure. In moving toward these goals, Charabanc did not, as they had earlier, invent their own identity. Instead, they adopted the generally available, generally hierarchial model provided by established theaters, and the division of labor interfered with the collaborative process that had led to their greatest successes.

Jones's increasing sense of herself as an individual writer seems, in fact, to have been one of the reasons for her departure from the company. In a 1994 interview she commented that "In Charabanc there were three people with equal power. . . . It was better that I went off and wrote what I wanted to" (1994b, 16). And in 1996 she recalled her early work with Lynch as individual work: "I asked him to write a play with some good women's parts in it, but he said 'Marie, write one yourself. . . .' It was great advice, and I took it" (1996a). In 1994 Lynch and other company members, including Jones, told me in separate interviews that Lynch's advice had been directed to the entire company, not to any one member. The typescript's designation of authors (Lynch and the company) and notes in the original program support this recollection. With Charabanc no longer in existence and her own reputation as an individual writer firmly established, however, Jones ceased to discuss herself as a member of a group.

At the end of 1993 and in early 1994, I spent time in the Charabanc offices, working as a volunteer. Artistic Directors Methven and Scanlan, the remaining founding members, worked creatively to move in the new directions appropriate to a changed company. The 1993 and 1994 International Workshop Festivals, for example, represented an effort both to broaden Belfast's somewhat provincial theatrical world and to make accessible to others some of the formal training that had been difficult for Charabanc's founders to obtain.

Acknowledging the failure of *The Illusionist*, Methven and Scanlan moved "back to Charabanc basics" and began to devise their own show. Optimism about the new-old direction was evident (Lojek 1994a, 1994b). Working with English playwright Sue Ashby and relying on research done by Scanlan and improvisation by actors, Charabanc developed *A Wife, a Dog, and a Maple Tree*, an examination of domestic violence in Northern Ireland, which takes place against the background of the more frequently analyzed violence of the Troubles. The production was a moderate success, despite the disaffection of audience members who had not understood recent Charabanc work, and it might have led to a rejuvenation of the company along lines closer to its founding, especially since it was followed by 1995's *Iron May Sparkle*, a rollicking two-hander written especially for Methven and Scanlan. In one surreal dream sequence they appeared as male dogs, treating audiences to biting observations made through the double filter of adopted gender and species. Financial management problems increased, however, and Scanlan and Methven, who had anticipated leaving the company in two years anyway, decided, with a mixture of regret and anticipation, to pursue other career opportunities. Scanlan, who had hoped to see Charabanc carry on in other hands, summarized her thinking: "We'd surmounted difficulties before, but there comes a point where you no longer have the energy to work non-stop to solve problems. The depth of commitment necessary for that is incredible"(Scanlan 1997). Charabanc ceased to exist as a company in 1995.

Full appreciation of Charabanc's contribution to theater (not just to women's theater) has been slow in coming, but it *is* coming. A 1995 roundtable discussion of "Irish Women as Theatre Artists" found woman after woman expressing gratitude for Charabanc's pioneering work.[3] Recent examinations of Irish theater by Roche and Murray laud Charabanc's contribution. The *Irish Times* recently described Charabanc as "one of the most important Irish theatre companies of the 1980s" (Jones 1996c, 12). The *Sunday Independent,* in a 1996 profile of Marie Jones, referred without explanation to Charabanc, expecting readers to recognize the name (Jones 1996b) — revealing reactions from a press that in 1983 had difficulty spelling the company name.

The impact of the company on the lives of the three individuals most involved with it was immeasurable. Jones continues to write and act with Dubbeljoint, whose popular productions regularly tour both Ireland and England; she recently completed a film script focusing on the killing of a joyriding Belfast teenager by a British soldier. Methven has concentrated on her acting career and has just completed filming *The Boxer,* directed by Jim Sheridan and starring Daniel Day-Lewis. She attributes her ease with the film's improvisational script development to training she got with Charabanc (Methven 1997). Scanlan credits the company with broadening her work as actor, director, writer (Scanlan 1997). She is teaching acting, studying at Queen's University, and continuing her stage and screen work; she too appears in *The Boxer.* Her short screenplay *Field of Bones* (based on Cathal O Searcaigh's poem "Gort na gCnamh") was filmed in the fall of 1997.

In 1994 Jones summarized her work with Charabanc: "At the time we were very much on the cutting edge . . . our stuff very much reflected what was happening to the working people of Belfast and how politics affected their lives. It was politics with a small 'p' in that it dealt with how social issues affected 'small' powerless people" (1994b, 16). Scanlan and Methven are equally aware of the plays' political importance. In separate interviews they focused on identical issues: the company's demonstration that actors, directors, and writers could make a living without going through establishment theaters, and its encouragement of the Arts Council to adopt a broader perspective (Scanlan 1997; Methven 1997). Much will no doubt be written about the company in the future; for now, however, it seems appropriate for these comments by Jones, Scanlan, and Methven to be the final words. The political reality is that Charabanc always was its own best interpreter.

Notes

1. The names of both Field Day and Charabanc are interesting parallels to Johan Huizinga's medieval definition of *play* as "a free activity standing quite consciously outside 'ordinary life' as being 'not serious' . . . an action connected with no material interest [that] proceeds within its own proper boundaries of time and space. . . . It promotes the formation of social groupings which tend to surround themselves with secrecy and to stress their difference from the common world by disguise or other means" (Turner 1987, 125).

2. John Wilson Foster (1991), however, suggests that in Ulster "The working class, I suspect, is the artistic descendant of the peasantry of the Irish revival," and notes a "connected reluctance to write about the middle class" in Ulster (274).

3. "Is Ireland a Matriarchy or Not? The Experience of Irish Women as Theatre Artists." American Conference for Irish Studies/Canadian Association for Irish Studies conference. The Queen's University of Belfast, June 1995. The panel was organized and chaired by Claudia Harris of Brigham Young University and included remarks by Liz Cullinane (designer, Glasgow), Katy Hayes (director, Glasshouse Productions), Lynda Henderson (University of Ulster/Coleraine and former editor of *Theatre Ireland*), Dierdre Hines (playwright, Letterkenny), Eleanor Methven (actor, artistic director, Charabanc), and Lynne Parker (artistic director, Rough Magic Theatre Company).

Works Cited

Brighton, Pam. 1994. Interview by author. 3 March. Belfast.

Charabanc Theatre Company. n.d. Charabanc Theatre Company pamphlet.

Conlon, Gerry. 1990. *Proved innocent: The story of Gerry Conlon and the Guilford four*. London: Hamish Hamilton.

DiCenzo, Maria R. 1993. Charabanc Theatre Company: Placing women center-stage in Northern Ireland. *Theatre Journal* 45:173–84.

Donoghue, Denis. 1985. Afterword. In *Ireland's Field Day*, by the Field Day Theatre Company, 107–20. London: Hutchinson.

Field Day Theatre Company. 1985. Preface to *Ireland's Field Day*, vii–viii. London: Hutchinson.

Foster, John Wilson. 1991. *Colonial consequences: Essays in Irish literature and culture*. Dublin: Lilliput.

Goodman, Lizbeth. 1993. *Contemporary feminist theatres: To each her own*. London: Routledge.

Hadfield, Paul. 1993. Field Day: over but not out. *Theatre Ireland* (Summer): 47.

Harris, Claudia. 1997. Telephone interview by author. 20 July. Provo, Utah.

Headrick, Charlotte. 1997. Telephone interview by author. 25 July. Corvallis, Oregon.

Jones, Marie. 1994a. Interview by author. 23 February. Belfast.

———. 1994b. Conscience crisis. *Irish Press*, 9 August.

———. 1996a. Crazy for the boards. *Sunday Belfast Press*, 29 September.

———. 1996b. The odd couple. *Sunday Independent*, 21 January.

———. 1996c. Speaking for the powerless. Interview by Luke Clancy. *Irish Times*, 20 February.

Kaplan, Caren. 1992. Resisting autobiography: Out-law genres and transnational feminist subjects. In *De/colonizing the subject: The politics of gender in women's autobiography*, edited by Sidonie Smith and Julia Watson. Minneapolis: University of Minnesota Press.

Lloyd, David. 1993. *Anomalous states: Irish writing and the post-colonial state*. Dublin: Lilliput.

Lojek, Helen. 1994a. Challenging cultural certainties: An interview with Charabanc's artistic directors. *Causeway* [Belfast] (Autumn):48–51.

———. 1994b. Seeding new writing, seeking more analysis: Belfast's Charabanc Theatre Company. *Irish Studies Review* 8 (Autumn):30–34.

Longley, Edna. 1990. *From Cathleen to anorexia: The breakdown of Irelands*. Dublin: Attic Press, LIP Publications.

Lynch, Martin. 1994. Interview by author. 10 March. Belfast.

Messenger, Betty. 1975. *Picking up the linen threads: A study in industrial folklore*. Austin: University of Texas Press.

Methven, Eleanor. 1994a. Interview by author. 2 February. Belfast.

———. 1994b. Interview by author. 26 May. Belfast.

———. 1997. Interview by author. 19 June. Belfast.

Murray, Christopher. 1997. *20th-century Irish drama: Mirror up to the nation*. New York: St. Martin's Press.

O'Toole, Fintan. 1985. Going west: The country versus the city in Irish writing. *The Crane Bag* 9:2. Reprinted in *The Field Day anthology of Irish writing*, 3:653–57. Derry: Field Day Company, 1991.

Roche, Anthony. 1994. *Contemporary Irish drama: From Beckett to McGuinness*. Dublin: Gill and McMillan.

Scanlan, Carol. [Carol Moore]. 1994. Interview by author. 26 May. Belfast.

———. [Carol Moore]. 1997. Interview by author. 17 June. Belfast.

Statement of Policy. 1983. Charabanc Theatre Company. Photocopy.

Turner, Victor. 1987. *The anthropology of performance*. New York: Performing Arts Journal.

Policing and the Northern Ireland Peace Process

The proposed Northern Ireland peace agreement, published on 10 April 1998, is much more comprehensive than many commentators expected. It is a lengthy, complex document that outlines, in considerable detail, proposals for the future governance of Northern Ireland and its relations with the Irish Republic and the United Kingdom. Yet one significant feature of much of the Northern Ireland peace process was the absence of constructive dialogue between the main parties on possible postconflict policy scenarios. After the paramilitary cease-fires were called in 1994, it was reasonable to expect that a whole range of issues that had been overshadowed by years of political violence might become the subject for debate. With certain exceptions, this did not happen. Most attempts to initiate policy debates were swallowed by the immediacy of temporal politics or were only dealt with briefly before interest shifted to another issue. Importantly, many of Northern Ireland's politicians and commentators refused to believe, in the absence of credible cease-fires and the decommissioning of paramilitary weapons, that loyalist and republican paramilitary organizations had permanently committed themselves to nonviolence.

More fundamentally, there was no shared conception of what the "peace process" entailed and what its end result might be. The tendency was for nationalists and unionists to interpret postconflict scenarios according to their preferences. Many unionists were inclined to view the process suspiciously as an exclusively nationalist vehicle. Their preferred unionist postconflict scenario was a strengthening of the union with Britain, and their preferred policy options reflected this. For nationalists, the preferred option was a dilution or breaking of the union and so policy issues were often discussed in terms of an Irish dimension. The result was that, for much of its duration, the peace process did not fuel sustained, dispassionate debates on credible policy options for a post–politically violent Northern Ireland. Policing is one issue that one would reasonably expect to be addressed in a political process attempting to agree on the future of a divided society. We should not exaggerate what isolating a single issue can reveal about a broader peace process. Nevertheless, an examination of the policing issue can help reveal how contentious issues are approached by the main parties to the Northern Ireland conflict.

The Background to Policing in Northern Ireland

Just as the state in Northern Ireland has been contested, so have its primary institutions, including the police force (Hamilton 1995; Hamilton and Moore 1995; Weitzer 1995). For many nationalists, the Royal Ulster Constabulary (RUC) is the first, and certainly the most visible, line of defense of a state that they have difficulty accepting as legitimate. They also tend to regard it as an "ethnic police force," as its overwhelmingly Protestant membership comes from Protestant centers of population, and polices Catholic areas with which it has little affinity. Furthermore, the "Ulsterisation" policy that the British government introduced in the mid-1970s gave the RUC a much greater security role (Brake and Hale 1992; O'Leary and McGarry 1993; Rolston 1991). Previously, the British army had shouldered the primary responsibility for security. In the 1980s, the RUC became intimately linked in the republican consciousness with a series of contentious issues, such as "shoot to kill" policies and the policing of paramilitary funerals, which reinforced the view that the police force was extremely partial and capable of repressive violence.

Unionists, on the other hand, have a high degree of attachment to the RUC. Most RUC members come from the unionist tradition, and the force's main mission, upholding the security of Northern Ireland, matches unionism's principal political goal. As the RUC became a major victim of republican violence in pursuit of this goal, unionist identification with the police force has strengthened.[1] The RUC, through its membership and its symbolism, also reflects core unionist values of the preservation of the existing order, and respect for monarchy and the British system of government.

Any debate on the nature of policing in a postconflict Northern Ireland is likely to face a number of important questions. One such question concerns the primary purpose of the police force. In a liberal democratic state, the primary purpose of the police is as an aid to the criminal justice system within the law. Northern Ireland's security situation has meant that the prevention of internal subversion has tended to overshadow this role. In a sense, the RUC has adopted the characteristics of a paramilitary force,[2] in the strictest definition of the term; it is heavily armed, is reinforced by permanent emergency legislation, and can take direct orders from the Northern Ireland secretary of state.[3] Furthermore, for every two members of the RUC in Northern Ireland, there are three members of the armed forces (*Hansard* 1994, 248: 1023).

The republican and loyalist paramilitary campaigns have meant that many RUC personnel have a range of skills wholly unsuited to "normal" policing duties, particularly as these duties must be carried out among politically and culturally sensitive communities. The British Home Office's Inspectorate of Constabulary Report for 1993 criticized the RUC for not having "an integrated crime strategy," a view that perhaps reflects the RUC concentration on antipolitical violence duties (*Sunday Tribune*, 1 May 1995). The necessity of ensuring the physical security of police personnel (through the use of armored vehicles or the construction of hugely fortified police barracks) has also meant that the police force has been physically removed from many people in Northern Ireland, thus preventing the development of accessible and responsive policing.

Another issue likely to attract attention in the debate on the future of policing is the structural organization of the RUC. The RUC is formally governed according to a tripartite arrangement among the secretary of state, the Police Authority for Northern Ireland (PANI),[4] and the RUC. In practice, however, the RUC has come under severe criticism for a lack of operational independence from political decisionmakers and a disregard for public accountability through the Police Authority (*Irish Times*, 17 and 25 May 1995; Committee on the Administration of Justice 1988; Brogdan 1997; Cook 1996). At a microlevel, the RUC is extremely large and top-heavy. The police-to-population ratio (if police overtime is taken into account) stands at 1:100 (*Sunday Tribune*, 1 May 1994), five times the average of other United Kingdom police forces, with the annual policing budget costing in excess of £600 million (*Irish Times*, 2 May 1996). With three regional headquarters and thirty-eight subdivisions, the RUC is also, in comparison with other

police forces in the United Kingdom, overbureaucratized (Tony Worth-
ington, *Belfast Telegraph*, 30 March 1996). A peaceful Northern Ireland would present significant opportunities for savings in the police
budget; because of the religious composition of the force, however, cuts
in RUC numbers would proportionately fall more heavily on the Protestant community. Furthermore, it is difficult to envisage how enough
Catholics could be admitted into RUC ranks to make a significant
impact on the force's religious composition if the size of the force was
being reduced.[5]

Perhaps the most sensitive issue to be addressed in a debate about a
postconflict police force for Northern Ireland will be its acceptability to
both communities. Traditionally, the RUC has been regarded as acceptable by most of the unionist community. Satisfaction with the RUC
remains extremely high among moderate unionists. Relations between
the police and more hard-line unionists soured during the protests
against the 1985 Anglo-Irish Agreement, and have again worsened
over the policing of contentious parades (Cochrane 1997). Changes in
the composition, role, and ethos of the RUC may further dilute police
acceptability to some unionists, particularly if they feel that the RUC is
being changed solely to accommodate nationalists (Weitzer 1995; *Belfast Telegraph*, 18 January 1996). The RUC's most fundamental acceptability problem, however, lies in its relations with the nationalist
community. In 1994, less than 8 percent of RUC officers came from the
Catholic community. While IRA targeting of police officers constituted
an obvious deterrent to Catholic recruitment, many Catholics had difficulty identifying with the ethos and symbolism of the RUC. One former
member of the Police Authority gave this damning assessment: "RUC
'canteen culture' is stubbornly male, Protestant, British, unionist and
laddish. . . . Orange and Masonic membership is widespread; only one
in 14 officers is from the Catholic faith; officers are required to swear an
oath of office pledging to 'well and truly serve our sovereign lady, the
Queen,' and symbols of Britishness—royal portraits, union flags and so
on—abound, to the exclusion of the minority tradition. . . . There is
thus compelling evidence that, by failing to create a neutral working
environment, the RUC has actually breached fair employment legislation" (Chris Ryder, *Irish Times*, 3 January 1996).

Any genuine reform of the RUC will have to include an effective
strategy to tackle the force's religious imbalance, and include measures
to make it easier for Catholics to identify with the force. Such reform

will also have to involve a reassessment of police complaints procedures, which currently seem to contain a high degree of indemnity for
police officers against official censure (*Irish Times*, 3 May 1996 and 18
April 1997).[6]

The Impact of the Cease-fires on Policing

The paramilitary cease-fires caused a number of changes in policing.[7]
For example, some RUC patrols in nationalist areas that had usually
been accompanied by military escorts, now patrolled alone. RUC officers began patrolling without flak jackets and the Police Authority
invested in a number of cars painted in "police" livery to complement
the fleet of ubiquitous gray Land Rovers. With the sharp decline in
paramilitary violence, the RUC was able to devote more attention to
other duties, particularly to drug-related crime, which was becoming
increasingly visible in Northern Ireland for the first time.[8] A less urgent
security situation also meant that RUC overtime was cut back 50 percent with a saving of £20 million (*Irish Times*, 15 December 1995).
Significantly, the number of Catholics applying to join the RUC increased from 12.2 percent to 21.5 percent of total applicants (*Irish
Times*, 25 May 1995), signaling that a peacetime RUC would be much
more acceptable to the Catholic community (*Irish Times*, 8 December
1995). One important role, which the RUC chief constable assumed
after the declaration of the paramilitary cease-fires, was that of interpreting the status or permanence of those cease-fires and then advising
the secretary of state of appropriate security responses. Decisions to
reopen roads between Northern Ireland and the Republic of Ireland,
and the removal of watchtowers or permanent checkpoints, were only
made after consultations with the chief constable and the army general
officer commanding. More generally, the chief constable, with access to
an intelligence network, was given the role of a modern-day soothsayer
who was expected to interpret paramilitary intentions (*Newsletter*, 5
July 1994; *Irish Times*, 5 October 1996, 3 January 1997, and 31 May
1997; *Belfast Telegraph*, 21 October 1996).

Political Reactions to the Cease-fires

The basic positions of Northern Ireland's political parties, in relation to
the policing issue, did not shift when the 1994 cease-fires were called.

Nor have they shifted since the formal breaking (and reinstatement) of the IRA cease-fire and the informal breaking of the Combined Loyalist Military Command cease-fire. In many respects, the issue of policing was not actually tackled in the multiparty talks. The April 1998 agreement defers many decisions on policing through the establishment of a Commission on Policing in Northern Ireland. During the peace process, issues of symbolism — for example, the oath of allegiance and the RUC badge — have attracted as much attention as substantive issues (*Irish Times*, 4 June 1997). The basic Sinn Fein position contained a demand that the RUC be disbanded, arguing that the force was unacceptable to nationalists and that any new policing service must start from a "clean slate" (*Irish Times*, 27 February 1995; *Belfast Telegraph*, 8 May 1996; 1997 Sinn Fein *Election manifesto*, http://www.irlnet.com/si...cuments/97manifesto.html). Constitutional nationalists argued that the RUC would have to undergo fundamental reforms, with one proposal suggesting the need for several police forces within Northern Ireland each of which would reflect the religious balance of a particular area.[9]

Many unionists simply did not see policing as an issue and were satisfied with existing police structures.[10] Others were loath to have the issue addressed for political reasons. They remained suspicious of the permanence of the paramilitary cease-fires, and were anxious that RUC force levels and powers were not reduced until guarantees about the end of paramilitary violence could be given. Essentially, however, many unionists interpreted proposals to change the RUC as part of a general trend of the diminution of the union. According to Democratic Unionist Party (DUP) Secretary Nigel Dodds, "Enough concessions have already been given to the IRA and their fellow travelers with nothing in return and such a move [changes to the RUC name and oath] would be regarded as a betrayal of all those RUC officers who have died or been seriously injured over 25 years of troubles" (http://www.dup.org.uk.ruc.htm).

Government Reactions

The notion that Northern Ireland's policing structures were in need of reform in the context of changes in the political and security environment was acknowledged by the British government, PANI, and by the

RUC soon after the IRA's 1994 ceasefire. All three bodies launched initiatives aimed at assessing the changes required. Taken individually, the proposed changes are modest. Taken together, as government ministers encouraged commentators to do, they are also modest (http://britain. nyc.ny.us/bistext/nireland/police.htm). The government approach to the policing issue (and to associated issues such as police complaints procedures and the use of plastic bullets) helps reveal wider British government strategy toward the Northern Ireland peace process, particularly up to the election of the Labour government in May 1997. While Sinn Fein, and to a certain extent other members of the loose nationalist coalition, tried to construct an open-ended, fluid political process, the British government, certainly under Prime Minister John Major, was anxious that the remit and timetable of the process be rigidly controlled. In the main, the government has approached contentious issues cautiously, through established procedural and legislative routes. The effect of dealing with contentious issues through review bodies and committees of experts has been to give the peace process an institutionalized character in which issues are dealt with slowly, in a compartmentalized fashion, and with a minimal risk of radicalism. Procedural mechanisms also have the effect of moving the focus of discontent away from central government and nearer the disputants.

British government attempts to make the peace process (and by extension reviews of policing and other issues) as unexceptional as possible are reinforced by two trends. The first is that recourse to review bodies and committees of experts has been extremely common throughout the Northern Ireland public sector in the form of nonelected boards or "QUANGOs."[11] The second is that, since the mid-1980s, a management consultancy culture has become endemic in government departments; in effect, institutionalizing review processes. The Irish government has remained largely silent on the policing issue, as it has on most policy issues connected with the peace process. Presumably, it has pursued the issue through the less visible channel of the Maryfield Secretariat, the consultation channel established between the British and Irish governments by the 1985 Anglo-Irish Agreement.

The Conservative government instituted a review of policing nine months after the declaration of the IRA cease-fire (*Belfast Telegraph*, 6 June 1995). The review was to be carried out internally by representatives from the Northern Ireland Office, the RUC, and PANI and was meant to contribute to a White Paper being prepared on the future of policing in Northern Ireland. The review panel was given the working assumption that the paramilitary cease-fires would hold, but that Northern Ireland's political leaders would be unable to reach a political settlement within eighteen months (*Independent*, 23 May 1995). Shortly after the declaration of the paramilitary cease-fires, the Northern Ireland secretary of state, Sir Patrick Mayhew, indicated that radical reforms of the RUC could be discounted. He told Parliament that "the police officers of the RUC face new challenges but also new anxieties, especially about their jobs. Those anxieties deserve our understanding and sympathy and a decent and worthy response from us. And they will get them. We shall not turn our backs on the people who have seen us through" (*Hansard* 248:1023).

In May 1995, the Police Authority embarked on its own consultation exercise, again with a view to contributing to the planned government White Paper on policing. It wrote to all of Northern Ireland's 600,000 households inviting written submissions on the future of Northern Ireland's police force.[12] Fewer than 8,000 replies were received. The consultation exercise, or more specifically the interpretation of its results, inflamed tensions within the Police Authority between the majority of members who favored a minimalist approach to reform of the RUC and the authority's chairman and another member who were in favor of more far-reaching reforms, particularly over the matter of the accountability of the RUC chief constable to the authority, and by extension, the public.[13] After a number of public rows, the authority gave a vote of no confidence in its chairman, David Cook, who refused to resign (*Belfast Telegraph*, 21 September 1995; *Irish Times*, 14 March and 10 May 1996). The secretary of state, who alone has power to make appointments to the Police Authority, was then faced with the decision to sack the chairman or face down the majority of members who were opposed to significant reform. He chose the former course of action. The subsequent Police Authority consultation report (*Everyone's Police* 1996) made no recommendations on changes to the RUC's name, uniform, and badge, and on the issue of attracting more Catholic recruits; its only proposal was a replacement of the oath of allegiance to the British monarch (*Irish Times*, 27 May 1996). Even so, the RUC's representative association condemned the consultation exercise as "ill-judged" and criticized the way in which the force had been "poked over, dissected and prodded" (*Irish Times,* 5 June 1996). One of Sir Patrick Mayhew's last acts as secretary of state for Northern Ireland was to reappoint the chair and vice chair of the Police Authority, thus limiting the room for maneuver for the new Labour administration.[14]

In May 1996, the government put forward details of its proposed White Paper. The *Foundations for Policing* proposals concentrated on clarifying the RUC's tripartite governing structure (shared among the RUC, NIO, and PANI). It also sought to "provide new mechanisms for greater community involvement in, and identification with policing." Significantly, the White Paper did not deal with issues of symbolism or wider reform issues. Instead, it noted that any future legislation on policing would "be informed by the forthcoming discussions on policing in the all-party political talks that [were] soon due to take place" (http://britain.nyc.ny.us...xt/nireland/rucbrief.htm). The RUC has itself put forward its own plans for a modernization (rather than reorganization) of the force. A *Fundamental review of policing,* published in January 1997, makes few recommendations for fundamental change. It notes that major changes in staffing levels will be almost entirely "security dependent" and is mainly confined to the introduction of new efficiency standards, information technology, and training programs (*Belfast Telegraph,* 16 January 1996).

Parades

One by-product of the Northern Ireland peace process has been a renewed emphasis on street demonstrations and politico-religious marches. This has had direct consequences for the RUC. Most controversy has been attached to Orange Order parades. The Order is exclusively Protestant and, given the divided nature of Northern Ireland, it has a strong political dimension.[15] Approximately 2,700 parades are held each year by Orange and related institutions. The vast majority of these parades pass without incident. Many Catholics find the parades intimidatory and offensive, and object to having to leave their areas or stay indoors during the marches. Supporters of the Orange Order argue that the parades are traditional, mainly religious, and have a right to use public highways.

There are perhaps seven reasons why the parades issue has become more politically charged in the 1990s. First, shifts in population have meant that, in some places, parades that traditionally passed through Protestant areas now pass through Catholic areas. This has led to calls for the rerouting of parades away from Catholic areas. Second, since the (February 1992) loyalist shooting of five Catholics in a book-maker's shop in the Lower Ormeau Road, Belfast, residents have be-come particularly sensitive to Orange and Apprentice Boys parades past that site (Mallie and McKittrick 1996). The Lower Ormeau Road parade has particular significance because it is one of the first major parades of the year and sets the tone for other parades.

Third, there seems to have been a conscious politicization of the parades issue among republicans and unionists. Many unionists believe that Sinn Fein took a deliberate decision to agitate on the parades issue and that nationalist residents groups are fronts for Sinn Fein — a claim the party denies (author interviews with senior members of Sinn Fein and the Ulster Democratic Party). According to one senior member of the Democratic Unionist Party, Sinn Fein is using the parades issue as a means of channeling the energies of its supporters at a time of wider political uncertainty (author interview with a senior member of the Democratic Unionist Party). Furthermore, the Ulster Unionist Party (UUP) has been particularly ready to take a stand on the parades issue. The prominent role that leading UUP member David Trimble played in the 1995 Orange Order-RUC standoff at Drumcree is thought to have been decisive in his subsequent election as party leader. No UUP MPs backed his election as party leader. Instead his power base is located in grassroots unionism; to maintain it, he is required to play a visible role in the parades issue.[16] A high profile on this issue also helps the UUP maintain its position of "defender of the Union" at a time when union-ists are faced with a wider electoral choice.[17]

Fourth, with the withdrawal of many professional and middle classes members, the Orange Order has become significantly more hard-line over the past twenty years (Walker 1996; *Sunday Business Post*, 9 July 1995). At the same time, however, it is worth noting that the parades issue placed the Orange Order, a large organic organiza-tion, under severe pressure and has revealed that it is not a monolithic force. Instead, the Order has moderate and hard-line opinion within its ranks (*Irish Times*, 9 and 20 May 1997; *Belfast Telegraph*, 6 and 27 May 1997). Fifth, the paramilitary cease-fires may have given many people in Northern Ireland confidence to engage in street politics —

something that they may have been cautious about when the paramilitary campaigns were ongoing (author interview with freelance journalist Malachi O'Docherty). Sixth, the parades issue was one of the few live issues during the peace process that gave nationalism and unionism the opportunity for direct, public confrontation. In a sense, the issue has had the capacity to become "the alternative troubles" (author interview with freelance journalist Malachi O'Docherty).

A seventh reason why the parades issue may have become more contentious during the 1990s relates to broader political change or perceived change. Crucially, many actors within both communities have come to regard the parades issue as an indicator of their treatment in any new political arrangement and the transitional phase that would usher it in. The nationalist readiness to protest may be related to a renewed confidence after the construction of a "nationalist coalition" (author interview with a senior Sinn Fein member), and the recognition of the equal legitimacy of unionist and nationalist identities by the British and Irish governments in the 1993 Joint Declaration. The unionist readiness to defend their right to march, on the other hand, may be linked to wider fears of an undermining of the union. According to Jeffrey Donaldson, assistant grand master of the Orange Order, "If nationalists cannot tolerate the culture and tradition of the Orange Order for 15 minutes in one year then I think we are entitled to ask what hope is there for the future?" (*Irish Times,* 4 July 1996). One unionist historian summed up the Orangemen's argument:

> For the past 25 years Protestants have felt themselves to be in a permanent retreat. They have experienced the loss of Stormont; the collapse of traditional and multinational firms which employed them; the most draconian fair employment legislation in western Europe which stops them being "spoken for" when seeking work; the imposition of an international "diktat" in 1985, when despite loyalist protest the Anglo-Irish Agreement gave the Republic a say in Northern Ireland's affairs; John Major's statement that Britain no longer had a strategic or economic interest in the region; and Tricolours and street signs in Irish no longer torn down by the RUC.
>
> In the past week litter bins over much of Belfast have sprouted neatly lettered labels saying Bruscar ("litter" in Irish the language). To Protestants, it seems like a sign of the times. Celebrations Orange marches may be, but increasingly they're a collective and determined attempt to hold the line. (Jonathan Bardon, *Irish Times,* 27 April 1996)

Mediation between residents' groups and the marching organizations has had little success in 1995 and 1996.[18] The rerouting of Orange parades away from nationalist areas in 1995 led to a three day
standoff between police and Orangemen at Drumcree, near Portadown
(Bryan et al., 1995; Jones et al., 1996). The issue inflamed sectarian
tensions, with an increase in arson attacks on churches and other iden-
tifiably "Catholic" and "Protestant" property (*Irish Times,* 17 July–23
August 1995). The 1995 pattern was repeated in 1996, though on
a much greater scale. Police attempts to block the Orange parade
at Drumcree prompted severe rioting and public unrest in Protestant
areas across Northern Ireland. Rioting broke out in many nationalist
areas when some days later the RUC, with considerable violence,
forced the parade along the mainly Catholic Garvaghy Road. There
followed, in the words of the secretary of state, "massive . . . civil
disorder . . . the worst set-back for many years" (http://148.100.56.24/
bis/nireland/ps150796.htm). Briefly, the violence sparked by the 1996
parades resulted in two deaths, a spate of arson attacks and intimidation, a deep polarization in community relations and a severe blow
to attempts to attract inward investment and tourism (North Report
1996, paragraphs 23–32; *Irish News,* 28 January 1997). The policing
bill for the marching season came to £13 million, while damage in
excess of this figure was caused (*Irish Times,* 13 September 1996; *Financial Times,* 11 December 1996).

Police handling of the parades issue has resulted in severe criticism
from both unionists and nationalists. Nationalist criticisms were all the
more serious given that the reduction in paramilitary violence had allowed the RUC to build better relations with some members of the
Catholic community. Not only was it left to the RUC to police the
parades (using Public Order legislation); the force was also given the
essentially political task of deciding whether or not parades should go
ahead. The extremely divisive nature of the parades issue means that
any decision is likely to incur the wrath of one community or the other.
RUC decisions to block or reroute Orange parades risk alienating the
RUC from the traditionally supportive unionist community, while decisions to allow marches through Catholic areas reaffirm nationalist
views that the RUC is pro-unionist and unreformable. At the height of
the Drumcree standoff in 1996, the Ulster Unionist Party's deputy

leader, John Taylor, noted that the majority community "was swinging very strongly" against the RUC (*Irish Times*, 10 July 1996). In 1995, one Church of Ireland minister had warned that if the RUC continued to allow itself to be used as a tool of the Northern Ireland Office to face down the Protestant population, and Orangemen in particular, then "all hell could break loose" in Northern Ireland (*Irish Times*, 23 August 1995). On the other hand, nationalists have accused the RUC of show-ing more relish in dealing with nationalist demonstrators (*Irish Times*, 13 July 1995 and 22 July 1996). According to one leading member of a resident's group, after protesters had been cleared off a road to allow an Orange parade to proceed, "There is no peace process. Nothing has changed for nationalists. The RUC has not changed. They laughed as they beat us. You could see by their faces they were really enjoying themselves" (*Irish Times*, 14 August 1995). Six thousand plastic bullets were fired by police in a ten-day period in July 1996, more than 90 percent of them at Catholics (*Irish Times*, 16 July 1996; http:www. serve.com/pfc/july96/whole.html).

After the RUC handling of the Drumcree standoff in 1996, the RUC chief constable admitted that the force had "lost ground with the na-tionalist community," and that "the rule of law has had a set-back" but was adamant that the RUC was not to blame for sparking the vio-lence.[19] Nationalist political leaders claimed that any improvement in relations between the RUC and the Catholic community that had taken place during the peace process had been swept away as a result of the RUC behavior.

Survey information supports this view. The number of Catholics in favor of reform of the RUC increased from 38 percent in 1995 to 46 percent in 1996, with the number calling for the replacement of the RUC increasing marginally to 32 percent. Seventy-five percent of Cath-olics felt that the RUC had treated Protestants better during the sum-mer's disturbances, with 65 percent believing that plastic bullets had been used more against Catholics than Protestants. Significantly, the proportion of Protestants in favor of reform of the RUC increased from 23 percent in 1995 to 32 percent in 1996.[20] The chief constable claimed that the parades issue had placed his force in an invidious position and that it was unfair to expect the police both to adjudicate on contentious parades and to enforce the decision. The government response, con-

tained in the North Commission, fitted the government pattern of referring contentious decisions to committees of experts.

It is important to be cautious when isolating specific issues associated
with the Northern Ireland peace process and then attempting to reach
broader conclusions about the process. That said, it is possible to reach
a number of conclusions.

First, there has been no preordained hierarchy of issues to be dealt
with in the peace process. In other words, there has been no automatic
sequence in which certain issues are likely to be dealt with, nor any
guarantee that some issues will be dealt with at all in the short-medium
term. The deferral of key decisions on policing suggests that the issue
was perhaps too sensitive to be dealt with, in a decisive manner, in the
final stages of the multiparty talks (author interview with a senior
member of the SDLP). The failure of the Major government to organize
structured and inclusive talks despite paramilitary cease-fires meant
that policing, and other policy issues, were only raised sporadically,
and usually through the unstructured fora of the media. Indeed, it was
another issue (parades) that attracted most attention to the policing
issue.

Second, there is a growing public perception of the necessity for
police reform, but unionists and nationalists disagree on the type
of reform required. Many nationalists believe the RUC should be reformed because of its connections with a state they have difficulty accepting. Increasing unionist calls for reforms stem from what they perceive as the heavy-handed policing of Orange parades and marches.
Unionists also remain wary of proposed changes in policing that they
believe are aimed at placating nationalists and that simultaneously
symbolize to them a diminution of the union. More optimistically,
changing perceptions of the RUC, particularly within the Catholic
community, have shown that opinions on contentious issues are not
necessarily set in stone. One of the most interesting questions is why
this nationalist fluidity of opinion has not been reflected by political
parties that have not altered their positions on policing.

Third, unionist and nationalist perceptions of policing are not monolithic. Subgroups within each community vary in their attitudes toward
police reform. Fourth, while nationalists have repeatedly throughout
the peace process accused the British government of "foot-dragging," it

is worth noting that the government, the PANI, and the RUC did take a number of initiatives on the policing issue since August 1994. While a number of these initiatives may have occurred in the course of normal organizational reviews, a number were introduced as a direct consequence of the changing political environment. At the same time, the procedural and determinedly unexceptional nature of the government initiatives reflected the government's discomfort with the concept of a fluid, open-ended peace process with no fixed outcome.[21] The government approach to policing reforms, via committees, review bodies, and existing legislative routes, has been replicated in other policy areas.[22] Crucially for nationalists, the British government has not explicitly recognized that the issue of policing has been one of the root causes of the conflict in Northern Ireland—although the mention in the April 1998 agreement of "the opportunity for a new beginning of policing in Northern Ireland" (*Agreement,* p. 22, paragraph 1) may amount to an implicit recognition.

Fifth, there has been no significant resistance to reform of the RUC from the force's rank-and-file membership. Admittedly, the RUC's representative association, the Police Federation, has consistently opposed proposed reforms, but these reforms have been tempered, in recent years at any rate, by an impotent Police Authority, a cautious government, and a supportive RUC management.[23] The fact that the April agreement increases the likelihood of large-scale changes in the RUC may change this rank-and-file compliance.[24]

Sixth, it is clear that continuing paramilitary violence is likely to place the emphasis on the necessity of security rather than the desirability of reform. In the April 1998 agreement, the British government aspires to "normal security arrangements in Northern Ireland, consistent with the level of threat" (*Agreement,* p. 21, paragraph 2). The existence of significant splinter groups, in both loyalist and republican communities, means that threat levels are likely to remain high.

The core argument of this essay is that a policy issue, the future of policing, was not discussed in a constructive manner during the Northern Ireland peace process. The April 1998 agreement pays considerable attention to policing and recognizes that both policing and the criminal justice system require an overhaul. Yet, for fear of jeopardizing the multiparty talks, and particularly the UUP's continued participation in them, detailed decisions on the future of policing have been deferred.

The Commission on Policing in Northern Ireland is due to report no later than summer 1999. The issue is extremely contentious. Many unionists have cited proposed changes to the RUC and proposed early release for paramilitary prisoners as the primary factors in their decision to oppose the agreement. The leadership of the Ulster Unionist Party claims that the union has been strengthened as a result of the multiparty talks. Sinn Fein claims that the union has been weakened and that any new political dispensation in Northern Ireland will be transitional, leading to a united Ireland. In other words, Northern Ireland's constitutional status is likely to remain contested for the foreseeable future. As the very nature of the state will be contested, it is reasonable to expect that the force protecting that state will remain contested.

Notes

1. According to RUC figures, 301 police officers have been killed since 1969 as a result of paramilitary violence; http://www.ruc.police.uk/press/statistics/deaths.html. Further casualty statistics are available in *Britain in the USA* website, "The Royal Ulster Constabulary," http://britain.nyc.ny.us...xt/nireland/rucbrief.htm.

2. A paramilitary force is defined as "denoting or relating to a group of personnel with military structure functioning either as a civil force or in support of military force," *Collins English Dictionary.* (Glasgow: HarperCollins, 1994), 1131.

3. The secretary of state for Northern Ireland is the member of the British cabinet with responsibility for Northern Ireland affairs.

4. An outline of the aims and functions of the Police Authority for Northern Ireland (PANI) is contained in *Everyone's Police* (1996), chap. 2, sec. 2. See also *Three years of Progress, 1985–1988: Working Together to Police Northern Ireland: The Work of the Police Authority for Northern Ireland and the Royal Ulster Constabulary* (Belfast: PANI, 1998).

5. The 13,000-strong RUC had an in-take of fewer than two hundred recruits per annum in 1994 and 1995. In all, only forty Catholics joined the RUC in this period. See the *Belfast Telegraph,* 30 March 1996.

6. The Labour government has said that it will revise Northern Ireland police complaints legislation in line with the 1997 Hayes Report. See the *Belfast Telegraph,* 27 May 1997.

7. The IRA announced a cease-fire on 31 August 1994 that lasted until 9 February 1996. It called another on 20 July 1997. The Combined Loyalist Military Command called a cease-fire on 13 October 1994.

8. A consultation exercise by PANI in 1995 revealed that 95 percent of respondents wanted to see an increase in anti-drug policing (*Everyone's Police* 1996).

9. Suggestion made by Social Democratic and Labour Party (SDLP) MP Seamus Mallon.

10. A *Belfast Telegraph* poll found that less than half the people in Northern Ireland believed that the RUC should be reformed as part of the peace process. See *Belfast Telegraph*, 18 January 1996. Neither the Ulster Unionist Party nor the Democratic Unionist Party 1997 General Election Manifestos mentioned police reform. Their only references to policing were with reference to greater security. See "Ulster Unionist's General Election Manifesto," http://www.uup. org/text/election/fulmanif.html and "DUP Manifesto 1997 — Democracy — Not Dublin Rule," http://www.dup.org.uk/manifesto1997.htm.

11. QUANGO stands for Quasi-autonomous non-governmental organization. Anne Marie Gray and Deirdre Heenan address the "vague and complex" selection procedures adopted by such public bodies as well as questions of competency in "The Significance of Public Bodies in Northern Ireland and their Representation of Women," *Administration* (1997), 43:57–75.

12. A number of public meetings were also held.

13. According to Andrew Hamilton (1995), "It is clear that the chief constable is not accountable to PANI in its role of representing the community in any meaningful sense" (236).

14. Brogdan (1997) refers to PANI as "unrepresentative and inexpert" and to its "chosen toothless stance" in relation to upholding police accountability (10).

15. Brendan O'Leary and John McGarry (1993) refer to the Orange Order, in a historical sense, as "often rabidly sectarian" (80); Brian Walker (1996) notes that, in the Stormont era, all of Northern Ireland's prime ministers and most Unionist MPs were members of the Orange Order. He also notes that the Order has provided a leadership for unionism (50, 91–99). See also, Cochrane (1996), 146–48; Nelson (1984), 33–34, 42–43; Whyte (1990), 30–32.

16. Drumcree is in David Trimble's constituency.

17. Political parties associated with loyalist paramilitary groups began contesting elections on a provincewide basis during the May 1996 elections to the Forum for Political Dialogue. The Ulster Democratic Party has links with the paramilitary Ulster Democratic Association and the Ulster Freedom Fighters while the Progressive Unionist Party has links with the paramilitary Ulster Volunteer Force. Another, more mainstream party, the United Kingdom Unionist Party, was also established in this period.

18. The 1997 marching season passed off comparatively peacefully, particularly in the light of predictions from many commentators. As far as can be told in early 1998, the more peaceful marching season had little to do with mediation.

19. See full text of "Chief Constable Sir Hugh Annesley interviewed by Barry Cowan on BBC Radio '7 days Programme' on Sunday 14 July 1996," on the *RUC* Website, http:www.nics.gov.uk/press/ruc/bcowan.htm. See also "Drumcree Setback for Rule of Law in Short Term, Says Annesley," *Irish Times,* 15 July 1996.

20. All figures from *A Partnership for Change: A Report on Further Consultation by the Police Authority for Northern Ireland,* annex 1. This survey was held in September 1996, after the Drumcree disturbances.

21. Sir Patrick Mayhew was uncomfortable with the term "peace process," instead preferring to use "political process" or later "talks process."

22. Most notably through the North Commission on the parades issue.

23. Former RUC chief constable Sir Hugh Annesley noted, "I do not start from the point of view that there is something wrong with the RUC and it needs to be changed." Remarks contained in "Annesley's Final Report Unyielding in Face of Demands for Reform of the RUC," *Irish Times,* 22 June 1996.

24. A sign of increasing rank-and-file frustration is illustrated by "RUC Members Warn Mowlam over Reform," *Irish News,* 4 June 1997, while government intentions may be gauged from "Mowlam Aims to Make RUC More Accountable and Effective," *Irish Times,* 16 May 1997.

Works Cited

Brake, M., and C. Hale. 1992. *Public order and private lives: The politics of law and order.* London: Routledge.

Brogdan, M. 1997. A new quangocracy. *Fortnight* 358:10.

Bryan, D., et al. 1995. *Political rituals: Loyalist parades in Portadown.* Coleraine, Northern Ireland: Centre for the Study of Conflict.

Cochrane, F. 1996. Meddling at the crossroads: The decline and fall of Terence O'Neill within the Unionist community. In *Unionism in Northern Ireland,* edited by R. English and G. Walker. London: Macmillan.

———. 1997. *Unionist politics and the politics of unionism since the Anglo-Irish Agreement.* Cork: Cork University Press.

Committee on the Administration of Justice. 1988. *Police accountability in Northern Ireland.* Pamphlet 11.

Cook, D. 1996. Doors that won't open. *Fortnight* 350:18–19.

Everyone's police: A partnership for change. A report on a community consultation undertaken by the Police Authority for Northern Ireland in 1995. 1996. Belfast: Police Authority for Northern Ireland.

Hamilton, A. 1995. Policing Northern Ireland: Current issues. *Studies in Conflict and Terrorism* 18:233–42.

Hamilton, A., and L. Moore. 1995. Policing a divided society. In *Facets of the conflict in Northern Ireland,* edited by S. Dunn, 187–98. London: Macmillan.

Jones, D. R., et al. 1996. *The Orange citadel: A history of Orangeism in Porta-down District*. Portadown: Portadown Cultural Heritage Committee.

Mallie, E., and D. McKittrick. 1996. *The fight for peace: The secret story behind the Irish peace process*. London: Heinemann.

Nelson, S. 1984. *Ulster's uncertain defenders: Loyalists and the Northern Ireland conflict*. Belfast: Appletree.

North, P. 1997. *Independent review of parades and marches*. Belfast: Stationary Office.

O'Leary, B., and J. McGarry. 1993. *The Politics of antagonism: Understanding Northern Ireland*. London: Athlone.

Rolston, B. 1991. Containment and its failure: The British state and the control of the conflict in Northern Ireland. In *Western state terrorism*, edited by A. George, 155–79. Cambridge: Polity.

Walker, B. 1996. *Dancing to history's tune: History, myth and politics in Ireland*. Belfast: Institute of Irish Studies.

Weitzer, R. 1995. *Policing under fire: Ethnic conflict and police-community relations in Northern Ireland*. Albany: State University of New York Press.

Whyte, J. 1990. *Interpreting Northern Ireland*. Oxford: Clarendon.

MÍCHEÁL D. ROE, WILLIAM PEGG, KIM HODGES,
AND REBECCA A. TRIMM

Forgiving the Other Side
Social Identity and Ethnic Memories
in Northern Ireland

The persistence of ethnic conflict and its resistance to traditional techniques of diplomatic or political intervention is widely recognized. One
reason for this intractability is the selective focus on the past of those
engaged in conflict. Images of the past are used to legitimate the present
social order, but social order presupposes collectively shared memories.
When memories diverge, a society's members can share neither experiences nor assumptions (Connerton 1989). It is not surprising that inter-
ventions to halt ethnic conflict, and subsequent attempts at long-term
peacemaking, often posit a revisiting of the history of each side and an
acceptance of responsibility for the past actions of one's own community (Montville 1993).

The political violence of Northern Ireland is a contemporary manifestation of centuries of conflict over Britain's control of the people
and resources of the island. This conflict thus predates by centuries the
Protestant Reformation in sixteenth-century Western Europe when coercion and violence became linked with religion. Since the partitioning
of Northern Ireland in the early twentieth century, significant periods
of political violence have broken out at different times with the most
recent beginning in the late 1960s (Whyte 1990). Also, over the years
intimidation has caused the relocation of tens of thousands of both
Protestants and Catholics, resulting in a patchwork of increasingly
segregated Protestant and Catholic working-class urban neighborhoods and rural towns (Boal and Douglas 1982; Darby 1986). This
long history of conflict has led to the emergence and maintenance of
Catholics and Protestants as distinct ethnic groups. The tendency of
Northern Irish Catholics and Protestants to selectively remember, construct, interpret, and celebrate their shared history results in distinct
social or ethnic memories (Wright 1988).

Historically, memory has been studied primarily as the experience of an individual with "social" factors providing background against which the individual remembers or forgets (Middleton and Edwards 1990). Today, it is recognized that even the cognitive information processing of individual memory is social in nature. That is, what is remembered or forgotten is socially influenced (Lyons 1994). Social memories are distinguished from individual memories in that social memories are shared by members of groups. They are articulated memories; that is, they must be capable of transmission, with transmission taking on verbal, visual, or kinesthetic modes (that is, as in physical ritual) (Fentress and Wickham 1992). They become context and content for what will be jointly recalled and commemorated in the future (Middleton and Edwards 1990) and as such raise questions about whether groups preserve or invent their pasts (Schuman and Rieger 1992). Similarly, collective forgetting is just as socially constructed as collective remembering with displacement or replacement processes substituting one version of the past for another (Irwin-Zarecka 1994).

Sociological and psychological writings on social memory are rich and diverse. However, they have received varied criticism for their lack of theoretical grounding or, alternatively, for their lack of empirical support (Devine-Wright 1996). Emerging from this literature is a new social psychological model of social memory that takes situations of group conflict explicitly into account (Lyons 1994). This model is based on four assumptions. First, groups have collective identities that are more than the simple sum of the identities of individual members. Second, collective identities can be conceptualized in a manner similar to individual identities. In particular, Breakwell's Identity Process theory is applied to group identity. Identity Process theory is framed around content and value dimensions, assimilation-accommodation and evaluation processes, and identity principles of distinctiveness, continuity, social value, and autonomy (Breakwell 1986, 1994). Third, social memory can be understood on the basis of what is known of remembering information about the self. Finally, social memory can only be understood by taking into account interactions between group identity processes and social context. In Lyons's application of Identity Process theory to social identity, it is argued that groups are likely to construct, sustain, and reconstruct memories in such a way as to show the group's continuity, collective self-esteem, distinctiveness, efficacy, and cohesion (Lyons 1994). This application provides a useful framework to explain the ethnic identities and relations between Catholic nationalists and Protestant unionists in Northern Ireland.

Continuity is demonstrated when members explain their group's present identity with consistent constructions of the past; for instance, unionists assert their "Britishness" by constructing their past with memories from Britain's history, while nationalists assert their "Irishness" by constructing their past with memories from the history of Ireland. Enhancing *collective self-esteem* is demonstrated, for example, in claiming famous persons as members of one's own ethnic group. Among unionists, this can be seen in their focus on the British crown, while the nationalist focus on early Irish chieftains and mythical heroes provides a comparative example. An interesting dynamic can occur between groups when both lay claim to the same personage. This leads to differing interpretations as to the figure's significance. Cuchulain provides one such example. Cuchulain was a mythical warrior-hero whose legendary exploits were passed along by generations of bards during Ireland's pre-Christian era. Because Cuchulain was also a part of Ireland's pre-British past, he has been an integral element in the communal memory of Catholic nationalists. A statue commemorating his heroic death stands in the Republic of Ireland's national post office building and his likeness has been painted on a number of wall murals in republican neighborhoods in the North. Recently, however, Cuchulain has been claimed by Protestant loyalists, too, because the kingdom for which he fought was in the North while the enemies against whom he fought came from the South. Today in Belfast stands a gable painting of the statue of that same Cuchulain found in the Republic's post office. What is noteworthy is that this painting is sited not in a Catholic nationalist neighborhood but in an area currently considered to be the heart of Protestant loyalism, where it adjoins other wall murals of armed, masked Protestant paramilitary members (see Rolston 1995, 17).

Distinctiveness guides the ritual processes of remembering the uniqueness of one's people. Marches, curb paintings, murals, and other commemorations of historical events and allegiances serve as reminders for both unionists and nationalists of their own uniqueness. Other examples include the annual Apprentice Boys' march in August and the year-round flying of the Irish tricolor in the Bogside area of Derry, or Londonderry (Rolston 1991, 1992, 1995). *Group sense of efficacy* is enhanced by memories of victories. Certainly the Battle of the Boyne serves such a role for unionists while Ireland's Easter Rising does the same for nationalists. Their annual commemorations bolster both group distinctiveness and group sense of efficacy (Loftus 1990, 1994). Finally, *group cohesion* is served when groups construct their past in ways that emphasize unity rather than internal division. Thus, nationalists when commemorating the Easter Rising of 1916 seldom focus on divisions within their own community at that time. Unionists, similarly, tend not to recognize the role of Protestants in nationalist causes, such as Wolfe Tone's involvement in the Rising of 1798 and Charles Stewart Parnell's work for home rule.

Montville (1993) has argued that in many ethnic conflicts memories of past violence and humiliations have not been acknowledged, or atoned for, by the aggressors or their descendants. He has further argued that this lack of acknowledgment results in deep pain, fear, and hatred in the victimized people. This process is complicated in those cases where groups in conflict have "competing psychologies of victimhood" (113) — as among Protestant unionists and Catholic nationalists in Northern Ireland. In this minority-minority relationship, Catholic nationalists feel threatened as a minority in Northern Ireland, while Protestant unionists feel threatened as a minority in all of Ireland, and increasingly, in Britain as well (Poole 1983; Whyte 1978). Alan Falconer (1988), formerly of the Irish School of Ecumenics in Dublin, posits a three-part model to address selective memories of pain and unatoned violence in Northern Ireland. According to Falconer, the reconciliation of memories that is needed to break out of the cycle of conflict involves a process of (1) seeking forgiveness, (2) accepting responsibility for past actions of one's own community, and (3) appropriating the history of the other community to learn from its experiences. Forgiveness is essential: "Through this process of forgiveness both [communities] are empowered to be and to enter a new relationship which is able to embrace the memories of the hurt and alienation" (Falconer 1988, 95).

Similarly, Enright and colleagues argue that forgiveness can be an intentional tool of intervention in ethnic conflicts within such diverse settings as Bosnia, the Middle East, South Central Los Angeles, and Northern Ireland (Enright 1994). This social concept of forgiveness entails a willingness to give up one's right to resentment, negative judgment, and indifferent behavior toward those who unjustly injure while simultaneously fostering the undeserved qualities of compassion, generosity, and even love, toward those same victimizers. It is more than simply moving on, or putting the past behind. Forgiveness makes room for victimizers. Paradoxically, as one abandons a focus on self and gives this gift of forgiveness to victimizers, one experiences psychological healing (Enright et al. 1994).

The present research tests Falconer's three-part model among adolescents in Northern Ireland who are at risk for participating in political violence. It is composed of two empirical studies that utilize quite different but complementary methodologies. The first study is quantitative and employs attitudinal survey techniques and psychometric scales. It examines the relationships between ethnic identity, attitudes toward accepting responsibility for the violent actions of one's own community, and forgiving the other side. This quantitative standardized data collection technique ensures that participants' attitudes are assessed on a broad range of concerns and uses relevant scales that have previously demonstrated reliability and validity. However, the quantitative approach precludes an in-depth examination of the "lived" personal experience of those who face political violence and who must respond to its perpetrators. The second qualitative study addresses this experiential dimension. It attempts to understand the process of forgiving a violent political act by listening to reported personal experiences. Hence, existential-phenomenological methods of analysis are applied to personal stories of forgiving (or not forgiving) actual life experiences of political violence. Such methods are based on the assumption that experience is objectively real for self and others, is existentially significant, and as such can elucidate our understanding of persons in process (Colaizzi 1978).

Methodology

Samples

Both the quantitative and qualitative studies were performed on subsets of subjects who had been participating in an evaluation research project associated with two ongoing reconciliation programs. One of these programs was a cross-border initiative and focused on children and youth from Northern Ireland and the Republic of Ireland. The other was a cross-community program for Protestant and Catholic youths from working-class neighborhoods in Belfast that also included cross-border experiences with Catholic youths in Dublin.

The subjects for the quantitative study (Study 1) were limited to Northern Irish youths from working-class areas in Belfast that suffer from low earnings and high unemployment. Many of the young people lived near interface areas between Protestant and Catholic estates. All were at risk for involvement in political violence and many had participated over the years in cross-community clashes. As participants in a cross-community reconciliation program, these subjects had been exposed both to positive cross-community contact experiences and to nonviolent conflict resolution techniques.

These subjects formed a small, opportunistic sample. They were not selected through a process that controlled for systematic bias and so threats to the external validity of this study do exist. On the other hand, as will be discussed below, their social circumstances, personal characteristics, and attitudes appear consonant with research on other working-class Northern Irish youths in similar social settings (see Bell 1990; Jenkins 1983; Roe and Cairns 1998). Also, it can be argued that what bias is present favors more positive attitudes and socially desirable responses. Therefore, at worst, these data represent an optimistic view of working-class adolescents at the time of the first cease-fire.

The qualitative study (Study 2) also utilized these same youths; in addition, however, adult leaders in Belfast cross-community programs were included to provide a comparison group from a contrasting developmental period. Like the youths, these adults were participants in the evaluation research of the reconciliation programs mentioned above. Consequently, they too formed an opportunistic sample and their experiences reflected those of persons actively committed to the struggle for peace at the neighborhood level in Northern Ireland. Threats to external validity were of less concern in this qualitative study since, in existential-phenomenological techniques, representativeness is claimed only for those whose stories are described. The purpose of such methodologies is to understand experiences in depth, not to generalize to a larger population, and validity is evaluated in terms of "fidelity to [the] phenomena" presented (Colaizzi 1978, 52).

The sample in Study 1 was composed of twenty-nine adolescents, from which two individuals were dropped due to insufficient data. Of the remaining twenty-seven participants, nine were Catholics, who resided in three different segregated urban housing estates, and eighteen were Protestants from five segregated urban housing estates. Six of the Catholics were female, and three were male; twelve of the Protestants were female, and six were male. Respectively, of these Catholic and Protestant youths, the mean ages were 15.8 years and 15.4 years, the mean educational levels were 12.0 years and 11.9 years, and the mean amounts of time in the reconciliation program were 1.4 years and 1.6 years.

Eight Catholics (four female and four male) and sixteen Protestants (six male and ten female) from Study 1 also participated in Study 2. The adult leaders in Study 2 consisted of five men and three women. For those on whom relevant data were available, ages ranged from thirty-four to fifty years with the exception of one who was twenty-two. This particular leader was an exception in other ways as well and his responses far more closely matched those of the Belfast youths than those of his fellow leaders.

Data Collection

All survey and interview data were collected around the period of the first cease-fire in safe locations within each person's own neighborhood, or outside the neighborhood in a neutral safe place. No youth data were gathered from within school contexts. The interviews and the instruments were individually administered in private settings. All subjects were assured that their responses would remain confidential.

The research team was cross-national and included members from Northern Ireland and the United States. This provided for "insider-outsider" analysis and provided a system of checks and balances. Most data were collected by North American social scientists in residence in Northern Ireland. Although research performed by Northern Irish social scientists benefits by insider understanding, it can be hampered by the researchers' own social identifications and their being identified by others as belonging to one or the other community (Cairns and Toner 1993; Cairns 1994; Heskin 1980; Taylor 1988).

The survey instrument for Study 1 contained several sections. These included: (1) demographic questions; (2) Likert-scaled items on national and sectarian identities that build from the research of Cairns (1989), Gallagher (1989), Moxon-Browne (1983), Rose (1971), Trew (1983), and Waddell and Cairns (1986); (3) Likert-scaled items on various political solutions to Northern Ireland's Troubles that build on Whyte's (1990) work; (4) Likert-scaled items on ethnic memory and corporate forgiveness that build from the studies of Falconer (1988), Working Party on Sectarianism (1993), and Wright (1988); and (5) formal religiosity scales, including the Credal Assent Scale (King 1967) and the Age Universal Religious Orientation Scale (Gorsuch and Venable 1983).[1] The former instrument is a simple measure of Christian orthodoxy and the latter is a measure of Allport and Ross's (1967) extrinsic and intrinsic religious orientations but at a reading level appropriate for older children and adolescents, as well as adults.[2]

In Study 2 semi-structured interviews covered two general content areas. First, questions and additional probes were presented regarding the effectiveness of the reconciliation programs. These focused on specific elements in the curriculum of the programs and on their perceived effects. Second, questions and additional probes were presented regarding forgiveness and experience(s) of political violence in which the subject, or someone close to the subject, was harmed. These questions and probes were formulated to reflect both the context of political violence in Northern Ireland and current research on the phenomenology of forgiving.

Methodological criteria and procedures followed the format suggested by Colaizzi (1978). They included the following steps:

A. Generating research questions to be submitted to the participants. Eight questions and associated probes were utilized in this study. Their formulation relied heavily on the phenomenological work of Rowe et al.(1989). They are displayed in Figure 1.

B. Collecting participants' stories or descriptive responses to the research questions. These are referred to as protocols and were collected through face-to-face, taped interviews that were later transcribed.

C. Reading through all the protocols to acquire a "feeling" for them.

D. Returning to each protocol to extract phrases or sentences that directly pertain to the process of forgiving political violence.

Figure 1. Interview Questions and Probes

1. Can you remember an experience of violence in which: (1) you were harmed in some way by a person or persons from the [Protestant or Catholic] community, and for which you finally (2) forgave those persons?

    alternative 1a: "in which a member of your family was harmed . . ."
    alternative 1b: "in which a close friend was harmed . . ."
    alternative 2a: if no forgiveness, then an experience of harm you have "put behind you"
    alternative 2b: if neither forgiveness nor a putting behind, then an experience of harm "you are still working through"

2. Please describe that experience.

3. What did you do and how did you feel at the time that experience occurred?

4. What did you do and how did you feel a short time after the experience occurred?

    probe: At times did you find yourself reliving the experience? Please describe.
    probe: At times did you find yourself remembering the hurt? Please describe.
    probe: At times did you feel anger? Please describe.
    probe: At times did you desire revenge? Please describe.
    probe: Did you attempt to explain to yourself the reason why those persons caused the harm? Please describe.

5. What led you to decide to forgive those persons? Please describe.

    alternative 1a: if no forgiveness, then "decide to put behind your hurt and anger toward those persons"
    alternative 1b: if neither forgiveness nor putting behind, then "what must happen before you will be ready to forgive or put behind"

6. If you decided to forgive, did you communicate this to the persons who harmed you? Please describe.

    probe: How did you communicate your forgiveness?
    probe: How did those persons respond?

7. How do you now relate to those persons who harmed you in the past and whom you have forgiven?

    probe: Do you think that you better understand those persons now?
    probe: How do you now feel and act toward those persons you forgave?

8. How has this experience of forgiving someone affected how you wish people would treat each other in this world? Please describe.

E. Formulating the meaning of each extracted statement.
F. Aggregating across protocols the formulated meanings into clusters of themes.
G. Integrating the results of steps A through F into an exhaustive description.
H. Returning to the participants to validate the description.

Analyses of the protocols were performed by three of the authors (independently of each other) through step F, clustering of themes. These analyses were then consolidated into single exhaustive descriptions. Unfortunately, the final step of returning to the participants was not possible.

Results of Study 1

Religiosity

Catholic subjects in this study both attended church more frequently and stated a preference for attending church more frequently than did the Protestants. In fact, over one-half of the Protestants attended church no more than once or twice a year. In spite of this difference, Catholics were not statistically significantly any more orthodox than Protestants, and both groups generally agreed with credal elements of the Christian faith. On a five-point scale, the Catholic and Protestant means and standard deviation for orthodoxy were $\bar{x} = 4.11$, $\bar{x} = 3.90$, and $s_x = .67$, $s_x = .85$ respectively. In addition, no statistically significant differences were found between Catholic and Protestant youths on the overall intrinsic and extrinsic nature of their religious experience, although the two groups notably deviated from each other in magnitude and variability on specific items. Again on a five-point scale, the Catholic and Protestant means and standard deviations for the intrinsic dimension were $\bar{x} = 3.23$, $\bar{x} = 3.17$, and $s_x = .67$, $s_x = .73$, respectively and for the extrinsic dimension, $\bar{x} = 3.08$, $\bar{x} = 3.00$, and $s_x = .53$, $s_x = .39$, respectively.

Social Identity

Social identity distinctives are demonstrated in Table 1. More than three-fourths of Catholic subjects thought of themselves as "Irish," while none of the Protestants did; in fact, close to 90 percent of Protestants actively disagreed with such an identification. In contrast, close

Table 1. National and Ethnic Identities

	Strongly Disagree	Disagree	Neither Agree/ Disagree	Strongly Agree	Agree	N
I think of myself as "Irish"***	Cath: 0 Prot: 61%	Cath: 0 Prot: 28%	Cath: 22% Prot: 11%	Cath: 44% Prot: 0	Cath: 33% Prot: 0	9 18
I think of myself as "British"**	Cath: 22% Prot: 0	Cath: 33% Prot: 17%	Cath: 44% Prot: 11%	Cath: 0 Prot: 39%	Cath: 0 Prot: 33%	9 18
I think of myself as "Northern Irish" ns	Cath: 11% Prot: 0	Cath: 22% Prot: 17%	Cath: 22% Prot: 17%	Cath: 44% Prot: 22%	Cath: 0 Prot: 44%	9 18
I think of myself as "Catholic"***	Cath: 0 Prot: 78%	Cath: 0 Prot: 22%	Cath: 0 Prot: 0	Cath: 11% Prot: 0	Cath: 89% Prot: 0	9 18
I think of myself as "Protestant"***	Cath: 56% Prot: 0	Cath: 44% Prot: 0	Cath: 0 Prot: 6%	Cath: 0 Prot: 22%	Cath: 0 Prot: 72%	9 18
I think of myself as "Unionist"*	Cath: 25% Prot: 6%	Cath: 12% Prot: 6%	Cath: 63% Prot: 22%	Cath: 0 Prot: 39%	Cath: 0 Prot: 28%	8 18
I think of myself as "Nationalist"**	Cath: 12% Prot: 50%	Cath: 0 Prot: 33%	Cath: 63% Prot: 17%	Cath: 0 Prot: 0	Cath: 25% Prot: 0	8 18
I think of myself as "Republican" ns	Cath: 33% Prot: 61%	Cath: 11% Prot: 22%	Cath: 44% Prot: 11%	Cath: 11% Prot: 6%	Cath: 0 Prot: 0	9 18
I think of myself as "Loyalist"**	Cath: 44% Prot: 0	Cath: 22% Prot: 17%	Cath: 33% Prot: 17%	Cath: 0 Cath: 33%	Cath: 0 Prot: 33%	9 18

*   Statistically significant Chi Square, d.f. = 4, p < .05
**   Statistically significant Chi Square, d.f. = 4, p < .01
*** Statistically significant Chi Square, d.f. = 4, p < .001
ns Not statistically significant
(Note: Due to small cell frequencies, interpretation of these Chi Square values must be done cautiously.)

to three-fourths of the Protestant subjects thought of themselves as "British," while none of the Catholics did. Catholics in turn were generally split between disagreeing and feeling neutral about "British" as an identification. "Northern Irish" elicited greater variability in responses from both groups of subjects, although two-thirds of Protestants agreed with it as an identification in contrast to less than one-half of the Catholics.

Two-thirds of the Protestant subjects thought of themselves as "Unionist," while no Catholics did. Only one-fifth of Catholics identified themselves as "Nationalist," with more than one-half feeling neutral about this identification. No Protestants identified themselves as "Nationalist"; in fact more than four-fifths of them actively disagreed with such an identity. Most of the Catholics were split between disagreeing or feeling neutral about the more militant identity of "Republican." Not surprisingly, most Protestants actively disagreed with this identity. Finally, two-thirds of the Protestants agreed with the more militant identity of "Loyalist." No Catholics so identified; in fact two-thirds of the Catholics actively disagreed with the identity.

Consonant with the patterns noted above in the identity data, most Protestants desired Northern Ireland to remain a part of the United Kingdom while most Catholics were neutral about this solution (see Table 2). Catholics varied in their attitudes toward the suggestion that the United Kingdom and the Republic of Ireland share in governing Northern Ireland, while most Protestants rejected such an arrangement. Two-thirds of Catholic subjects agreed with the statement that Northern Ireland should be a part of the Republic of Ireland and most Protestants, in contrast, disagreed. Finally, both Protestant and Catholic subjects varied in their attitudes toward Northern Ireland becoming an independent country.

Ethnic Memories and Forgiveness

Catholic subjects did not feel that either the Catholic community as a whole, or the Protestant community as a whole, should accept responsibility for terrorist acts committed by individual members (see Table 3). Protestants were more variable in their attitudes, with only about one-half feeling as strongly as the Catholics. Both Catholic and Protestant subjects were variable in their responses regarding Catholics and Protestants, as whole communities, seeking forgiveness from each

Table 2. Political Solutions for Northern Ireland

	Strongly Disagree	Disagree	Neither Agree/ Disagree	Strongly Agree	Agree	N
Northern Ireland as part of United Kingdom**	Cath: 0 Prot: 6%	Cath: 22% Prot: 6%	Cath: 78% Prot: 6%	Cath: 0 Prot: 28%	Cath: 0 Prot: 56%	9 18
Republic of Ireland and U.K. govern Northern Ireland*	Cath: 0 Prot: 17%	Cath: 22% Prot: 61%	Cath: 33% Prot: 6%	Cath: 44% Prot: 6%	Cath: 0 Prot: 11%	9 18
Northern Ireland as part of Republic of Ireland**	Cath: 0 Prot: 56%	Cath: 0 Prot: 22%	Cath: 33% Prot: 0%	Cath: 44% Prot: 6%	Cath: 22% Prot: 17%	9 18
Northern Ireland as independent country *ns**	Cath: 11% Prot: 17%	Cath: 33% Prot: 11%	Cath: 56% Prot: 33%	Cath: 0 Prot: 28%	Cath: 0 Prot: 11%	9 18

*   Statistically significant Chi Square, d.f. = 4, p < .05
**   Statistically significant Chi Square, d.f. = 4, p < .01
*** Statistically significant Chi Square, d.f. = 4, p < .001
ns Not statistically significant
(Note: Due to small cell frequencies, interpretation of these Chi Square values must be done cautiously.)

other. Protestants, however, were stronger in their attitudes, with about one-half disagreeing with this suggestion.

Catholic subjects were basically split between disagreeing or feeling neutral about the suggestion that Protestant and Catholic communities cease celebrating historical events in which they were in conflict with each other. Protestants, in contrast, were both more uniform and stronger in their protest of such a curtailment. The vast majority of Protestants rejected the cessation of Protestant celebrations; in fact, only one of the Protestant subjects was willing to consider the stopping of such activities as a positive move. Although a smaller portion of the subsample, still a majority of Protestants disagreed with the cessation of Catholic celebrations. Finally, both Catholics and Protestants varied

Table 3. Ethnic Memory and Forgiveness

	Strongly Disagree	Disagree	Neither Agree/ Disagree	Strongly Agree	Agree	N
Catholics as comunity accept responsibility *ns*	Cath: 78% Prot: 33%	Cath: 11% Prot: 22%	Cath: 0 Prot: 17%	Cath: 11% Prot: 22%	Cath: 0 Prot: 6%	9 18
Protestants as community accept responsibility *ns*	Cath: 63% Prot: 22%	Cath: 25% Prot: 28%	Cath: 12% Prot: 22%	Cath: 0 Prot: 28%	Cath: 0 Prot: 0	8 18
Catholics as community seek forgiveness *ns*	Cath: 11% Prot: 22%	Cath: 33% Prot: 28%	Cath: 11% Prot: 33%	Cath: 44% Prot: 17%	Cath: 0 Prot: 0	9 18
Protestants as community seek forgiveness *ns*	Cath: 12% Prot: 22%	Cath: 25% Prot: 33%	Cath: 25% Prot: 28%	Cath: 38% Prot: 17%	Cath: 0 Prot: 0	9 18
Catholics not celebrate historical events of conflict *ns*	Cath: 22% Prot: 39%	Cath: 22% Prot: 22%	Cath: 44% Prot: 22%	Cath: 11% Prot: 17%	Cath: 0 Prot: 0	8 18
Protestants not celebrate historical events of conflict *ns*	Cath: 25% Prot: 61%	Cath: 12% Prot: 22%	Cath: 50% Prot: 11%	Cath: 12% Prot: 6%	Cath: 0 Prot: 0	9 18
Catholics learn more of Protestant history *ns*	Cath: 0 Prot: 6%	Cath: 12% Prot: 22%	Cath: 50% Prot: 28%	Cath: 38% Prot: 33%	Cath: 0 Prot: 11%	8 18
Protestants learn more of Catholic history" *ns*	Cath: 0 Prot: 11%	Cath: 12% Prot: 33%	Cath: 50% Prot: 17%	Cath: 38% Prot: 39%	Cath: 0 Prot: 0	9 18

* Statistically significant Chi Square, d.f. = 4, p < .05
** Statistically significant Chi Square, d.f. = 4, p < .01
*** Statistically significant Chi Square, d.f. = 4, p < .001
ns Not statistically significant
(Note: Due to small cell frequencies, interpretation of these Chi Square values must be done cautiously.)

in their attitudes toward learning more of the history important to the other community.

Results of Study 2

The clusters of themes emerging from three independent analyses of the protocols were quite similar. These three independent clusters were then consolidated into a single set of clusters for each of the groups assessed. The clusters from the Belfast Catholic and Protestant youths were almost identical and so were further consolidated into a single set. This set is displayed in Figure 2 and provides the framework for this accompanying commentary. Direct quotes from the protocols are used extensively as the social processes described can be better understood in the participants' own words than in the researchers' paraphrases. (The number in parentheses following each quote refers to the subject's identification number in Study 2.)

Protestant and Catholic Youths in Belfast

The reported first responses of these Belfast youths to experiences of political violence included feeling sick, disgusted, scared, and humiliated. Some also felt hate, anger, and a desire to retaliate in kind. Often these young people qualified their comments by stating that the violence occurred for no reason, other than that the victim was Catholic (or Protestant):

> Sick. It was terrible, because he wasn't doing anything. He was just sitting at the front of the bus minding his own business and got beat up for nothing—just because he was Catholic. (1)

> Disgraced. I didn't understand why they had to hit her just because she was a Catholic. . . . Very, very angry. That time that she got beaten up I kept saying I hated Protestants and I hated all the violence. (14)

> I was only young at the time and they [Catholics] were all older than me—about the same age as I am now. I didn't think that was right. After that I hated them. . . . Lying on the ground I wanted to be bigger and have all my friends and have a big stick just to get up and get back into them and do what they were doing to me. Give them all the pain that I had, but I couldn't at the time. (15)

Some youths argued for the importance of forgiveness; most, however, appeared to have little understanding of it. They discussed it pri-

Figure 2. Clusters of Themes: Protestant and Catholic Youth in Belfast

I. First responses to an act of political violence
    a. Sick, disgusted, scared, humiliated
    b. Hate
    c. Anger and desire to retaliate in kind

II. Ambivalence regarding forgiveness
    a. Little understanding of forgiveness; discussed primarily in terms of putting event behind
    b. Others speak of forgiveness as not possible, or irrelevant

III. Importance of putting event of political violence behind, and moving on
    a. Not dwell on past, but get on with life
    b. Anonymity of victimizers facilitates putting event behind

IV. Understanding reasons for political violence
    a. Ultimately political violence has no valid reason
    b. Each community is the same in terms of perpetuating violence and in terms of suffering from violence
    c. Each community socializes next generations toward political violence
    d. Being victimized by political violence leads to participating in political violence
    e. Actively identifying with one community and not the other community contributes to political violence
    f. Constant background of the Troubles desensitizes

V. Role of revenge for acts of political violence
    a. Satisfaction from, particularly when immediately following an event of political violence
    b. Knowing who the victimizers are increases motivation for retaliation
    c. Recognition that revenge only leads to more problems

VI. Harboring of bitterness
    a. Degree of bitterness is contingent on relationship to victim and the severity of the injury
    b. Not knowing persons from other side permitted stereotyping and prejudice

VII. Reasons for not harboring bitterness
    a. Violent individuals do not represent entire community
    b. Political violence comes from both sides
    c. Empathy with the other community

marily in terms of putting the violent event behind them, not dwelling on the past, and getting on with life. They also noted that anonymity of the victimizers facilitated putting the event behind. Others spoke of forgiveness as not possible, or irrelevant:

> There's a lot of people who would need to be forgiven. There's families and that who I'm sure will find it hard to forgive. The problems here would have killed some of their sons, brothers, and members of their family, but they're fighting people and they don't even know them. If people were just a little more forgiving and loving, then they wouldn't have to forgive. Does that make sense? (26)

> It is important to forgive. If you don't forgive it's going to go on like this for many more years, but if you get a lot of people forgiving from both sides, if everybody forgives and forgets about the stuff that's happened before, then it should be alright. (15)

> I have forgiven them because now they're probably involved in something like this [cross-community program]. They may not be, then if they never have been, they're just doing what they believed in. (15)

> I put it behind me. It doesn't bother me. I mean if I saw her in the street, I wouldn't hold it against her. Probably forgive them. (26)

> Well, I don't know who it was, so I don't know who to hold the grudge against. . . . Well, I don't really think about that, about forgiving anybody. (20)

> You just move on. Put it behind you. Why should you forgive them if they're throwing bricks and bottles at you. It's just useless. (21)

Ultimately these youths recognized that there was no valid reason for the political violence, at least in terms of specific acts directed against them. There was little evidence that they saw beyond their evaluations of these "illegitimate" personal actions to questions regarding the legitimacy of larger constitutional issues in Northern Ireland. This may be simply an artifact of the methodology in that they were asked to focus their attention on a specific event of violence. On the other hand, this apparent failure to generalize from their own immediate experience to more ultimate issues in Northern Ireland may also reflect concrete thinking processes (discussed below) and is congruent with motivations to maintain distinct social identities. Questioning the legitimacy of the political stance of one's own community would appear to weaken group continuity and group cohesion (see Lyons 1994).

The youths did attempt to understand motivations for political violence. They realized that both sides were similarly involved in the violence and that both sides were socialized to identify with their own community and to respond with violence toward the other. They recognized that being the victim of political violence can lead to participation in the same actions. Growing up in Northern Ireland desensitized them to such violence and set a standard of normalcy that included political violence. In contrast, they also realized that all in the community are not like those who commit violence:

> They'll hit and beat everyone they see the same as I would have done and that most of my friends are probably still doing. It's not really their fault. It's the way they were brought up. If they see a Protestant and they have a stick, they'll hit them with it hard. They were just being silly, they didn't really know. They thought beating a kid, beating a Protestant kid was something that they were supposed to do and had to do. They just didn't know in their own minds what to do. (15)

> Disgusted at them. I wouldn't say I didn't like Catholics because of it, you know, because that happened, because they're all different. I mean because like there's Protestants that would beat up Catholics. The same things happen on either side. (2)

> If I went back up and I seen a ten or eleven year old kid, probably I would go over and do the same as they did [to me] at the time. [Being beaten] changed me, because before I wouldn't have done anything like that. (15)

> Well, I have been beaten up by Catholics, but I don't really have any bitterness because we did the same. (23)

> Well, at the time I was brought up, you just heard things on the street, and we just got to dislike Protestants. (32)

A Catholic participant described an encounter with a Protestant girl with whom she was acquainted as follows:

> [The Protestant girl shouted] "I'm not a Fenian. I'm a Protestant and that's what I'm proud to be." I looked at her, and said "fair enough, if you're proud, that's okay, I don't mind." But we sorta kept our distance then, and it wasn't that I minded her shouting "I'm not a Fenian." It was afterwards we just couldn't talk to each other properly. Now we're okay ... but it was just then ... I can understand if she has been brought up in a Protestant community, and I've been brought up in a Catholic community. It's only right that she has to stick up for herself. (31)

Although these youths recognized that revenge only leads to more problems, many expressed their satisfaction with retaliation, particularly immediately following a violent event. They also noted that knowing who the victimizers were increased their motivation for retaliation. The degree of their bitterness was contingent on how close the victims were to their families, how well liked the victim was, how many were injured, and how severe the injuries were:

> I still hate him. If I met him I would throw myself at him or something. Sometimes think if I had a gun I'd put it to his head and shoot him. . . . I'll never forgive him. I could maybe forgive him if the person he beat up wasn't so close to me, but because it was my sister, I can never forgive him. Even if he had a wife and kids, I could never forgive him. (14)

> Even if it meant killing myself, I would want revenge. . . . Because that's my family, and they've no need to do that. They've taken my blood away . . . [revenge] wouldn't bring peace, but I would be happy. (18)

> Just because they're bitter, and they've nothing to do. They just think they can do anything they want to. . . . You kinda know who it is, and would recognize them. . . . You want to run over and flippin' kill them. (21)

> Well, I saw her once, and I was on the bus and she had a child, and I felt I could get up here and jump her. She can't do much because she has the baby, but I felt "No, what's the point, because [she] would be left and I'll probably be dead." . . . I wouldn't do anything now. If she wants to be stupid like that, it's up to her, just as long as I don't get hurt, I don't mind. (26)

These youths delineated many reasons for not harboring bitterness. Most of these have been presented in the previous discussion about understanding motivations behind political violence. Young people recognized that the two communities were similar; that violence came from both sides; and that violent individuals did not represent their entire community. Cross-community experiences were particularly relevant to this latter point. One Protestant participant, after he was beaten up in error by peers from his own community, developed a particular empathy for the other side:

> That was done by Protestants, because they thought that I was a Catholic. That was the worst one ever, and that made me see how my side got on, and I didn't like it . . . 'cos they used like weapons and that, and they went really bad because they thought I was a Catholic. (23)

Leaders of Cross-Community Programs in Belfast

In reflecting back on experiences of political violence during childhood and/or adolescence, the leaders of the Belfast cross-community programs recalled shock, fear, darkness, and pain (see Figure 3). Some desired to retaliate in kind. One remembers feeling a sense of glory in his injury, since he had "suffered a bit for the cause."

> Fear. Shock. I just felt totally sad and I burst into tears, and thought, why is he doing this to me? (35)

> All I felt was fear and darkness and pain. But mostly fear, fear was the big one. Really frightened that I wasn't going to get out alive. (39)

As adults experiencing current political violence, they suffered deep feelings of sadness, anger, and numbness. No longer did they feel a desire for revenge. They felt empathy for victims and their families, and a heightened commitment to work for peace:

> [if the attack had been twenty years ago] I either would have shot someone or burned someone out. . . . [Now, I would like to] be able to introduce myself and shake their hands. And ask them why. I would like to have that opportunity. (41)

> I felt numb, you know. I really felt numb, and I thought we have to get on with this work. This work is necessary, and the kids thank God, weren't really bitter about it 'cos that was my worry. (37)

The adult leaders spoke of their willingness to forgive and of the difficulties of teaching the process to young people who may not know what forgiveness is. They noted that forgiveness follows empathy and understanding, and that it is necessary to separate the person from the violent act. Three of the leaders noted the role of their Christian faith in motivating them to forgive and work for reconciliation:

> What I do is separate the individuals from the act, so I hate the act with a passion, so it's important to condemn that and I'd be outspoken about it, especially to [my] own community. . . . If I met the person I could forgive them, like Ron for instance who just shot Catholics. . . . I hate what he did but I could have done it as well, but I like him as a person and even if he's still active, I could separate it. He's worth trying to reach as a person at least. (39)

> I tried to build up an anger within myself, but it wasn't justified in any way, it was just me trying to say, "they've killed my brother, I'm going to take revenge," you know. It was something I was trying to build up rather

Figure 3. Clusters of Themes: Leaders of Cross-Community Programs
in Belfast

I. First responses to an act of political violence
    a. Remembering childhood experiences of political violence
        1. Shock, fear, darkness, pain
        2. Desire to retaliate in kind
        3. Glory in suffering for the cause
    b. Experiences of political violence today as an adult
        1. Deep sadness, anger, numbness; no desire for revenge
        2. Heightened commitment to peace
        3. Empathy for victims and their families
II. Willingness to forgive and forgiveness understood
    a. Process of forgiving political violence include empathy and understanding
    b. Effects of forgiving political violence are experienced at the personal and community levels
III. Understanding reasons for the political violence
    a. Ultimately political violence has no valid reason
    b. Each community is the same in terms of perpetuating violence and in terms of suffering from violence
    c. Each community socializes next generations toward political violence
IV. Importance of putting events of political violence behind, and moving on
    a. Reliving the experience of political violence brings bitterness to the surface
    b. No value in dwelling on past incidents of political violence
V. No role for retaliation against perpetrators of political violence
VI. Taking positive action in response to political violence
    a. Empathizing with victim, and with victimizer or victimizer's community
    b. Actively attempting to see both communities' points of view
    c. Responding with dialogue
    d. Responding with cross-community peace work

---

than being a natural sort of thing. No there was nothing there, just deep sadness. . . . I believe it was just God's hand upon the whole situation which has given me that peace. (34)

Forgiving perpetrators of political violence resulted in changed personal attitudes. As one leader stated, "I didn't see them as enemies anymore. I saw them as friends to be won." Personal spiritual healing followed, as did healing of relationships:

You could actually genuinely care about them and of course they picked that up. So that's how the healing could take place. . . . I do believe that there is a language of the psyche that we all talk and so if there is unforgiveness in my life, I think their spirit senses that and they're uncomfortable, whereas if they sense forgiveness, then it enables them somehow to forgive as well. So it's how healing works. (39)

Ultimately the adults realized that there was no valid reason for the political violence; on the other hand, they understood its origins. They noted that each side was as violent as the other, and this balance itself was evidence of the futility of violent political strategies. Both sides consisted of persons with human needs and desires, who hurt equally from loss:

> I still feel that it doesn't matter who killed him. All that matters is that his life has been taken. He didn't need to die. There was no cause for that, for him to be taken . . . it's such a waste that a lovely boy like that had to die, but there's so many people in so many homes that feel that way. (38)

They recognized that violent persons from both sides were socialized toward political violence through no fault of their own, and that these persons often were misguided and desperate:

> I just thought, "That was stupid." I got caught behind enemy lines, so what could I expect. It wasn't like they shouldn't have done that to me, that was the most natural thing for them to do. (39)

> . . . something that he'd probably got caught up in through no fault of his own, just the situation that he was brought up in, born into. (34)

> Just blamed it on the Troubles. It's just the times we were living in. (37)

The cross-community leaders recognized the importance of putting events of violence behind, and moving on. If one continually relived the experience, then bitterness was maintained and reports of new violence brought anger back to the surface. As illustration, the following quote is taken from the protocol of the twenty-two-year-old leader mentioned earlier. His anger, desire to retaliate, and continuing bitterness more closely fit the profile of Belfast adolescent data, than leader data.

> My feelings were "bastards, send the army in, just bastards. They know who they are, just take them and put them up against the wall." I'm sorry but I just felt "get them, knock the fuck out of them, kill them, death's too good for them, bastards, you know?" . . . If ever something

happens on the news it'll bring it back a bit because I know at the end of the day these people are cowards behind their guns. (33)

In general, though, adults saw no value in dwelling on past incidents. These incidents were unpleasant and such preoccupations resulted in personal bitterness and bigotry, ruined relationships, and in energy drained from other positive efforts. They also recognized that Northern Ireland's Troubles were due to dwelling on centuries of just such past experiences. Likewise, they saw no role for revenge. Retaliation did not solve the problem; it only created another. As mentioned above, giving up feelings of hate or revenge permitted personal spiritual healing:

> I felt for my own spiritual healing that it was important that I let those feelings go. Because that would make it a lot easier to forgive and love. (39)

These leaders saw an active role for empathy, not only with the victims, but also with the victimizers. Perpetrators of violence, they realized, were no different from themselves; all had darker sides. While they noted that forgiveness followed empathy and understanding, they also recognized that empathizing with victims of political violence made it difficult to seek reconciliation with the victimizers and their community. They also noted that one must attempt to see both sides' points of view:

> She remembers seeing the guy's face and his body buckling in pain and agony and just bleed and scream, and she just thought, "Jesus, that's somebody's husband, that's somebody's dad." (33)

> I can't distance myself from the paramilitaries and say that they're not me, they were never me, and I can never be like them. So I can't do that, because I know the darker side of me as well as the parts that's good. (39)

> I was that much more determined that I wouldn't be caught up in that atmosphere where I would be leaning so far to one side that I wouldn't be able to see the other person's point of view. (34)

They saw the importance of making something good out of violent experiences, and they rekindled their commitment to dialogue and cross-community peace work:

> I'm horrified by [the Shankill Road bombing of 1993] and I keep saying to myself, "if that person belonged to me, how can they forgive

them? How can those people go out and do what they're doing?" That bomb was so horrific, you know, to see that guy right now out being able to go out and to, you know, inspire peace in his own community and different groups, I think that's sort of incredible . . . I think people like that in Northern Ireland are very inspirational. (36)

Discussion

Religiosity

The religiosity scales provided opportunities to explore the nature of religious beliefs and motivations in the adolescents, and to move beyond the commonly cited and limited role of religious labels as no more than social identities. In terms of performances on the intrinsic and extrinsic dimensions of religiosity, Catholic and Protestant youths did not differ significantly from each other, and their actual intrinsic and extrinsic scores were quite moderate in magnitude. On the credal scale, both Catholic and Protestant youths, many of whom continued to express sectarian opinions and to participate in cross-community violence, indicated rather firm agreement with the basic tenets of Christian orthodoxy. This apparent incongruity between belief and behavior can be explained in part by their limited endorsement of intrinsic religious motivations. As discussed earlier, intrinsically motivated faith implies a personalizing and internalizing of faith-related values. Although the adolescents appeared orthodox in their beliefs, it did not seem that they had internalized to any great extent the implications of those beliefs.

These adolescents' general credal orthodoxy and church attendance patterns were consonant with analyses by Cairns (1992) who noted that in Northern Ireland, adult attendance and membership in churches remained relatively high in comparison with the rest of the United Kingdom and Western Europe. He also found a slight drop in the number of adults attending church each week, with this latter finding most marked among Protestants; Catholics were much more frequent in their church attendance, and their attendance was much more consistent across generations and social class than it was for Protestants.

Similar results were found when Northern Irish adolescents were specifically assessed in two studies that investigated changes in religious behavior and belief during the period of the Troubles. Turner, Turner, and Reid (1980) studied Catholic and Protestant adolescent boys in

1969 and again in 1979. They found that attitudes toward church, doctrine, and religious practices were consistently more positive, at all ages and times of measurement, among Catholic youths than among Protestant youths. Turner et al. noted, however, that despite their lower ratings, Protestant youths still retained moderately positive religious attitudes. That is, they continued to endorse such statements as "I believe the teachings of my church" and "God knows all my thoughts and movements." Greer (1990) studied Protestant adolescent boys and girls in 1968, 1978, and 1988, and found a steady decrease in weekly church attendance. In contrast to attendance trends, Greer found evidence of unchanged or increased orthodoxy on a number of indices of religious belief.

As noted above, political violence in Ireland originated long before religious labels were associated with the communities in conflict; however, the conclusion that the Troubles of today are exclusively ethnic and political is also an inadequate characterization (see Falconer 1988; 1990; Interchurch Group on Faith and Politics 1993; Liechty 1993; McSweeny 1989). Clearly the dominant role of religion and religious symbols in the Troubles is as a definer of group identity; in this role it has been associated with social stratification, social attitudes, and social control (Benson and Sites 1992; Fulton 1991; McAllister 1982, 1983). However, for some subgroups, religious beliefs are directly related to sectarian attitudes and conflict (Bruce 1986), and for many, the exclusive and apparent alien nature of religious practices of the other community perpetuates identity distinctiveness. This is concretely demonstrated weekly in segregated worship. On the other hand, it is the churches that have publicly and most consistently condemned the political violence of the Troubles, as they have exhorted their members to seek reconciliation, not revenge (Morrow 1991, 1995).

Social identity

The social identity data present clear distinctions between the two groups of adolescents, not only in what they identify with, but also from what they distance themselves. In line with Social Identity theory, both Weinreich (1982) and Cairns (1983) have provided similar data that show a pressure in adolescent identity development to disassociate from the other group, resulting in a tendency to exaggerate or even create differences between the two groups. Ethnic discrimination differs from racial discrimination in that the cues are less obviously perceptual. Ethnic cues tend to be more cognitive (that is oversimplified generalizations or beliefs) so that mastering ethnic discrimination appears to take longer than learning racial discrimination. In Northern Irish children, ethnic discrimination appears at about eleven years of age (Cairns 1980, 1989; Jahoda and Harrison 1975). Thus, for many of these subjects, a fully developed ethnic identity was a relatively recent experience.

Sectarian social identities are expected to be particularly strong in settings of intergroup conflict such as Northern Ireland (Cairns 1982); however, the situational nature of social identities is such that variance in the degree of adherence may exist (Gallagher 1989; Waddell and Cairns 1986). Related to this variance are observations from this and other studies of working-class adolescents in segregated neighborhoods who regularly participate in cross-community sectarian violence. Friendly relations, even romantic ones, may exist between Protestant and Catholic youths; however, this is more likely to occur if the relations are not with members of geographically adjacent housing areas between which sectarian violence is common (Bell 1990). In addition, superordinate identities may at least temporarily override the influence of sectarian social identities. Bell noted in his observations of working-class adolescents that, even in the midst of a sectarian riot, the arrival of the Royal Ulster Constabulary led the two battling groups to join forces and fight the police, only to return to fighting each other when the police left. We observed a similar role for superordinate identity among a subgroup of the adolescents in the present study. When these youths later traveled to the United States to learn about and live within U.S. ethnic minority communities, they used their shared Irishness (North and South) to define themselves when among African-American or Native American peoples.

Forgiveness

The qualitative data from Study 2 revealed experiences similar to the phenomenology of forgiveness described by Rowe and colleagues. In their study, Rowe et al. (1989) delineated a process that began with the perception that one has been unjustly wronged by another who is culpable. This perception was followed by reliving the experience and remembering the hurt, anger, and desire for retribution or revenge;

attempts at explanations to make the experience more understandable; the desire to feel peaceful rather than haunted by the experience; letting go; becoming personally changed; and finally shifting one's understanding of (and relationship to) the other, one's self, and the world. In general, Belfast adolescents reacted to political violence first with hurt, shock, fear, or anger. This was followed by desires for retribution, seeking explanations to make their experiences more understandable, recognizing the need to let go in order to be at peace with themselves, and then putting the events behind them. Most of the Belfast adults moved further and completed the process by shifting their understanding of, and their relationship to, the victimizer and themselves, and ultimately forgiving.

The quantitative data from Study 1 revealed a reticence among the adolescents both to accept communal responsibility and to seek forgiveness for past actions. They also revealed an ambivalence toward forgiving members of the other community for current acts of political violence. Finally, they revealed an opposition to relinquishing commemorations and celebrations of historical events in which Catholics and Protestants were in conflict. These remembrances were considered elements of their ethnic cultures and were often simply fun events in which to participate.

A number of explanations offer themselves for this apparent hesitancy to embrace the other community and live integratively in peace. First, the youths were socialized toward sectarian attitudes and conflict (Cairns 1987; Dunn 1995). They experienced segregated education, housing, and employment. Both formally and informally, they were taught selective ethnic histories; they commemorated events of conflict; and they observed sectarian attitudes and behavior in the adults of their respective communities:

> . . . they're doing what they believed in. They'll hit and beat everyone they see the same as I would have done and the most of my friends are probably still doing. It's not really their fault, it's the way they were brought up (15).

Second, because it gave emotional salience and credence to each community's selective ethnic memories, the pervasive and personal experience of the Troubles perpetuated sectarian attitudes and conflict. Consider again the words of a Northern Irish adolescent girl whose sister was beaten by a Protestant man for no other reason than she was Catholic:

> I still hate him. If I met him I would throw myself at him or something. Sometimes I think if I had a gun I'd put it to his head and shoot him. . . . I'll never forgive him. I could maybe forgive him if the person he beat up wasn't so close to me, but because it was my sister, I can never forgive him. Even if he had a wife and kids, I could never forgive him (14).

Related to ethnic memory and direct experience was the difficulty these adolescents had in fully understanding personal forgiveness, and the symbolic aspects of communal responsibility and communal repentance and forgiveness. Forgiveness is a challenging abstract concept. Questions such as, "What does it mean truly to forgive?" "What consequences follow forgiveness?" and "How is forgiveness different from putting an experience behind oneself?" require some facility with formal operational thought (that is, abstract reasoning). The reasoning of many, if not most, of these adolescents was quite concrete in form; in fact, in a separate comparison described in Roe et al. (1997), it was found that this difficulty in understanding was more pronounced for these Belfast adolescents than for a comparable group of adolescents living in a Dublin working-class estate.

The adolescents' greater difficulty in forgiving appears consonant with Enright's observation regarding concrete operational thinking. Enright (1994, 75) predicted that persons at the level of concrete operations "would be more situational in their practice of forgiveness. They may be more swayed by the concretely experienced features of the problem, especially when deeply hurt." This also helps explain the distinction between the protocols of the Dublin and Belfast youths; the Northern Irish adolescents were facing levels of serious threat to their lives or limbs that were far beyond the Dublin adolescents' experience (Roe et al. 1997).

In contrast to the cognitive operation of *reciprocity* in forgiveness (Piaget 1965) is the cognitive operation of *identity* in forgiveness (Enright 1994); that is, the understanding that a person as a human being is not altered when surface features change, as occurs in violent actions. This understanding makes possible the moral principle of *inherent equality,* which is lived out in Northern Irish settings of political violence through the recognition that, regardless of how people treat each other, they are equal as human beings. "This recognition may be quite difficult for a forgiver to achieve because there are so many features on which to focus — one's own emotional hurt, the apparently unjust behavior of the other, one's own belief about unfairness, and the characteristics self and other possess beyond the hurtful event" (Enright 1994, 74).

The sequence toward forgiveness observed in the Belfast adults, and in the Belfast and Dublin adolescents, substantiates a developmental progression (see Enright and the Human Development Study Group 1991; Enright et al. 1992). Increased proficiency with formal operational thought is expected from adolescence on into adulthood. In this study, as might be predicted, true understanding and enactment of forgiveness occurred most often among the adult participants, even though they were living in the midst of political violence. Although formal operations are emerging, concrete reasoning dominates adolescent thought, and so it is not surprising that both the Dublin and Belfast youths displayed concrete thinking in their descriptions of forgiving. That such thinking was more prevalent among the Belfast youths is also expected, given the pervasiveness of their ethnic identities, sectarian attitudes, and the immediacy and severity of their experiences with political violence.

Finally, although the lessened paramilitary violence of today is welcome, sectarian attitudes and clashes between the two communities remain to clarify identity boundaries. The unionist identity is particularly vulnerable, as long-term political solutions involve some level of distancing from the United Kingdom and closer ties with the Republic, but adolescents from both communities were reticent to give up sectarian symbols, rituals, and celebrations. As Connerton (1989) argued, such symbols and rituals do not simply provide remembrances of the past; one of their defining features is the explicit claim of commemorating *continuity* with the past. Thus, when these adolescents were asked about their willingness to give up a ritual, they were not simply considering the cessation of a remembrance; they were considering the cessation of a claim to continuity with their past. The potential loss of such a claim was quite likely threatening to the adolescents' ethnic identities. Also relevant here is the social concept of *tradition;* that is, the belief that a ritual has taken place in the same manner over a long period of time, with this belief in turn providing justification for continuing the ritual into the future (Bryan, Fraser, and Dunn 1995). Ritual, as tradition, has potential for the legitimization and protection of power "for in suggesting that something is right because it has always been that way, it is part of what the participants are. Since it is part of the participant's identity, opposition to the ritual [that is, the tradition] becomes an attack upon both the individual and his or her community" (Bryan, Fraser, and Dunn 1995, 10).

Returning to Lyons's (1994) social application of Identity Process theory in closing, two hypotheses appear particularly applicable to this discussion of threatened ethnic identities. First, "when a group's identity is threatened by challenges to its values and what it stands for, then the continuity and cohesiveness principles will dominate" (36). A focus on continuity and cohesiveness leads to an emphasis on the past and to entrenchment of identities. In Northern Ireland, commemorations, rituals, and symbols serve both those functions; thus, since the continuity and cohesiveness principles would be stymied, consideration of their cessation raises dissonance. The recent series of "sieges" in 1995, 1996, 1997, and 1998 near the Drumcree Parish Church outside Portadown, the associated clarion call for "no surrender" and the consequent riots appear to substantiate this hypothesis.

The second hypothesis emerging from this model states that "where the group's identity is threatened in terms of recognition of its existence by others, then the distinctiveness principle will dominate because what makes a group distinct is likely to provide the rule of inclusion and exclusion for the group" (Lyons 1994, 36). This hypothesis calls into question the efficacy of forgiveness as intervention into the political violence of Northern Ireland, as long as ethnic identities are perceived to be threatened. It also provides additional insight into the reticence of the Belfast youth to forgive. Forgiveness by its very nature is counter to the distinctiveness principle. In the forgiveness process, those who forgive must look beyond violent acts to the humanity they share with their victimizers and recognize the inherent equality between them. Ultimately in the process of forgiveness, the cognitive operation of identity, as presented by Enright (1994), threatens the social operation of distinctiveness and as such may not receive any widespread welcome in Northern Ireland until there is a decrease in investment in ethnic identity.

Notes

1. The items on ethnic memory and corporate forgiveness were sufficient in internal consistency to form a scale with a Cronbach's coefficient alpha reliability of 0.81. The reliability coefficient for the Credal Assent Scale was 0.97, and for the intrinsic and extrinsic dimensions of the Age Universal Religious Orientation Scale, 0.84 and 0.75 respectively.

2. Individuals with extrinsic orientations tend to perceive religion in utilitarian terms. They may find religion useful in attaining status, maintaining social ties, or in providing security or solace. In contrast, individuals with intrinsic orientations internalize the beliefs and values of their religion and attempt to live in harmony with them. "The extrinsically motivated individual uses his religion, whereas the intrinsically motivated lives his" (Allport and Ross 1967, 434).

Works Cited

Allport, G., and J. Ross. 1967. Personal orientation and prejudice. *Journal of Personality and Social Psychology* 5:432–43.

Bell, D. 1990. *Acts of union: Youth culture and sectarianism in Northern Ireland*. Hampshire: MacMillan.

Benson, D. E., and P. Sites. 1992. Religious orthodoxy in Northern Ireland: The validation of identities. *Sociological Analysis* 53:219–28.

Boal, F. W., and J. N. Douglas. 1982. *Integration and division: Geographical perspectives on the Northern Ireland problem*. London: Academic Press.

Breakwell, G. M. 1986. *Coping with threatened identities*. London: Methuen.

———. 1994. Identity processes and social changes. In *Changing European identities: Social psychological analyses of social change*, edited by G. M. Breakwell and E. Lyons, 13–27. Oxford: Butterworth-Heinemann.

Bruce, S. 1986. *God save Ulster: The religion and politics of Paisleyism*. Oxford: Oxford University Press.

Bryan, D., T. G. Fraser, and S. Dunn. 1995. *Political rituals: Loyalist parades in Portadown*. Coleraine, Northern Ireland: Centre for the Study of Conflict, University of Ulster.

Burton, F. 1978. *The politics of legitimacy*. London: Routledge and Kegan Paul.

Cairns, E. 1980. The development of ethnic discrimination in young children in Northern Ireland. In *Children and young people in Northern Ireland: A society under stress*, edited by J. Harbison and J. Harbison, 115–27. Somerset: Open Books.

———. 1982. Intergroup conflict in Northern Ireland. In *Social identity and intergroup relations*, edited by H. Tajfel, 277–97. Cambridge: Cambridge University Press.

——— 1983. The political socialisation of tomorrow's parents: Violence, politics and the media. In *Children of the Troubles: Children in Northern Ire-*

land, edited by J. Harbison, 120–26. Belfast: Learning Resources Unit, Stranmillis College.

———. 1987. *Caught in crossfire: Children and the Northern Ireland Conflict.* New York: Syracuse University Press.

———. 1989. Social identity and intergroup conflict: A developmental perspective. In *Growing up in Northern Ireland,* edited by J. Harbison, 115–30. Belfast: Stranmillis.

———. 1992. Political violence, social values and the generation gap. In *Social Attitudes in Northern Ireland: The Second Report, 1991–1992,* edited by P. Stringer and G. Robinson, 149–60. Belfast: Blackstaff.

———. 1994. Understanding conflict and promoting peace in Ireland: Psychology's contribution. *Irish Journal of Psychology* 15:480–93.

Cairns, E., and I. J. Toner. 1993. Children and political violence in Northern Ireland: From riots to reconciliation. In *Psychological effects of war and violence on children,* edited by L. A. Leavitt and N. A. Fox, 215–29. New York: Erlbaum.

Colaizzi, P. F. 1978. Psychological research as the phenomenologist views it. In *Existential-phenomenological alternatives for psychology,* edited by R. S. Valle and M. Kin, 48–71. New York: Oxford University Press.

Connerton, P. 1989. *How societies remember.* Cambridge: Cambridge University Press.

Darby, J. 1986. *Intimidation and the control of conflict in Northern Ireland.* Dublin: Gill and MacMillan.

Devine-Wright, P. 1996. Memory and ethnic conflict: A multi-disciplinary review of social-scientific theory and research. Unpublished manuscript. Londonderry, Northern Ireland: INCORE, University of Ulster.

Dunn, S., ed. 1995. *Facets of the conflict in Northern Ireland.* London: MacMillan.

Enright, R. D. 1994. Piaget on the moral development of forgiveness: Identity or reciprocity? *Human Development* 37:63–80.

Enright, R. D., E. A. Gassin, T. Longinovic, and D. Loudon. 1994. Forgiveness as a solution to social crisis. Paper presented at the conference, Morality and Social Crisis, Institute for Educational Research, Beograd, Serbia.

Enright, R. D., E. A. Gassin, and C. R. Wu. 1992. Forgiveness: A developmental view. *Journal of Moral Education* 21:99–114.

Enright, R. D., and The Human Development Study Group. 1991. The moral development of forgiveness. In *Handbook of moral behavior and development* 1, edited by W. Kurtines and J. Gewirtz, 123–52. Hillsdale, N.J.: Erlbaum.

Falconer, A. D. 1988. The reconciling power of forgiveness. In *Reconciling memories,* edited by A. D. Falconer, 84–98. Blackrock, County Dublin: Columba.

———. 1990. From theologies-in-opposition towards a theology-of-interdependence. *Life and Peace Review* 4:11–13.

Fentress, J., and C. Wickham. 1992. *Social memory.* Oxford: Blackwell.

Fulton, J. 1991. *The tragedy of belief: Division, politics, and religion in Ireland.* Oxford: Clarendon.

Gallagher, A. M. 1989. Social identity and the Northern Ireland conflict. *Human Relations* 42:917–35.

Gorsuch, R. L., and G. D. Venable. 1983. Development of an "age universal" I-E scale. *Journal for the Scientific Study of Religion* 22:181–87.

Greer, J. 1990. The Persistence of Religion: A study of sixth-form pupils in Northern Ireland, 1968–1988. *Journal of Social Psychology* 130:573–81.

Heskin, K. 1980. *Northern Ireland: A psychological analysis.* Dublin: Gill and McMillan.

Interchurch Group on Faith and Politics. 1993. *Breaking down the enmity: Faith and politics in the Northern Ireland conflict.* Belfast: Belfast Interchurch Group on Faith and Politics.

Irwin-Zarecka, I. 1994. *Frames of remembrance: The dynamics of collective memory.* New Brunswick, N.J.: Transaction.

Jahoda, G., and S. Harrison. 1975. Belfast children: Some effects of a conflict environment. *Irish Journal of Psychology* 3:1–19.

Jenkins, R. 1983. *Lads, citizens and ordinary kids: Working-class youth lifestyles in Belfast.* London: Routledge and Kegan Paul.

King, M. 1967. Dimensions of religiosity in "measuring the religious variable." *Journal for the Scientific Study of Religion* 6:173–90.

Liechty, J. 1993. Roots of sectarianism in Ireland: Chronology and reflections. Paper commissioned by the Working Party on Sectarianism. Belfast: Northern Ireland.

Loftus, B. 1990. *Mirrors: William III and Mother Ireland.* Dundrum, Northern Ireland: Picture Press.

———. 1994. *Mirrors: Orange and green.* Dundrum, Northern Ireland: Picture Press.

Lyons, E. 1994. Coping with social change: Processes of social memory in the reconstruction of identities. In *Changing European identities: Social psychological analyses of social change,* edited by G. M. Breakwell and E. Lyons, 31–39. Oxford: Butterworth-Heinemann.

McAllister, I. 1982. The devil, miracles and the afterlife: The political sociology of religion in Northern Ireland. *British Journal of Sociology* 33:330–47.

———. 1983. Religious commitment and social attitudes in Ireland. *Review of Religious Research* 25:3–20.

McSweeney, B. 1989. The religious dimension of the Troubles in Northern Ireland. In *Religion, state, and society in modern Britain,* edited by P. Badham, 67–83. Lampeter, Wales: Edwin Mellen Press.

Middleton, D., and D. Edwards, eds. 1990. *Collective remembering.* London: Sage.

Montville, J. V. 1993. The healing function in political conflict resolution. In *Conflict resolution theory and practice: Integration and application,* edited by D. J. D. Sandole and H. van der Merwe, 112–27. Manchester: Manchester University Press.

Morrow, D. 1991. *The churches and inter-community relationships*. Coleraine, Northern Ireland: Centre for the Study of Conflict, University of Ulster.

——. 1995. Church and religion in the Ulster crisis. In *Facets of the conflict in Northern Ireland*, edited by S. Dunn, 151–67. London: Macmillan.

Moxon-Browne, E. P. 1983. *Nation, class and creed in Northern Ireland*. Aldershot: Gower.

Piaget, J. 1965. *The moral judgment of the child*. New York: Free Press.

Poole, M. 1983. The demography of violence. In *Northern Ireland: The background to the conflict*, edited by J. Darby, 151–80. Belfast: Appletree Press.

Roe, M. D., and E. Cairns. 1998. Adolescents and political violence: A case of Northern Ireland. In *Adolescents, cultures and conflicts: Growing up in Europe*, edited by J. E. Nurmi. New York: Michigan State University Press and Garland Publishing.

Roe, M. D., W. Pegg, K. Hodges, and R. A. Trimm. 1997. Selective ethnic memories and forgiveness of political violence in Northern Ireland. Paper presented at the annual meeting of the American Conference for Irish Studies, Albany, New York.

Rolston, B. 1991. *Politics and painting: Murals and conflict in Northern Ireland*. London: Associated University Presses.

——. 1992. *Drawing support: Murals in the North of Ireland*. Belfast: Beyond the Pale Publications.

——. 1995. *Drawing support 2: Murals of war and peace*. Belfast: Beyond the Pale Publications.

Rose, R. 1971. *Governing without consensus: An Irish perspective*. London: Faber and Faber.

Rowe, J. O., S. Halling, E. Davies, M. Leifer, D. Powers, and J. van Bronkhorst. 1989. The psychology of forgiving another: A dialogal research approach. In *Existential-phenomenological perspectives in psychology*, edited by R. S. Valle and S. Halling, 233–44. New York: Plenum.

Schuman, H., and C. Rieger. 1992. Collective memory and collective memories. In *Theoretical perspectives on autobiographical memory*, edited by M. A. Conway, D. C. Rubin, H. Spinnler, and W. A. Wagenaar, 323–36. Boston: Kluwer Academic.

Taylor, R. 1988. Social scientific research on the Troubles in Northern Ireland: The problem of objectivity. *Economic and Social Review* 19:123–45.

Trew, K. 1983. A sense of national identity: Fact of artifact? *Irish Journal of Psychology* 6:28–36.

Turner, E. B., I. F. Turner, and A. Reid. 1980. Religious attitudes in two types of urban secondary schools: A decade of change. *Irish Journal of Education* 14:43–52.

Waddell, N., and E. Cairns. 1986. Situational perspectives on social identity in Northern Ireland. *British Journal of Social Psychology* 25:25–31.

Weinreich, P. 1982. Identity development in Protestant and Roman Catholic adolescent boys and girls in Belfast. Paper presented at the 10th International Congress of the International Association for Child and Adolescent Psychiatry and Allied Professions, Dublin.

Whyte, J. 1978. Interpretations of the Northern Ireland problem: An appraisal. *Economic and Social Review* 9:257–82.

———. 1990. *Interpreting Northern Ireland.* Oxford: Oxford University Press.

Working Party on Sectarianism. 1993. The report of the Working Party on Sectarianism: A discussion document for presentation to the Irish Inter-Church Meeting. Belfast: Department of Social Issues of the Irish Inter-Church Meeting.

Wright, F. 1988. Reconciling the histories of Protestant and Catholic in Northern Ireland. In *Reconciling memories,* edited by A. D. Falconer, 68–83. Blackrock, County Dublin: Columba.

MAUREEN S. G. HAWKINS

Brenton's *The Romans in Britain* and Rudkin's *The Saxon Shore*

Audience, Purpose, and Dramatic Response to the Conflict in Northern Ireland

Historical drama, according to Christopher Murray, "has always been concerned with power, identity, and the national consciousness" (1988, 269). It suits this purpose because, as Hugh says in Brian Friel's *Translations,* "it is not the literal past, the 'facts' of history, that shape us, but images of the past embodied in language" (1984, 445). These images shape our communal consciousness, dictating how we should perceive ourselves and behave as members of a community — usually the nation[1] — rather than as individuals.[2] Historical playwrights attempt to influence their audience's self-image and resultant behavior by dramatizing past events in order (usually implicitly) either to validate the audience's present behavior or to criticize it and establish an alternate model. As a result, historical drama is directed to a specific audience: the audience that embodies the "national consciousness" the playwright perceives as creating the present with which he or she is concerned and/or as having the power to create the future that he or she desires.

The past that the historical playwright dramatizes to effect this end is the targeted audience's own past, even when only metaphorically so. For example, in the nineteenth and early twentieth centuries, a common metaphor (used by the English and Irish alike and exploited by Irish nationalist playwrights such as Lady Gregory and Oliver St. John Gogarty)[3] for the British occupation of Ireland was the Roman occupation of the Holy Land. In the 1980s, under the impetus of the Troubles in Northern Ireland, two playwrights, Howard Brenton (writing for an English audience) and David Rudkin (writing for a Northern Irish loyalist audience) changed that metaphor, dramatizing their responses to the British presence in Northern Ireland in terms of the Roman occupation of Britain, focusing on the period when Rome was withdrawing and the Saxons invading.

This change is significant in a number of ways. Shifting Ireland's metaphorical locus from the Holy Land to Britain desacralizes the cause of Irish independence, moving the conflict from the spiritual to the secular sphere. This allows both playwrights to avoid portraying the republican or loyalist movements or the conflict itself as sectarian and allows them to deny traditional Romantic nationalism's sectarian definition of "Irishness," even though both playwrights acknowledge and exploit the religious differences that mark their combatants. Shifting the object of imperial occupation from Palestine to Britain permits Brenton to draw on his English audience's patriotism in lieu of divine sanction to advocate Northern Irish independence in *The Romans in Britain*, which premiered at London's National Theatre in October 1980. Although Rudkin did not design *The Saxon Shore* for the London audience at the smaller Almeida Theatre where it finally premiered in February 1986, the shift from the Holy Land to Britain serves the same function for that audience as it would have for the Northern Irish loyalist audience for which he wrote the play. Finally, setting their plays primarily during the period in which Rome was withdrawing from Britain allows both playwrights to bestow an aura of historical inevitability on British withdrawal from Northern Ireland and, thus, on the eventual triumph of the republican movement.

Although both dramatists imply the inevitablility of British withdrawal from Northern Ireland, significant differences, dictated by both their chosen audiences and their political agendas, exist in their arguments. Brenton, a British dramatist, is writing for an English audience about the English presence in Northern Ireland that he regards as the primary source of the Troubles there and whose withdrawal he regards as providing at least a partial solution to those Troubles. However, he knows that his English audience would, only a year after Mountbatten's 1979 assassination, be disinclined to view Irish republicanism favorably. Furthermore, given Britain's recent experience with Northern Ireland, the audience would see the British role there as beneficial, providing a divided and violent people with much needed protection from themselves. To convince them that "all empire is bad; the Republican cause is just; the border is a crime" (Oakes 1980, 39) and that the British should withdraw from Northern Ireland, Brenton imputes fascist characteristics to the British troops in Northern Ireland by portraying them as brutalizing the locals and by having Julius Caesar, transformed into a contemporary British officer in Second Part, quote the first two lines of "Long-legged Fly," a late poem written by Yeats when he was flirting with fascism.

More important, Brenton encourages his English audience to empathize and identify with the Northern Irish republican movement even as he characterizes the English as imperialist invaders in Northern Ireland. He portrays early British history as a succession of brutal invasions from the Belgic incursions that overwhelmed the earlier Celtic inhabitants, to the Roman invasion that oppressed both, to the Saxon influx that devastated the Romanized Britons. He makes his allegory explicit through (a) the transformation at the end of Part 1 of Caesar and his troops in England into British troops in Ireland and (b) the central character of Part 2, Thomas Chichester, a British agent "from an old English Army family" (Brenton 1980, 97) whose father was killed in another British possession, Cyprus. Although Chichester claims "Anglo-Irish parentage" (88), he asserts to himself that "home" is "England" even as he realizes that the Northern Irish field in which he is waiting to assassinate a Northern Irish republican leader is "the dead likeness of the Old Acre. A field back home, on the family farm" (69). While he waits, he witnesses events (which the audience also sees) during the Roman and Saxon invasions of Britain that make him question where his loyalties should lie and that are intended to lead the audience to see the British presence in Northern Ireland as imperialist, oppressive, exploitative, violent, and destructive.

However, Brenton is not simply anti-imperialist; he is also a Marxist who, with David Edgar, Tony Bicat, Brian Clark, Francis Fuchs, David Hare, and Snoo Wilson, had already written *England's Ireland* (1972), "which used British imperialism to illustrate the oppressive nature of class society" (Innes 1992, 190). Because his plays, Brenton says, are written "unreservedly in the cause of socialism" (Stine and Marowski 1985, 56) and he believes that "if you're going to change the world, . . . there's only one set of tools, and they're bloody and stained but realistic" (Rusinko 1989, 132), *The Romans in Britain* postulates revolutionary socialism as a historically inevitable successor to and means of ending abusive hierarchical systems including imperialism, slavery, racism, classism, and patriarchy. As Robert Gross puts it, the play enacts a single "story of the genesis of revolutionary consciousness, and the necessary role of violence in the development of that consciousness"

(1992, 75). Its "three historical segments . . . [are] coordinated . . . within a single, over-arching narrative that begins with the depiction of a society's inability to resist imperialist oppression, through increasingly powerful acts of revolt, to the tentative formation of an alternative society, articulating for the first time the myth of its golden age. . . . The First Part reiterates the defeat of the less powerful at the hands of those more powerful than they: the fugitive Irishman killed by the Celts, the Celts killed by the Romans, the female slave raped by the male criminal, the Irish girl shot by the British soldier. . . . The Second Part shows the defeat of authority figures by those beneath them in the social hierarchy" (Gross 1992, 72–74). In it, the Steward kills and robs his aristocratic Roman mistress, Adona, as Corda does her sexually abusive father, and Corda vows to become "a mother of killers. . . . Children brought up right" to "[k]ill the Saxons" (Brenton 1980, 101). To that end she enlists the aid of her sister, "all the men and women we can find," and the cooks turned poets who will inspire them all with their story of Arthur, the "King who never was . . . a golden age, lost and yet to come" (102).

Lest the audience miss the point that Arthur is the champion of the invaded, oppressed Celtic inhabitants of the British Isles and of their/ Brenton's idealized alternative society—and *not* of the modern, imperialist England that claims him—Chichester tells Maitland that the field in which he has been waiting is "like one on my mother's farm, not far from Colchester. The Roman city of Camulodunum. . . . And Camulodunum could be the site for Arthur's last battle. King Arthur! Celtic warlord. Who fought twelve great battles against the Saxons. That is, us. . . . Very fashionable, the Celts, with the arty-crafty. . . . But show them the real thing—an Irishman with a gun, or under a blanket in an H-block and they run a mile. If King Arthur walked out of those trees, now—know what he'd look like to us? One more fucking mick" (Brenton 1980, 75). The English have a right to him only if they embrace the principles of his imagined reign: "His government was the people of Britain. His peace was as common as rain or snow. His law was as natural as grass, growing in a meadow. And there never was a Government, or a peace, or a law like that" (102). They can be created, Brenton implies, but not by a hierarchical society which demands, as Adona does, "Restore the Empire! . . . Appoint magistrates. . . . Set up gibbets in the fields to punish deserters." England must realize, as the cooks do, that "the Romans left Britain a hundred years ago" (95), that the age of "Rome, invaders, Empire" (97) is over, and that it is time to begin the age of Arthur in Britain as well as in Ireland.

Unlike Brenton, Rudkin, though born in England, may validly be considered as "Irish" a playwright as any other product of the diaspora who turns his attention to Irish issues. Of English and Northern Irish Evangelical Protestant parentage, Rudkin has stated that he perceives himself as having two identities: a "Northern Irish Protestant identity [and an] English one" (Etherton 1989, 26); he considers rural Ulster dialect his childhood tongue, and he has, in several of his major plays, addressed important Irish issues: British repression of Ireland in *Afore Night Come* (1962); the nature of Irish nationalism and the vexed question of Irish identity—especially for Northern Irish Protestant Republicans like himself—in *Cries from Casement as His Bones Are Brought to Dublin* (1973); metaphorical effects of the Troubles in the North in *Ashes* (1974); and, as in *The Saxon Shore* (though in a more veiled fashion), the self-destructive effects of the Scots-Irish rejection of union with the mere Irish[4] in his adaptation of Euripides' *Hippolytus* (1978).

In the early 1980s, the directors of Field Day according to Marilynn Richtarik, "in keeping with their goal . . . to question old assumptions in the interest of forging a more inclusive notion of Irish identity[,] . . . were especially anxious to present the work of Protestant dramatists who might approach the issue of Irish identity from an angle that differed from traditional [that is, Romantic] nationalist feelings about it" (1994, 191), so they asked Rudkin to write a play for them intended, like all their plays, for premiere in Derry. Rudkin, though surprised by their request because "he assumed that they were green [that is, Romantic] nationalists who would not be interested in the kinds of things he had to say about Ulster" (Richtarik 1994, 192), was delighted by "the opportunity to take part in a dialogue about the future of what he still regarded as his country" and as well as by the opportunity "to articulate dramatically how it felt to be an Ulster Protestant."

The resulting play, *The Saxon Shore,* in which Rudkin analyses the origins and effects of what he calls the Ulster Protestant loyalist "plantation mentality" (Richtarik 1994, 193), is obviously written for a Northern Irish audience, for whom, as Richtarik says, "certain words, phrases, and speeches would [be] politically resonant" (195), but it is directed particularly toward Northern Irish Protestant loyalists, thus suggesting that Rudkin sees their reaction to their largely Catholic republican compatriots as a primary cause of the Troubles in the North and that he believes that persuading them to change that reaction would help to resolve the Troubles. Unfortunately, Field Day declined to produce *The Saxon Shore* on the grounds that it had insufficient resources to stage the play, though Rudkin insists that the rejection was based on political considerations; specifically, Richtarik says, "that [Field Day was] not as interested in the Protestant viewpoint as they professed to be. . . . [and] that the directors were afraid of what 'their' (that is, nationalist) audiences would make of it" (197). Some critics, such as Brian McAvera and Shaun Richards, apparently agree with Rudkin (see Richtarik 1994, 303 n. 9), which supports Richtarik's supposition that Field Day's rejection of the play was likely to have offended Northern Irish Protestants, an ironic outcome, given that, as she persuasively argues, Field Day may have rejected it to avoid their being offended by its criticism of them (198–202).[5] Determined to bring the play to the audience for which he had conceived it, Rudkin then offered the play to Belfast's Lyric Theatre, which also declined it.

Whether one knows its production history or not, it is evident that Rudkin's intended audience is Northern Irish, particularly Northern Irish loyalists of planter stock, and that he is casting his argument in the context of their anxieties following the previous year's Hillsborough Agreement (1985), which exacerbated their "sense of crisis, of insecurity, and of being dependent on the whim of an imperial power that does not care about them" (Richtarik 1994, 194). According to the "Historical Note" to *The Saxon Shore,* beginning around 367, Rome "planted" Saxon tribes on Britain's North Sea coast as a first defense against Celtic invasions of Romanized Britain (Rudkin 1986, vii), a practice that Richtarik states "was usual imperial practice" (193). The play creates an analogy between these tribes and Northern Ireland's Protestant "garrison," an analogy that Richtarik says that Lynda Henderson has demonstrated "is precise" (193). Richtarik adds that "Rudkin reinforces the parallel . . . through language and accents" (1994, 194) as well as through his depiction of the Saxons' anxieties about the intentions of Rome and of their Celtic neighbors.

Through this analogy, Rudkin implies that the loyalists must accept that England has manipulated them against their mere Irish compatriots, brutalizing them and denying them an Irish identity that the mere Irish would have extended to them through bonds of love. Furthermore, he implies that, just as Rome withdrew from Britain, abandoning her Saxon "planters," Britain will withdraw from Northern Ireland and abandon *her* planters, forcing them either to become totally dehumanized, like the play's Saxons who become werewolves at night to attack their Celtic neighbors, or to create a new, assimilated, Irish identity — with the second possibility becoming ever more remote because of their belligerent intransigence and the extent of the hatred to which their actions drive their Irish compatriots.

To create his analogy, Rudkin draws careful parallels between his characters and those groups that have and/or have had an interest in Northern Ireland. That Rome equals England is evident, and the Roman NCO's despising of Athdark and the other planted Saxons suggests that the English, including British troops currently garrisoning Northern Ireland, similarly despise the Northern Irish Protestant loyalists, just as Rome's withdrawal from Britain forecasts England's withdrawal from Northern Ireland.

In the play, the Romanized Celtic squire, Litorius, and his wife, Priscillina, correspond to the Anglo-Irish. Rudkin's portrayal of them implies that Ascendancy unionists like Carson have exploited the Ulster loyalists to ensure their own security and prosperity — or, in the event of successful rebellion, to give them time to get themselves and their wealth safely out of the country — and that they will abandon them as the couple abandon the Saxons. This parallel is made even stronger by Litorius's use of conventional Orange Lodge rhetoric to encourage the Saxons to rebuild the breached wall; he refers to "Our Covenant. . . . Our Sovereignty. Our legacy of three centuries. Our Heritage" (Rudkin 1986, 26) — which, significantly, becomes "*your* heritage" (my emphasis) near the end of the play when he urges the Saxons to fight while he and Priscillina escape. Just as, especially after the Act of Union, the Anglo-Irish filled administrative roles throughout the British Empire, the couple have served in other parts of the Roman Empire: Hungary, Egypt, and Spain, in every one of which there was "trouble" and their house was "burned down" (48), thus implying that Northern Ireland is but the latest of many British colonies to rebel — and that, like the others, it will achieve independence.

Rudkin's Saxons have the same problems of identity experienced by

Northern Irish Protestant loyalists. Richtarik points out that "Athdark expresses the curious envy the Saxons have of the dispossessed native British: 'They know who they are. Who am I?' " and adds that "like the (British) Northern Irish Protestants, who need all four words to describe their condition, the Saxons cannot take refuge in any simple notion of their cultural identity. They do not feel as though they belong anywhere. They are not accepted by the Romans as Roman citizens with the same rights as those at home, but they are regarded as part of the imperial enemy by the Celtic tribes who seek to reconquer the entire island" (196). Agricola, their pastor, says that they are Roman by covenant, Saxon by stock, and British by "land, dwelling, and husbandry," though he denies that this last identity makes them any kin to the Celts (Rudkin 1986, 7). However, though both Agricola and the Old Farmer make a virtue of being more loyal to Rome than "the perfidious Romans" (46), the latter accepts a hyphenated Saxon-British identity but rejects a Roman one, just as some modern Northern Irish Protestant loyalists identify themselves as Scots-Irish but, feeling betrayed by what they perceive as England's abandonment and betrayal of them, refuse to consider themselves English or British.

Religiously, Rudkin's Christian Saxons differ from their pagan, goddess-worshiping Celtic neighbors, and much of their religious/ political rhetoric is that of the dominantly Scots-Irish Presbyterian Orange Lodge. Agricola's sermon on the biblical story of Ahab, Jezebel, and Naboth suggests a covenanting ideology, and, unlike Naboth, the preacher implies, the Saxons *will* defy the king and will not allow themselves to be dispossessed without a fight. Agricola's choice of text suggests a distrust of Rome analogous to the growing Northern Irish loyalist distrust of England in the wake of the Hillsborough Agreement. That Jezebel, whom Agricola identifies with the local Celts, is successful in falsely persuading the authorities to convict Naboth of blasphemy in order to obtain his garden for Ahab implies a fear that England will grant their "garden" to the Irish nationalists. However, Agricola's insistence that the Saxons will not respond peacefully as Naboth did may imply that, unlike him, they really *will* be guilty of "cursing God" (Rudkin 1986, 6) by their use of Christianity to justify their midnight werewolf raids on their Celtic neighbours.

Finally, Rudkin equates the British Celts with the mere Irish. Most live north of Hadrian's wall, which Litorius implicitly parallels with the border between Northern Ireland and the Republic of Ireland by saying of the land beyond it, "we gave them that. Whole new country, all to themselves. Leave 'em alone, and they'd leave us alone. You'd think" (27), though Lugovelin makes it clear that the Celts are far from satisfied with this "gift": "Rome is soon gone. . . . Oh then the Kingdom. Lost to us so long. Comes to fall, into our hands. In our time" (24).

The Celts' worship of a virgin goddess whom they call "Our Lady" (14) not only stresses the religious difference between them and the Christian Saxons but also suggests what to many Protestants is a signal difference between their faith and that of Roman Catholics: devotion to the Virgin Mary. That Ceiriad is both heir to the Celtic throne and priestess of the goddess links her with the Lady's attributes: "Mercy[,] . . . Healing[, and] Grief" (14), thus fitting her, despite their long history of bitter, violent enmity, for the role of mediatrix between the Celts and the Saxons. That she is the banished daughter of Llyr (Shakespeare's King Lear) connects her to Shakespeare's Cordelia, further rendering her an embodiment of martyred, selfless love (as the etymology of both names, Cordelia and Ceiriad, suggests). Her saving, healing, and love of Athdark suggests that the mere Irish could have welcomed, loved, and assimilated the Scots-Irish through marriage had the latter been willing to accept that love and dissociate themselves from English imperialism.

Ceiriad's connection with Shakespeare's Cordelia also reinforces the parallel Rudkin draws between Ireland and Celtic Britain to enlist British/Northern Irish loyalist patriotic support for Northern Irish independence from Britain. Furthermore, that Cordelia brought a French army into Britain to help her father and end Britain's bloody civil war both suggests and exculpates Ireland's history of seeking aid from France and Spain and implies the possibility that Ireland could have driven out both the English and the Scots-Irish had it not been for internal dissension.

Athdark's murder of Ceiriad suggests that the Scots-Irish have only themselves to blame for mere Irish enmity. Indeed, despite that murder and that enmity, the Celts still hold out hope of reconciliation if the Saxons will become loyal to Britain; Sulgwen translates Lugovelin's final challenge: "Saxons! What is your title to the land you have taken? Who are your people now? Now to what land is your desire? . . . Until you answer, here is our answer. (*Raise each a clawlike hand in blood-*

stained salute above the dead)" (43). However, Rudkin himself seems to doubt the possibility of such reconciliation. Although it is clear in the play that the Celts and Saxons speak different languages, until this point the audience "hears" both in English.[6] But in this scene, Lugovelin's speech, delivered in a reconstructed form of Cumric which, Rudkin says, "should sound grim, and alien, and frightening" (1986, 52), is unintelligible both to the Saxons and to the audience — whom Rudkin had intended to be Northern Ireland's Scots-Irish loyalists, the Saxons' analog. This menacing linguistic change makes it clear, Rudkin writes, that the Saxon raid on Dinas Maros and the murders of Ceiriad and the others "have finally alienated the Celts, and [made] the separation between the two cultures [and therefore their languages] unbridgeable" (51). Richtarik says that Rudkin has described *The Saxon Shore* as a "play about a man [Athdark, whose bent posture as a result of the wound 'he received as a wolf . . . illustrates dramatically his stunted personality'] learning to stand" (Richtarik 1994, 197), but the Saxons' alienation of the Celts and Athdark's solitude at the end of the play, when he finally stands upright, suggest that Rudkin believes that Northern Irish loyalists will have to rely on their own form of Sinn Fein before they can hope to become, like Athdark, *"the beginnings of a man"* (Rudkin 1986, 49) and convince their neighbors that they are willing to "look to the land in which they live for their future, together with the people with whom they share it" (Richtarik 1994, 197).

Although his characterization of Ceiriad romanticizes the Celts, Rudkin balances his treatment of them somewhat through his characterization of the other Celts. Sulgwen, who declares that "it's kingdoms that marry" (Rudkin 1986, 32), is as pragmatic, materialistic, and dismissive of love as the Saxon Widow Flax, who declares that "it's acres wed" (11). Though Ceiriad is in love with Athdark, Sulgwen can see him only as an enemy. Her vision of him is shared by the old male Celt — whose look of hatred changes Athdark's perception of Ceiriad from an "angel" (31) to a "Whore of Ahab" (43) and fills his own eyes with reciprocal hatred — as well as by the warlike Lugovelin, whom Sulgwen thinks a fitter husband for Ceiriad and whose policy of revenge against the Saxons will become the order of the day after Athdark murders her.

Far from romanticizing the Celts, Brenton uses the First Part of his play to present them as just as oppressive, brutal, and violent as the invading Romans, Saxons, and English. When the two Irish criminals encounter an Irish slave girl, they have no hesitation about killing her to keep her from betraying them to her British owners. When her owner's sons finally capture them, they peremptorily kill one, bless their fields by slitting his throat and pouring his blood on the earth, and hunt the other with hounds.

Meanwhile, their family's matriarch, caught between two Belgic tribes, the Catuvellauni and the Trinovantes, rejects a Catuvellaunian embassy asking her to ally with them to resist the advance of Julius Caesar and his troops because she hopes that her alliance with the Trinovantes, who have made a truce with the Romans, will protect her people. Neither resistance nor truce, however, avails. Historically, it is known that Caesar defeated the Catuvellauni and exacted hostages and tribute from them (Scullard 1979), and, though historically the truce did protect the Trinovantes, it does not protect the matriarch's people. Three Roman soldiers, separated from their unit and heading for a swim in the river, encounter her three sons, murder two, and attempt to rape the third, Marban, a young man in training to be a Druid. Two cohorts, similarly separated from the Roman army, encounter the matriarch's village and, as Caesar puts it, have "some fun" (Brenton 1980, 50) massacring its inhabitants.

Though Caesar is annoyed at this "tiny stupidity" (Brenton 1980, 52), he orders the prisoners killed and their fields sown with salt because "even a little massacre must look like policy. They'll take it as a warning. Or that we knew these people were traitors. Probably leave a little local war behind us — no bad thing" (57–58) — which implicity substantiates the Irish republican woman's (Moraed) later charge that all "the *British* Empire [gave] the people it enslaved [was t]ribal wars" (98; my emphasis). When Marban is brought before him, Caesar orders him humiliated and released bound *because* he is a Druid; sectarian brutality is simply an effective weapon of war to terrify the enemy.

Found by other survivors, Marban, before committing suicide, tells them that "we must . . . [c]hange ourselves into animals . . . an animal not yet heard of. Deadly, watching, ready in the forest. Something not human" (60) — an apt description of the children Corda later vows to raise to kill Saxons and of the Irish republican operatives, especially Moraed, who kills Chichester. As in *The Saxon Shore*, if the Irish/Celts are brutal terrorists, it is because they have been taught to be so. Even

Chichester, who, as O'Rourke describes him, is "an honourable man
. . . [an] assassin, humanized by his trade" (98) because he has come to
realize that "in my hand there's a Roman spear. A Saxon axe. A British
Army machine-gun" (97), has no right to expect otherwise of them.
They find his liberal conversion irrelevant — and rightly so because it is
merely sentimental and self-serving; when he discovers that they mean
to kill him anyway, he falls back on his previous stereotype of them,
cursing them as "murdering bastards" (98) before he dies.

Despite their differences, however, Brenton and Rudkin are united
in condemning patriarchy as the root both of imperialism and of the
Troubles in Northern Ireland. Rudkin's Christian Saxons perceive
themselves as more civilized than their British neighbours because they
try to live by Roman standards and worship god as a father whose law
they obey by enduring pain and exercising "Will" to raise themselves
"above the beasts" (Rudkin 1986, 6). However, Rudkin implies that
their imperialistic values and patriarchic conception of god, which lead
them to equate slaughtering Celtic women and children with being
civilized and doing "God's Work," inverts their ideals and perverts their
Christianity and their humanity. Their repressed animal nature erupts
in their nocturnal transformation into werewolves, one of whom is
ironically named Agnes. When they are werewolves, their leader as-
sures them that they are superior to "mere men." It is as werewolves
that they are both most violent and most patriarchic/hierarchic, calling
their leader "Master" and "Lord" (2) and viewing the "feminine" principle as a Kali figure embodied in the moon as a "Lady Mother" who
presides over their attempts to destroy the humanity as well as the
bodies of the Celts, which they rend until they are "unknowable for
pieces of Man" (39).

Nor, though he postulates the Celts as represented by Ceiriad as
offering a "feminine" alternative to patriarchy, are most of Rudkin's
Celts, especially the males, less patriarchically violent. When Sulgwen
reminds Ceiriad that the Celts are her kingdom's enemy, Ceiriad point-
edly replies, "My *father's* enemy" (22; my emphasis), and Lugovelin is
eager for war despite Ceiriad's desire for peace.

Whether Celt, Roman, English, or Irish, the men in Brenton's play,
as Gross points out, "kill with objects they have crafted as instruments
of death": knives, shields, and rifles; "knives are associated with erec-
tions" throughout the play, and male violence is visually linked with

male sexual behaviour by the Second Soldier's use of a knife to cut Marban's shoulder and buttocks in the scene in which the soldiers try to rape him (1992, 76–77). Conlag, having murdered a man, has no compunctions about raping the Irish slave girl, and Cai, who sexually abuses his daughters, has no compunctions about slitting the Saxon's throat to make a blood offering to his conception of the "feminine" principle (a conception very like that of Rudkin's werewolves), the pre-Christian goddess to whom he has made such offerings before.

Though both playwrights postulate the Celts as providing a "feminine" alternative to patriarchy, Rudkin's view of it is more romanticized than Brenton's. Ceiriad's goddess is linked to nature through being worshiped in an oak grove (which also suggests a parallel to the city of Derry, which is named for an oak grove); her will is healing rather than enduring pain, and she sends love to those who ask for it. When Athdark enters Celtic territory, his patriarchic perceptions are inverted: nature appears heavenly, not a realm of beasts to be conquered; women are angels; and everyone, not merely the elect, is saved. His later conviction that hearing "the voice of the God of my fathers" (Rudkin 1986, 37) made him revert to patriarchic values, is ironic: what caused his reversion was seeing the old male Celt's hatred-filled eyes, later mirrored by his dead mother's "accusing eyes" (Rudkin 1986, 37), which he associates with his divine, pastoral, and biological fathers. This irony reinforces Rudkin's message that patriarchy, not ethnicity, is the real cause of the Troubles—a point further reinforced by his doubling of roles: one actor plays Cambyses, the leader of the werewolves; the Old Farmer, the leader of the Saxons; and Llyr, the warlike king of the Celts. Similarly, a single actor plays both Agricola and Lugovelin, the patriarchic war-leaders of the Saxons and the Celts; and the same actress plays the three women who accept the values of patriarchy: the Saxon Widow Flax, the Celtic Sulgwen, and the Romanized Priscillina.

Brenton's "feminine" alternative to patriarchy is also embodied by Celtic women: the matriarch, the Slave, Corda, and Moraed, but his feminine principle and its avatars are not devotees of peace, love, and reconciliation like Rudkin's Ceiriad and her goddess. Although, unlike Brenton's patriarchal figures, they do not craft instruments for killing, they have no hesitation about shedding blood in their own defense or to benefit their land or people, and their ability to do so increases as the play progresses. Though it is Marban who kills Daui, it is his mother who offers the Irishman's blood to her fields. The Slave and Corda both kill their abusers with stones (a more "natural" way to kill than with a weapon crafted for the purpose), and though the Slave is immediately thereafter killed by British soldiers, Corda survives to become a "mother of killers" (Brenton 1980, 101) like Moraed, who refuses even to think of peace as long as British troops are in her country.

Though both plays were written to persuade their intended audiences, neither was given the opportunity to do so because they ended up with little or no access to those audiences. Because *The Saxon Shore* was rejected both by Field Day, which had commissioned it for initial production in Northern Ireland, and by Belfast's Lyric Theatre, it did not reach its intended audience. Although it was well reviewed in London, there is no doubt that its London audience, which was unlikely to know of, much less understand, the differences between the Anglo-Irish, the Scots-Irish, and the mere Irish, failed to understand Rudkin's allegory[7] (and, even had they understood it, not being Northern Irish loyalists, they would have been unable to effect the change the playwright desired). Furthermore, Christopher Innes argues that "the traumatic degree of human suffering and assault on human sensibilities" in Rudkin's later plays is "counter-productive; and [that therefore] none of [them, including *The Saxon Shore*] has reached a wide public" (1992, 426), thus lessening the chance of its ever reaching its intended audience.

Brenton's play exhibits a similar "traumatic degree of human suffering and assault on human sensibilities," and its production experience forces us to wonder whether Rudkin's play would have been allowed to "reach" his intended audience had it been performed for them. *The Romans in Britain* was widely reviewed and well attended, but Brenton's message was lost in the furore that Mary Whitehouse provoked over the scene of Marban's attempted rape. Keith Peacock may well be correct that it was not that scene so much as the criticism of Britain's role in Northern Ireland delivered from "the Olivier stage of the National Theatre" that upset her and "the Political Right" (1991, 128) — an assertion that seems justified by James Fenton's review of the play. Fenton rightly says that Brenton's strategy is to make his audience feel guilty by persuading them that they "are imperialist pigs who do not care two hoots about the crimes the British Army is committing in

[their] name" if they are "bored" by the play and/or find it "repug-
nant." Having encouraged the English audience to indulge in "a little
calm self-questioning" about whether they "care" about "the Celtic
criminal who is strung up by the feet while his throat is cut" or whether
"the odd Roman soldier sodomized the odd Druid," Brenton directs his
readers to the "proper" response: "[W]hat is that to us?" he asks, and
replies, "Nothing" (qtd. in Evans and Evans 1985, 240).

Though the court case Whitehouse instigated against Michael Bog-
danov, the director of Brenton's play, for offenses under Section 13 of
the Sexual Offenses Act was eventually dropped by the prosecutor (see
Roberts 1992, 67), it effectively ensured that no subsequent professional productions were undertaken, that "two of the three proposed
university productions in the 1980s were cancelled" (Lane 1992, 85),
and that no English audience would again have an opportunity to be
persuaded by *The Romans in Britain*. Following Field Day's rejection
of his play, Rudkin's lack of access to the Northern Irish loyalist audience he crafted it for ensured that his intended audience would have
no opportunity to be persuaded by it. Neither Brenton's assertion that
the English can resolve the Troubles in Northern Ireland nor Rudkin's
assertion that the key to resolution lies with the Northern Irish loyalists
had any chance to be tested, nor had either writer the opportunity to
persuade his targeted audience to make the changes he advocates. Auden may be right that "poetry makes nothing happen" (1945, 50), but
neither play was allowed the freedom to try to prove the contrary.

Notes

1. Obviously the community need not be one that defines itself as a "nation" in the modern sense as, for example, religious plays dramatizing significant events in religious groups' histories (mythological or otherwise) from all
over the world indicate; however, in the modern West, at least, most historical
drama is concerned with the history of the nation.

2. Even historical plays that prioritize the needs of the individual over those
of the nation, such as Dryden's *All for Love,* serve this function by implicitly
defining what we should see as the proper relationship between them.

3. See, for example, Lady Gregory's *The Deliverer* or Gogarty's *A Serious
Thing.*

4. The term "mere Irish," which derives from the Elizabethan meaning of
"mere" (that is, "pure"), designates those of "Gaelic Irish" descent, with the

added implication of Roman Catholic religious affiliation. Because such terms as "Gaelic" and "Celtic" (both of which are linguistic rather than ethnic categories) or "ethnically Irish" imply an exclusivist Romantic nationalist ideology that is inappropriate in the context of Rudkin's plays (which champion the United Irish inclusivist ideological definition of "Irishness"), the archaic term "mere Irish" is used herein to designate those whom Rudkin's chosen Ulster Protestant loyalist audience for *The Saxon Shore* would perceive as embodying it.

5. Richtarik supports her analysis with comments made to her by two of Field Day's directors, David Hammond, who said that he "thought that the image of northern Protestantism was a bit askew" (1994, 200), and Stephen Rea, a Protestant who said that, being a Catholic, Brian Friel might "have been more sensitive about them [Northern Irish Protestants] being portrayed as ravening wolves . . . than I would" (1994, 201). She adds that Tom Paulin, another director, "felt that the play suggested that the Saxon characters, who were analogous to the loyalists in Northern Ireland, did not have a right to their land, and he firmly resisted any implication that Protestants in the North should still be regarded as colonial 'settlers' " (1994, 201). Rea's statement that the political message of the play is "a bit over-stated" (Richtarik 1994, 200) suggests the alternate/additional possibility that the Field Day directors may have found the play too *overtly* political (rather than objecting to its politics) in a period in which they "were concentrating . . . on keeping the focus of their dramatic work, as opposed to their publishing, strictly theatrical, with the 'politics' implicit rather than explicit" (Richtarik 1994, 215).

6. There are a "few snatches of Latin" and a "few isolated words of Cumri language" (Rudkin 1986, 51) heard earlier in the play, but they are always translated and/or made clear by context.

7. Richtarik notes that although *The Saxon Shore* "received favourable, albeit puzzled reviews" when it premiered in London, "hardly any of the critics made the connection with Northern Ireland" (1994, 197). Other than Michael Billington and Richard Allen Cave, the critics, she says, "tended to see the play as an exploration of the *English* national character" (1994, 303 n. 12).

Works Cited

Auden, W. H. 1945. In memory of W. B. Yeats (*d. Jan. 1939*). In *The collected poetry of W. H. Auden*, 48–51. London: Random House.

Brenton, H. 1980. *The Romans in Britain*. London: Eyre Methuen.

Etherton, M. 1989. *Contemporary Irish dramatists*. New York: St. Martin's.

Evans, G., and B. Evans, eds. 1985. *Plays in review, 1956–1980: British drama and the critics*. London: Batsford Academic and Educational.

Friel, B. 1984. *Translations*. In *Selected plays*, 377–451. Irish Drama Selections 6. Washington, D.C.: Catholic University of America Press; Gerrard's Cross, Bucks., United Kingdom: Colin Smythe.

Gogarty, O. n.d. *A serious thing.* In *The plays of Oliver St. John Gogarty,* edited by J. Carens, 59–73. Newark, Del.: Proscenium.

Gregory, I. A., Lady. 1979. *The deliverer.* In *The tragedies and tragic-comedies of Lady Gregory, being the second volume of the collected plays,* edited by A. Saddlemyer, 255–77. 4 vols. Gerrards Cross: Colin Smythe.

Gross, R. 1992. *The Romans in Britain: Aspirations and anxieties of a radical playwright.* In *Howard Brenton: A casebook,* edited by A. Wilson, 71–84. New York: Garland.

Innes, C. 1992. *Modern British drama: 1890–1990.* Cambridge: Cambridge University Press.

Lane, H. 1992. "Infirm of purpose": Dynamics of political purpose in Thirteenth Night. In *Howard Brenton: A casebook,* edited by A. Wilson, 85–100. New York: Garland.

Murray, C. 1988. The history play today. In *Cultural contexts and literary idioms in contemporary Irish literature,* edited by M. Kenneally, 269–89. Studies in Contemporary Irish Literature 1; Irish Literary Studies 31. Totowa, N.J.: Barnes and Noble; Gerrard's Cross, Bucks., United Kingdom: Colin Smythe.

Oakes, P. 1980. Caesar on the South Bank. *Sunday Times* [London], 12 October.

Peacock, D. 1991. *Radical stages: Alternative history in modern British drama.* Contributions in Drama and Theatre Studies 43. New York: Greenwood.

Richtarik, M. 1994. *Acting between the lines: The Field Day Theatre Company and Irish cultural politics: 1980–1984.* Oxford: Oxford University Press.

Roberts, P. 1992. The trials of The Romans in Britain. In *Howard Brenton: A casebook,* edited by A. Wilson, 59–70. New York: Garland.

Rudkin, D. 1986. *The Saxon shore.* London: Methuen.

Rusinko, S. 1989. *British drama, 1950 to the present: A critical history.* Boston: Twayne.

Scullard, H. 1979. *Roman Britain: Outpost of the empire.* London: Thames and Hudson.

Stine, J., and D. Marowski. 1985. Howard Brenton. In *Contemporary literary criticism,* edited by J. C. Stine and D. G. Marowski, 31:56–69. Detroit: Gale Research.

Yeats, W. B. 1989. The long-legged fly. In *The poems: Revised,* edited by R. Finneran, 339. *The Collected Works of W. B. Yeats* 1. New York: Macmillan.

WILLIAM A. HAZLETON

· ·

Local Government and the Peace Process

Until the historic breakthrough of the peace talks that on Good Friday, 1998, endorsed a new British-Irish Agreement, efforts to reestablish a regional government, one that is inclusive and responsive to the
needs and aspirations of all the inhabitants of Northern Ireland, had
foundered in the absence of consensus. But for Catholics and Protestants who are willing to accept in principle, if not heartily endorse, a
Northern Ireland Assembly,[1] the task ahead is more than simply one of
implementing a political agreement that embodies institutional safeguards and guarantees. The question, rather, is how to obtain cross-
community consent for what by necessity will have to be a consensual
working arrangement. Irreconcilable objectives regarding Northern
Ireland's future, combined with a lack of trust and tolerance both between and within the unionist and nationalist traditions, provides scant
optimism that political representatives, inexperienced as they are in the
art of accommodation and compromise, will be capable of constructing
a new set of political arrangements.

The democratic process is arguably the best route to intercommunal
cooperation. But the people of Northern Ireland have developed an
attenuated view of democracy that focuses less on the rules and procedures for making decisions than upon engineering—better yet con-
trolling—what the outcome of those decisions will be. Democracy's
relationship to the principle of popular sovereignty has historically
been viewed very narrowly in terms of majority rule; that is, the expec-
tation that the community with the greatest number should prevail.
This creates an obvious need for protecting minorities from majority
abuses; in a more profound way, however, it further elevates the importance of a border that determines which majority, unionist or nationalist, shall rule. Subjectively applied, democracy under these conditions
becomes a vehicle for stronger ethno-nationalist communities to im-
pose decisions, or for weaker ones to veto decisions, rather than allowing individuals a voice in determining their future (Wilson 1996; Horowitz 1994).

Northern Ireland's existence has historically been contested. As Catholic civil rights protests and Protestant counterdemonstrations became increasingly violent in the early 1970s, British ministers and civil servants replaced local authorities and assumed direct responsibility for making and administering public policy. Thus, the immediate solution to restoring peace without consensus was to insulate the "business of government" from politics. Direct rule not only maintained essential services, enabling Northern Ireland to function as a governmental entity, but also expedited the implementation of major reforms to combat religious and political discrimination. However, removing power and responsibility from locally elected officials also meant that they had fewer incentives and less need to accommodate intercommunal differences. Under direct rule, these matters have been decided for them by the Northern Ireland Office or through negotiations between Dublin and London.

I argue here that institutional arrangements and guarantees to bridge Northern Ireland's divisions such as those contained in the proposed British-Irish Agreement (http://news.bbc.co.uk) will meet with only limited success unless the two communities develop the skills, desire, and motivation to think and act politically; that is, to resolve their differences through compromise and accommodation. A careful and controlled expansion of the powers and authority of local government can advance the broader aims of the peace process by encouraging greater cross-community consensus through enhanced popular accountability. This proposition is an approach to conflict resolution, not a solution. It seeks to reduce the "democratic deficit" in Northern Ireland, and in so doing, to complement rather than replace other initiatives to achieve cooperative politics.

Traditionally, calls for ending the democratic deficit have come from unionists in the form of proposals to reestablish a devolved assembly at Stormont (Ulster Unionist Party 1996; Judge 1997). But a wider application of the term refers to the effects of direct rule by British ministers and the Northern Ireland Office at all levels of local government. As Richard Jay (1995, 68) observes, the "democratic deficit" has "detached people and political leaders from the machinery of government," leaving them with "neither power or responsibility, in a mire of political rhetoric." Such conditions breed dependency and fatalism and assure further political polarization. This essay explores the reasons, proposals, and prospects for expanding the power and responsibilities of Northern Ireland's twenty-six, democratically elected District Councils. By strengthening the piers supporting local government, it may be possible over time to bridge the democracy gap and aid in the construction of a more inclusive framework for consensual politics.

Political Impasse

The infernos ignited annually at Drumcree and other marching sites offer sobering examples of the rigidity of Northern Ireland's political fault lines. The right to march through contested areas raises legitimate concerns; but with little understanding of—much less sympathy for—the other side's position, demonstrations of communal identity usually become a matter of principle and a test of communal power over which there can be no concessions. Fueled by fear and frustration, the inflexibility of one side has often been matched by the intransigence of the other, each deeply aggrieved and resolute in its quest for what threatens to be a Pyrrhic victory.

Recurrent violence has reinforced the view of Northern Ireland as a "failed state" that cannot be made to work. Principal among the causes of this perceived failure has been the repeated use of bombs, assassinations, mass disobedience, boycotts and other forms of protest by extremists, from both sides, bent on making the region ungovernable. Threats to withhold cooperation have passed for political debate, to the point that one columnist has claimed that "storming out" is the "war dance of Ulster politicians" (Jenkins 1995, 18).

Reason dictates that dialogue and compromise are needed to resolve situations like Drumcree and in negotiating the region's future. Yet, given a choice, impassioned elements on both sides would minimize political contact to avoid surrendering too many unionist or nationalist aspirations. Therefore, unionists generally prefer not to talk, especially to Sinn Fein; nationalists prefer the added voices of Dublin, London, and Washington; and fringe groups have often found that exclusion brings greater publicity and political rewards than involvement. In terms of consensus-building, Northern Ireland not only lacks a political center; its political culture normally eschews negotiation, thus making what passes for political discourse often resemble "a disengaged flywheel—plenty of motion but no outcome" (Wilson 1996, 50).

Blame for the political impasses that have characterized political life in Northern Ireland has been leveled at terrorists and/or Northern Ireland's politicians who are broadly depicted as unrepresentative, unimaginative, and self-serving. Calls for new reinvigorated leadership, greater grassroots participation, and popular referendums find support in the belief that those who make their life outside the political sphere are more rational and moderate than experienced politicians (McGarry and O'Leary 1995). Yet, when opportunities for changing elected leaders arise, results reflect fairly consistent voting patterns along ethnically differentiated (or sectarian) lines.

Competing communal identities, not the politicians who represent them, give Northern Ireland's multiparty system its "dual character" (McAllister and Nelson 1979; Mitchell 1995). Antipartition parties see little advantage in wooing votes from unionists, or vice versa. Therefore, real electoral competition occurs within each ethno-religious group: the Social Democratic and Labour Party (SDLP) is pitted against Sinn Fein for the Catholic vote; and the Ulster Unionists (UUP) and Ian Paisley's Democratic Unionist Party (DUP) are the chief contenders for Protestant support (Mitchell 1991; Diskin 1984; Irvin and Moxon-Brown 1991).

The logic of intraethnic competition generally creates an incentive for "ethnic outbidding" or "flanking" through the articulation of strident and extremist positions (Welsh 1993). Small changes in support between the UUP and the harder-line DUP, or more recent shifts between the latter and the paramilitary-linked loyalist Progressive Unionist (PUP) and Ulster Democratic Parties (UDP), serve as a barometer of Protestant angst; Sinn Fein's electoral gains serve as indicators of republicanism's increased legitimacy within the Catholic community. By playing on deep-seated prejudices and fears of a "sellout," DUP makes their co-confessional rivals reluctant to appear too accommodating. Consequently, until the recent agreement, party politics in Northern Ireland have primarily been a zero-sum game, in which election results follow sectarian lines and politicians are rarely punished for damaging cross-community relations (Evans and Duffy 1997).

The Withholding of Consent

In Northern Ireland, clashing views of territorial sovereignty and self-determination have taken a toll on self-government. While elections are held for district councillors, members of Parliament, and members of the European Parliament, those elected have had no real power over important day-to-day decisions affecting their constituencies, nor can they hold accountable those who do. On one hand, this means that politicians have freely ignored most substantive issues over which they have little or no control. On the other hand, the absence of responsibility has allowed them the luxury of supporting anything and everything they or their supporters have desired. Elected officials have generally not been forced to consider different options, to weigh potential consequences, or to meet financial obligations. All of that has been largely done for them by appointed regional authorities and the Northern Ireland Office. Thus, an unintended consequence of direct rule has been to make the role of elected representatives principally one of championing grievances, whether of individual constituents or their respective communities, which has resulted in a "responsibility gap" of staggering proportions (Wilson 1996; Hazleton 1995).

Arguably, self-government, or popular accountability in a more meaningful sense, will require both communities, and their leaders, to assume greater responsibility for their actions. To avoid the discrimination and injustice experienced by the nationalist minority in the past, parliamentary and administrative acts have strengthened minority rights, thus providing greater equity in the administration of policies and the allocation of public resources (Livingstone and Morison 1995). However, antidiscrimination measures inevitably fall short in that they can ensure neither strict equality nor just outcomes in every case. The challenge, then, has been to incorporate the principle of equality between the two communities into a set of political arrangements that, with appropriate safeguards, will allow the return of regional self-government.

The negotiations leading to the April 1998 agreement addressed this concern by making it clear that any new constitutional arrangements would need the support of both communities. The result was an understanding among the participants in the multiparty talks that "nothing was agreed until all was agreed" in the form of a comprehensive agreement. In its provisions for a new assembly, the proposed agreement (Strand 1, paragraph 5) qualifies majoritarianism by arrangements to ensure that key decisions are taken on a cross-community basis, either through parallel consent or a weighted majority. Moreover, the chair and the deputy chair of the assembly are to be elected on a similar basis, and ministers, committee chairs, and committee memberships will be allocated in proportion to party strengths. The proposed agreement (Constitutional Issues, paragraph 1) also recognizes the principles of "equality of civil, political, social and cultural rights, of freedom from discrimination for all citizens, and of parity of esteem and of just and equal treatment for the identity, ethos, and aspirations of both communities."

While the parties to the agreement (Declaration of Support, paragraph 5) will "endeavor to strive in every practical way towards reconciliation and rapprochement," the acknowledgment of "substantial differences between [their] continuing and equally legitimate political aspirations" will make consensual decisionmaking problematic, to say the least, in the proposed new assembly. Respect for, and equal treatment of, individuals and groups with different religions, cultures, and identities are fundamental tenets of political equality. The impasse comes when the expressions of those differences involve incompatible national allegiances and competing political aspirations rule out political accommodation. In such cases, expressions of identity become more assertive than persuasive, thus inhibiting cross-community consensus-building. Moreover, failure to respect and/or preserve parity of esteem is often a matter of subjective judgment that depends largely upon whose interests and aspirations are being furthered or thwarted by particular political initiatives.

Parity of esteem, the recognition of an Irish identity, and inclusion of an Irish dimension is designed to win nationalist support for the agreement. The larger question is whether both communities are willing to participate in a political process that includes a regional assembly and cross-border arrangements with the Republic of Ireland. Unionist acceptance of an all-island ministerial council is contingent upon the majority of the people of Northern Ireland having to consent to any change in the region's constitutional status. For Irish republicans and many nationalists, this guarantee amounts to a unionist veto, rather than a recognition of the majority's right to remain in the United Kingdom, if that is their choice. According to Martin Mansergh (1996), senior adviser to Taoiseach Bertie Ahern, the consent principle is specific and quite limited, especially in comparison to what unionist majorities could veto in the past. Under the agreement, each community will in effect have a veto because the concept of consent cuts both ways: it provides a basic guarantee for unionists; it also, however, needs to be won through political concessions to nationalists and republicans if democratic institutions and procedures are to be accepted and stability returned to Northern Ireland.

As greater self-government returns to Northern Ireland, representatives to local councils and the new assembly must view cross-community consent, not simply as narrow institutional and procedural prohibitions, but more broadly and positively as a way both communities can influence and make decisions by means of political persuasion and efforts at compromise. Yet, as the *Irish Times* commentator Dick Walsh (1996) has observed, in Northern Ireland consent like compromise is what is expected of the other side. The sad truth is that both communities tend to see consent, not as a practical necessity, but in a much narrower and more defensive light. Consent is generally not something that is freely given or gained through voluntary acceptance, but rather something that is withheld. With the "right to say no" enshrined as principle, consent becomes a potential impediment to the political arrangements outlined in the Good Friday agreement.

Direct Rule's Impact on Local Government

In many respects, the democratic deficit in Northern Ireland is an unintended by-product of administrative reforms that were overtaken by the Troubles. The need to modernize local government and rationalize the delivery of services became increasing apparent in the 1960s, and the civil rights movement underscored the importance of eliminating sectarian abuses of power at the local level. Popular accountability for the new administrative arrangement was, primarily, to be regionally based. Stormont's subsequent collapse did not deter the transfer of local authority to administrative bodies that were now subject only to Westminster's oversight. Public services improved in terms of efficiency, overall quality, and equity, but left locally elected officials with little power and no incentive to bridge the sectarian divide.

Since partition, there have been administrative structures for Northern Ireland, including a Northern Ireland civil service, that are separate from the British administrative system. According to John Loughlin

(1992, 64), the old Stormont government was "rather extravagant and over-blown" for a population of one and a half million, but the powers in London "devised it this way as a means of ensuring that the Northern Ireland problem did not impinge upon politics in Great Britain." This system was subject to abuse, however. Responding to civil rights protests in the 1960s, the Cameron Commission Report (1969) cited inequities in housing allocation, discrimination in appointments, gerrymandered boundaries, and a restricted franchise, all of which were attributed to unionist domination of most local councils. In response, Labour Home Secretary James Callaghan intervened and created a centralized housing executive, thus removing this contentious issue from the hands of local government. Shortly thereafter, another commission, headed by Sir Patrick Macrory (1970), recommended a major reorganization of local government.[2]

The growth of the public sector in the 1960s had outpaced local resources. Local governments were usually underfinanced, lacking in professional or technical staff, and left woefully unprepared to provide additional services. Under the administrative reforms, the number of local entities was reduced from seventy-three to twenty-six. Most of their major functions—housing, education, libraries, social services, planning, roads, and water—were transferred to advisory bodies, "next step" agencies, nominated boards called quasi-autonomous non-governmental organizations (QUANGOS), or to administrative departments of the parliament at Stormont. This left the new district councils with few residual powers except for environmental matters; in colloquial terms, "drains, bins, graves and sports centres."

The idea behind the reorganization was to make the formulation and execution of policy more efficient and effective by removing it from the cockpits of sectarian strife; in other words, to take the politics out of policymaking and administration at the local level. The QUANGO and agency advisory system was to be accountable to Northern Ireland's parliament, but this part of Macrory's proposals was quickly overtaken by the proroguing of Stormont in 1972, when direct rule was imposed to prevent civil war. Because the suspension was assumed to be temporary, the planned reforms and reorganization went ahead. Depoliticizing issues like housing, education, social services, and industrial development successfully distanced most service areas, except policing, from the Troubles and allowed regional and local authorities to function, even in times of severe crisis. The price, however, was a truncated and largely unaccountable system of local government.

Under direct rule, most legislation for Northern Ireland has been carried into effect by Orders in Council at Westminster (Hadfield 1991). Executive responsibilities are in the hands of the secretary of state for Northern Ireland, who along with other government ministers, oversees the operations of the Northern Ireland Office and various regional departments. Beneath them is a layer of statutory bodies that includes 161 QUANGOS, 7 executive agencies, 38 advisory bodies, and 15 tribunals (Weir 1995; Livingstone and Morison 1995). These bodies are appointed by the Northern Ireland Office and serve under the policy direction and financial control of the regional departments. "To put it at its most absurd," said Kenneth Bloomfield (1991, 16), the former head of the Northern Ireland Civil Service, "it is the cabinet in London which is ultimately responsible for dealing with potholes in the roads of Northern Ireland." The prominence of London officials and reliance upon appointed bodies has caused direct rule to be characterized as "helicopter rule," and "government by expert" or government by "the great and the good."

The lack of popular accountability, direct participation, and public debate accounts for much of Northern Ireland's democratic deficit under direct rule. Critics (Morison and Livingstone 1995) cite the absence of substantive discussion of social and economic policies in political forums, the kind of debate that might have redirected energies away from the constitutional question in Northern Ireland. Policies are driven by "elite-based, bureaucratic priorities" and, as a result, are "paternalistic" and "inaccurately targeted" (Jay 1995, 68). Public participation and transparency are lacking in that QUANGO meetings are not open, nor are minutes published for most, and such bodies are not always required to consult with voluntary and community groups. Direct rule is roundly attacked by local politicians, resentful of the interference of British ministers. Ulster Unionists (1992) have been especially critical of "quango rule." In a submission to the Opsahl Commission (1993, 197), a local UUP officer wrote: "Direct rule makes our rulers arrogant, deters our best brains from entering politics, breeds servility in the population, promotes clientelism in local politicians, prevents elected representatives from learning how to govern, and absolves voters from accepting responsibility for their actions. Direct rule is a recipe for political stagnation in which the terrorist thrives."

The effects of direct rule and the Macrory reforms have not been all negative, however. Not only have services been provided during the Troubles, but the quality of these services has greatly improved since 1972. Although disparities in treatment persist, service delivery is more equitable, and several administrative agencies have played a key role in combating sectarian discrimination. Appointees to boards and QUANGOS are representative of the locality's political and religious makeup, thus empowering groups who might be excluded under more democratic methods of selection. District and regional appointed bodies are not totally isolated from the public, as frequently witnessed by their flexibility on policies and pragmatic responses to local pressure (Carmichael, Knox, and Osborne 1997). Emphasis on technocratic decisionmaking has made public agencies better informed, advised, and managed. This has allowed them to initiate, as well as respond to, social change. Good administration, however, does not necessarily win universal allegiance or confer legitimacy upon the state. As Michael Connolly (1993, 95–96) has observed, "the substitution of administration for politics has helped to contain the Northern Ireland conflict," but "it has not produced a solution."

The budgets of the Northern Ireland Office and related agencies dwarf those of local government.[3] Limited responsibility and diminished powers have deterred new political recruits from seeking office and, correspondingly, eroded the public's trust of local councillors. When a major crisis such as the 1981 hunger strike or the 1995 Anglo-Irish Agreement arises, local elections take the form of regional referendums. However, when this is not the case, campaigns are characterized by complacency and cynicism, with little attention devoted to local bread-and-butter issues, and a poorer turnout reflects the electorate's weariness of the same old politics.[4]

Because the district councils have few responsibilities, and little authority, they have often been reduced to their sectarian roots and exploited as outlets for protest. In 1985, when Sinn Fein councillors first won seats, vitriolic battles erupted over their presence in council chambers, with UUP and DUP councillors seeking to adjourn all business (Knox 1990b). The Anglo-Irish Agreement later that year brought an even larger wave of unionist protest. Eighteen unionist-controlled councils adjourned and refused to strike a district rate (that is, a local tax) in a symbolic "withdrawal of consent" for what they saw as Northern Ireland's subjection to a "joint authority system" (Knox 1990a, 47–48). The impact on services proved to be minimal due to the actions of council staff and central government officials and, ultimately, of many unionists who exercised a degree of restraint. Ironically, the protests convinced some councillors of "the sterility of adversarial politics," and deliberate steps toward power-sharing began in a number of councils (Beirne 1992, 37).

Moves toward Local Cooperation

Although greater civility is evident in most council chambers today, a preoccupation with divisive issues that have nothing to do with local government is frequently evident. As former Dungannon District Councillor Ken Maginnis admitted, "excursions into such territory, where there is no opportunity to directly influence matters, are invariably recriminatory, futile, and destructive. Hence, the difficulty of achieving consensus is increased, not by the misuse of power but by the lack of it."[5] Since lack of power has eliminated the need for politics in a practical sense, local councils fail to provide a necessary training ground in which to acquire and practice the art of compromise. So long as "direct rulers carry the burden of compromise," Simon Jenkins of the *Times* has argued, "local leaders need only defend group interests" (http://www.sunday-times.co.uk. 17 July 1996).

While a few councils, like the Belfast City Council and Craigavon Borough Council, have been sharply divided along communal lines, others evidence cooperative working relationships and take a more constructive approach to local concerns.[6] Of Northern Ireland's twenty-six councils, twelve had some type of responsibility-sharing arrangement in 1998. The most common form was office-sharing by nationalist and unionist councillors; that is, the regular rotation of the position of council chair and vice chair; or, in Derry and Belfast, of lord mayor and vice mayor. The other form of responsibility-sharing that has often accompanied office-sharing was an intercommunal proportional arrangement for assigning committee chairs and/or membership. Electoral considerations and party support are important factors in explaining which councils adopt responsibility-sharing. Three "hung" councils, Belfast, Dungannon, and Moyle, had responsibility-sharing arrangements in 1998, as did seven of nine councils controlled by nationalist parties. Of the fourteen councils controlled by unionist parties, only two experimented with office-sharing. Among those councils not employing responsibility-sharing, nine had substantial unionist majorities that allowed them to avoid it, and two had no nationalist councillors to make it possible.[7]

Despite allegations that councils do not have enough work to keep them out of mischief, councillors argue that they are busy responding to constituents' complaints about services. The public expects them to liaise, or put in a "fix" on their behalf, with QUANGOS, local boards, or central government offices, even though the matter in question is beyond the councillor's competence. Because most issues are routinely referred to civil servants, or local MPs, the general impression is that councillors duck their responsibilities; most councillors, on the other hand, express frustration with their limited powers (John 1993; Birrell 1983).

Central government has a statutory obligation to consult local authorities over planning, roads, and water and sewerage services. Planning issues are the greatest sources of friction, with councils lobbying civil servants and departments on behalf of local applications. Because councils cannot create local authorities to develop planning policies, their role is reduced to that of a pressure group for local special interests. In addition, the number of the services provided by local councils was further reduced by the former Conservative government's switch to competitive tendering for such services as refuse collection.

A key factor in a district council's level of activity and success is its chief executive. The energy and skill of a chief executive must be directed not only at managing the council's affairs and promoting the district's interests, but also at avoiding the political pitfalls and tension that can incapacitate a council. Success also depends, of course, on how willing the councillors are for their chief executive to play an active role.

A Rowntree Foundation study (John 1993, 18) found that district councils were "in search for a role," and that many councillors desired "greater responsibilities," especially in the area of economic development. While the seriousness and effectiveness of these efforts vary, most councils have created committees to encourage economic investment and development. Following the lead of Armagh and Fermanagh, district councils have become proactive in persuading government departments and agencies to undertake infrastructure initiatives, and in lobbying for European Union funds. Because economic development is a noncompulsory function for local councils (that is, they have no formal powers in this area), these bodies have acted to facilitate and manage local association and interest group networks so as to influence regional and central government agencies. Local authorities, playing a pivotal role as brokers, have forged social partnerships to mobilize representatives of the voluntary sector, business community, trade unions, and statutory agencies in support of local initiatives to attract European-funded programs (Knox 1997b; Sweeny 1997). Their public, private, and community-based composition has served to undermine traditional unionist-nationalist cleavages in local decisionmaking and gain wide public support for this type of social partnership.

Community relations are another arena in which councils have successfully initiated local projects. However, here the impetus came from central government. In the late 1980s, grants became available to those district councils in which the Northern Irish constitutional parties would agree to implement a community relations program. (Sinn Fein was initially excluded to preempt unionist objections.) The intention was to promote "consensus at the political level and in turn, by example, to the community" (Knox and Hughes 1995, 50). By 1993 every council had adopted a community relations policy statement, appointed a community relations officer to administer the scheme, and begun to fund projects, all of which required cross-party agreement. The budget for these programs remains relatively modest, and the scheme's objective of promoting cooperation through better understanding rules out "quick fix" results. Not surprisingly, those councils that already had community service departments and ongoing relations with community groups have benefited the most from this new function.

In the areas of community relations and economic development, most councillors have learned that minimizing partisan conflict can get things done and achieve tangible rewards in the form of grants, jobs, and community improvements. Willingness to cooperate on specific initiatives has not erased, or necessarily softened, fundamental political differences over Northern Ireland's constitutional future. But for a number of councils, district partnerships and other initiatives have encouraged greater trust and cooperation and created a more workable environment for agreement and compromise on local issues.

Proposals for Greater Local Accountability

While Northern Ireland's democratic deficit presents serious problems, most analysts would not agree with Stuart Weir (1995) that "the first priority of the peace process, in terms of democratisation, should be the restoration of local democracy." Proposals to strengthen local government incite strenuous opposition, especially from sections of the nationalist community, in that such reforms would result in the return of control over many local services to unionist-dominated councils. Incidents of discrimination still exist, and Sinn Fein (1992) argues that sectarian practices, especially in hiring public employees, have not changed since the 1960s. SDLP also cites continued discrimination and the lack of proportional committee membership in most councils. In its view, the existing system of ministerial appointments to local boards and QUANGOS is more representative of the minority community. As for possible changes, Eddie McGrady (1991), SDLP MP for South Down, has argued that the provision of most local services should be on a multidistrict or regional basis, with popular accountability residing in the hands of a Northern Ireland assembly that is accompanied by new North-South structures of cross-border cooperation.

The relatively small size of Northern Ireland's twenty-six districts presents practical problems. Unless their areas were increased, most rural local councils could not efficiently manage or provide services like education and transportation. A more important question is whether the councils generally are capable of shouldering additional responsibilities. If the absence of real power has made responsibility-sharing and cross-community cooperation possible, the granting of additional functions could conceivably reverse this process. While there is reason to hope that cross-party cooperation will not only continue but advance, legitimate concerns remain over sectarian tensions and communal divisions, from which local authorities will not be immune.

Warnings of partisan bickering and political deadlock are voiced by voluntary groups that are rooted in local communities and that represent special interests in Northern Ireland. Estimated to number five thousand (McDonagh 1996), groups like the Rural Community Network, Committee on the Administration of Justice, Women in Politics, and Enniskillen Together, see themselves as intermediaries, pressing grassroots concerns at different administrative levels. In an age of downsizing, privatizing, and contracting-out, many of these voluntary groups either supply or supplement services formerly provided by the public sector. Consequently, voluntary agencies are apprehensive about increasing the executive functions of local elected authorities because such a change could undermine their position (Meehan 1996). Interest-group politics, in their view, is better tailored to meet Northern Ireland's needs because it deliberately isolates the allocation and delivery of services from rancorous debates over the constitutional question.

Expanding the powers of local government also raises questions regarding its future relationship to the new devolved Northern Ireland assembly to be put in place following the April 1998 British-Irish agreement. The future of district councils has largely been ignored in the peace process and in the recent agreement. Simon Jenkins (1997), an outspoken proponent of increased democratic accountability at the local level, has argued that British government efforts to reestablish a regional assembly continually fail because power-sharing is inherently unworkable when applied to the context of an assembly at Stormont. The solution, in Jenkins's mind, is to encourage accountable majorities by devolving as much administrative responsibility as possible to local authorities. According to Jenkins (1994, 15), "the essence of political reform in Ulster is to acknowledge segregation — even the fact of ethnic cleansing — and try to construct tolerant self-governing communities across the divide. The way lies not through artificial, enforced power-sharing but through the power that is shared by local compromise, by the give-and-take of citizens who know each other."

Jenkins's assessment of the practical benefits of local self-government is unrealistic given Ulster's sectarian prejudices and ideological divisions. More to the point, the degree of decisionmaking responsibility that he proposes to grant local government is politically unacceptable to London, Dublin, the nationalist community, and even to a majority of unionists. However, his central tenet that local councils are underutilized as forums for learning the art of conciliation and accommodation does have a bearing on making the political settlement work. Bargaining over substantive issues and greater democratic accountability at the local level could play a constructive role in building political relationships. Peaceful coexistence between Northern Ireland's warring factions is unlikely to be solely and successfully engineered from the top down, nor, as Jenkins has argued, be achieved from the bottom up; rather, the challenge is to construct an overall working arrangement through a series of consensual agreements. Democratizing local government becomes politically attractive when it is part of a multilayered, comprehensive approach that addresses a broad range of communal concerns including expressions of identity, power-sharing and cross-border ties, both North and South and East and West.

In this context, some questions that are already being asked about ameliorating the democratic deficit at the local level are (1) How much, and in which areas, should executive responsibility be turned over to local authorities? (2) Under what conditions, and by whom, should local governments be held accountable for performing these functions? and (3) What are the potential consequences of providing more services at the district council level?

A few "integrationists" have proposed giving district councils the same powers as are exercised by councils elsewhere in the United Kingdom. However, most recommendations (Bloomfield 1993; John 1993; Opsahl 1993) take Northern Ireland's unique conditions into account and advocate a more limited and gradual approach; that is, some type of rolling devolution in which councils might win back powers. Among the first functions to be returned to district councils are local planning, library boards, additional environmental measures, and the maintenance of local roads. If councils prove successful in performing these services, it might be possible in the future to transfer to their authority other functions like primary education, housing, social services, and local health services.

In these proposals, rolling devolution is made conditional on the council's willingness to cooperate across the sectarian divide. Responsibility-sharing, to be meaningful and effective, would have to go beyond the rotation of council offices. Weir (1995, 23), for example, suggests that "new rules for minority representation on councils and all committees — possibly with rights of veto or appeal for outvoted minorities — could be introduced." A code of conduct, regulating the behavior of councillors, could offer protection for minority parties against arbitrary government or simple majoritarianism (Connolly 1992). No doubt, under any scheme, central government would have a strong

supervisory role, and an appeals process would have to be established
to address minority concerns. Watchdog bodies, including the Equal
Opportunities Commission and other QUANGOS already in place,
might be used to monitor and check discrimination and sectarian bias
in council policies. Through consultative procedures, and possibly
more formalized arrangements, the Irish government would presumably offer an additional avenue of oversight. The ultimate safeguard is
that the Westminster Parliament or a new devolved Northern Ireland
assembly could always revoke the powers that it had bestowed if local
authorities are unable to function in a fair and efficient manner.

One consequence of restoring popular accountability to local government is the effect it would have on the plethora of voluntary groups
and community organizations that act as "the people's" intermediaries
to QUANGOS and other public agencies. On the one hand, it is quite
possible that their influence over policy decisions and implementation
would diminish as district councils gained control over more functions.
On the other hand, new social partnerships between these groups and
local government could emerge, whereby community organizations become even more active participants, working with local authorities to
find ways of utilizing each other's capabilities (McDonagh 1996;
Sweeny 1997). Through partnership in the broader political process,
voluntary associations and community-based organizations not only
can continue to influence administrative and policy decisions; they can
spur Northern Ireland's elected representatives to adopt substantive
positions across a wider range of issues.

The prominence accorded to power-sharing in the return of functions to local government is likely to produce mixed results. Power-
sharing, in purpose and design, recognizes that people in Northern
Ireland do not hold common political aspirations, and that minority
interests need to be protected. Yet, if power-sharing is viewed solely
from the perspective of defending "two traditions," it threatens to become a mechanism, not for cooperation and tolerance, but for per-
petuating sectarian and political divisions. Thus, while power-sharing
and protection of rights must be at the core of any internal arrangement
for Northern Ireland, it becomes equally vital, in very practical terms,
that they be designed to further the creation of a nonsectarian society
(Farry 1998).

A related concern is that granting more functions to district councils may move Northern Ireland toward cantonization, with concentrations of Catholics and Protestants in different subregions. Increases in residential segregation are already apparent in most areas, with terrorism and harassment being the primary cause of sectarian ghettoization.[8] That a district has a clear unionist or nationalist majority should not, in theory, disqualify its inhabitants from assuming responsibility over their affairs, just as it should not, in practice, give the majority license to ride roughshod over the minority. The challenge here will be for the majority to gain minority confidence (that is, consent) through its actions. In cases where there is no clear majority, the challenge will be to find ways for local nationalists and unionists to work together. To reverse Northern Ireland's sectarian divisions, the answer is not less local self-government, but rather less suspicion and fear so that communal representatives gain the confidence to address local issues with the thought of conciliating competing interests in making policy decisions.

Additional rules and procedures can be put in place to curb the abuses of majoritarianism at all levels of government in Northern Ireland. But institutional safeguards alone will not make the political process work, particularly when such devices are most effective as prohibitions that allow minorities, as well as majorities, to withhold consent. A workable political solution will require a political center, composed of elements from both traditions who are amenable to compromise and accommodation. It will necessitate a change of attitude and outlook on the part of many, if not most, participants in the peace process, a tall order even under the best of circumstances. At a minimum, popular consent and democratic accountability require a willingness to share a multiethnic and multicultural Northern Ireland (Wilson 1996; Corrigan 1994); otherwise, no consensual agreement will work because one side or the other will fear that such an agreement jeopardizes its national identity.

The time has come to reduce the democratic deficit and to stop governing Northern Ireland in terms of administering public services. While ministers, bureaucratic mandarins, and QUANGOS have improved the daily lives of most people in the North, they have had little success in moving them toward reconciliation. In part, the benefits of direct rule are to blame. Neither community has been more than peripherally involved in the actual business of government; that is, in deciding "who gets what" and being accountable for the outcome. Instead, these decisions are largely made for them, and imposed on them, in the hope of restoring peace. The problem with this strategy is that unionists and nationalists, those who have been spared the task of making hard decisions, are now being expected to resolve complex and deeply divisive constitutional issues as part of a negotiated agreement.

The implementation of a comprehensive settlement requires capable and responsible political leadership from both sides. These leaders must be able to formulate objectives that incorporate not only what their respective communities desire, but also what they may be willing to give up. For those inexperienced in reconciling different interests and hammering together compromises, political accommodation appears to be too great a price for peace, because it comes at the expense of their illusions of victory (Crick 1990).

If the political leaders of Northern Ireland are to make difficult choices that their communities will be expected to live with, they must have the self-confidence and self-reliance that comes from practicing responsible self-government. For them and their followers, more accountability requires more independence at the local level; more rights demand more responsibility. In other words, accommodation must be recognized as a means for self-preservation and, more hopefully, mutual survival.

Granting greater responsibility and increased accountability to local government is an approach, not a solution, to important questions that concern the nature of the state, national allegiances, and the legitimacy of governmental authority. Through much of its troubled history, Northern Ireland has been a constitutional experiment (McCrudden 1994). Strengthening local government should become part of that experiment, not just to help bridge the democratic deficit, but to move the principle of consent closer to the acceptance of accommodation and compromise in Northern Ireland's search for peace.

Notes

I express my appreciation for the insights and information provided by Colin Knox and the comments made by Alan Ward, who read an earlier version presented at the 1996 American Political Science Convention.

1. According to a poll carried out by Market Research (Northern Ireland)

in December 1997, 86 percent of Protestants and 80 percent of Catholics deemed an assembly acceptable (Hadden 1998, 12–13).

2. The Macrory Report was generally welcomed by unionist ministers at Stormont. Opposition parties also endorsed it, except for the voting provisions that did not prescribe proportional representation.

3. Local government spending accounts for roughly 2.7 percent of the total government expenditure in Northern Ireland (Knox 1997a, 2).

4. By way of comparison, the turnout for the 1981 local elections was 66.2 percent; for the 1997 local elections was 54.7 percent.

5. Councillor Ken Maginnis, speech given at Inchigeela, County Cork, 5 August 1991.

6. With the unionists' loss of control in 1997 and the election of the first nationalist lord mayor, Alban Maginness, Belfast City Council embarked upon a responsibility-sharing arrangement that was controversial because it allegedly excluded Sinn Fein.

7. In 1997–98, the following councils were engaged in responsibility-sharing: Armagh, Belfast, Derry, Down, Dungannon, Fermanagh, Limavady, Lisburn, Magherafelt, Moyle, Newry and Mourne, and Omagh.

8. Based on the 1991 census, estimates are that out of Northern Ireland's population of 1.5 million, only 110,000 live in religiously mixed areas (McKittrick 1993).

Works Cited

Beirne, M. 1992. Local government in Northern Ireland: Cooperation across the communal divide? Oxford University, B.A. (Hons.) thesis.

Birrell, D. 1983. Local government councillors in Northern Ireland and the Republic of Ireland: Their social background, motivation, and role. In *Contemporary Irish studies*, edited by T. Gallagher and J. O'Connell, 95–110. Manchester: Manchester University Press.

Bloomfield, K. 1991. Who runs Northern Ireland? *Fortnight* (Belfast) 300:14–17.

———. 1993. Closing the gap. *Fortnight* (Belfast) 315:18–19.

Cameron Commission. 1969. *Disturbances in Northern Ireland: Report of the commission appointed by the Governor of Northern Ireland.* Belfast: HMSO.

Carmichael, P., C. Knox, and B. Osborne. 1997. Research report: Mapping the pubic sector in Northern Ireland. In *Review of Northern Ireland administrative arrangements*, 1–7. Belfast: Chief Executive Forum.

Connolly, M. 1992. Learning from Northern Ireland: An acceptable model for regional and local government. *Public Policy and Administration* 7:31–46.

———. 1993. Public administration in a conflict situation. *Governance* 6:79–98.

Corrigan, P. 1994. Acting locally. *Fortnight* (Belfast) 328:20–21.

Crick, B. 1990. The high price of peace. In *The elusive search for peace,* edited by H. Giliomee and J. Gagiano, 261–75. Capetown: Oxford University Press.

Diskin, M. 1984. *The development of party competition among unionists in Ulster, 1966–82.* Strathclyde, Scotland: University of Strathclyde Centre for the Study of Public Policy, 129.

Evans, G., and M. Duffy. 1997. Beyond the sectarian divide: The social bases and political consequences of nationalist and unionist party competition in Northern Ireland. *British Journal of Political Science* 27:47–81.

Farry, S. 1998. Multiple communities. *Fortnight* (Belfast) 368:9–10.

Frameworks Documents. 1995. *Frameworks for the future.* Belfast: HMSO.

Hadden, T. 1998. An "acceptable" settlement. *Fortnight* (Belfast) 368:12–13.

Hadfield, B. 1991. Northern Ireland affairs and Westminster. In *The Northern Ireland question: Myth and reality,* edited by P. J. Roche and B. Barton, 130–50. Aldershot, England: Avebury.

Hazleton, W. 1995. A breed apart? Northern Ireland's MPs at Westminster. *Journal of Legislative Studies* 1:30–53.

Horowitz, D. 1994. Democracy in divided societies. In *Nationalism, ethnic conflict, and democracy,* edited by L. Diamond and M. F. Plattner, 35–55. Baltimore: Johns Hopkins University Press.

Irvin, C., and E. Moxon-Browne. 1991. Not many floating voters here. *Fortnight* (Belfast) 295:7–9.

Jay, R. 1995. Democratic dilemmas. *Social exclusion, social inclusion, Democratic dialogue* (Belfast) 2:68–71.

Jenkins, S. 1994. The ethnic cleansing of Ulster. *The Spectator* (London) 8634: 13–16.

———. 1995. Squaring Ulster's circle. *The Times* (London), 22 February, p. 18.

———. 1996. Zulu lessons for Ulster. *The Times* (London), 17 July (http://www.sunday-times.co.uk/).

———. 1997. In place of Stormont. *The Times* (London), 4 June (http://www.sunday-times.co.uk/).

John, P. 1993. *Local government in Northern Ireland.* York, England: Joseph Rowntree Foundation.

Judge, T. 1997. UUP calls for an end to "democratic deficit." *Irish Times* (Dublin), 8 October (http://www.irish-times.ie/).

Knox, C. 1990a. Local government in Northern Ireland: Adoption or adaptation? In *Public policy in Northern Ireland: Adoption or adaptation,* edited by M. E. H Connolly and S. Loughlin, 35–53. Belfast: Queen's University and the University of Ulster, Policy Research Institute.

———. 1990b. Sinn Fein and local government elections: The government's response in Northern Ireland. *Parliamentary Affairs* 43:448–63.

———. 1997a. Local government in Northern Ireland: Emerging from the bearpit of sectarianism? *Occasional Papers. School of Public Policy, Economics and Law, University of Ulster.* Jordanstown, Northern Ireland.

———. 1997b. Local government, its operation since the Macrory report and its potential for the future. In *Review of Northern Ireland administrative arrangements*, Essay 2. Belfast: Chief Executive Forum.

——, and J. Hughes. 1995. Local government and community relations. In *Facets of the conflict in Northern Ireland*, edited by S. Dunn, 43–60. New York: St. Martin's.

Livingstone, S., and J. Morison. 1995. An audit of democracy in Northern Ireland. *Fortnight* (Belfast) 337 (supplement).

Loughlin, J. 1992. Administering policy in Northern Ireland. In *Northern Ireland: Politics and the constitution*, edited by B. Hadfield, 60–75. Buckingham, England: Open University Press.

Macrory, P. 1970. *Report of the review body on local government in Northern Ireland*. Belfast: HMSO.

Maginnis, K. 1991. Local democracy in Northern Ireland. Speech delivered at Inchigeela, County Cork, 5 August.

Mansergh, M. 1996. Manufacturing consent. *Fortnight* (Belfast) 350:13–15.

McAllister, I., and S. Nelson. 1979. Modern developments in Northern Ireland's party system. *Parliamentary Affairs* 32:279–316.

McCrudden, C. 1994. Northern Ireland and the British constitution. In *The changing constitution*, edited by J. Jowell and D. Oliver, 323–75. Oxford: Clarendon Press.

McDonagh, R. 1996. Community actions. *Fortnight* (Belfast) 352:23–24.

McGarry, J., and B. O'Leary. 1995. Five fallacies: Northern Ireland and the liabilities of liberalism. *Ethnic and Racial Studies* 18:837–61.

McGrady, E. 1991. Local democracy in Northern Ireland. Speech delivered at Inchigeela, County Cork, 5 August.

McKittrick, D. 1993. Apartheid deepens on streets of Ulster. *Sunday Independent* (London), 21 March.

Meehan, E. 1996. Democracy unbounded. *Reconstituting politics, Democratic dialogue* (Belfast) 3:23–40.

Mitchell, P. 1991. Conflict regulation and party competition in Northern Ireland. *European Journal of Political Research* 20:76–92.

——. 1995. Party competition in an ethnic dual party system. *Ethnic and Racial Studies* 18:773–93.

Morison, J., and S. Livingstone. 1995. *Reshaping public power: Northern Ireland and the British constitutional crisis*. London: Sweet and Maxwell.

O'Leary, B. 1995. Afterword: What is framed in the framework documents? *Ethnic and Racial Studies* 18:862–72.

Opsahl Commission. 1993. *A citizens' inquiry: The Opsahl report on Northern Ireland*, edited by Andy Pollak. Dublin: Lilliput Press.

Sinn Fein. 1992. *Discrimination in local government: A record of abuse*. Belfast, February.

Sweeny, P. 1997. Achieving a more participative and inclusive form of democracy in Northern Ireland. In *Review of Northern Ireland administrative arrangements*, Essay 5. Belfast: Chief Executive Forum.

Ulster Unionist Party. 1992. Quangopus government. *Unionist Voice* 7:1–4.

————. 1996. The democratic imperative: Proposals for an elected body for Northern Ireland (http://www.uup.org/).

Walsh, D. 1996. Small steps fan peace hopes in dark days. *Irish Times* (Dublin), 10 August (http://www.irish-times.ie/).

Weir, S. 1995. Aloof in quangoland. *Fortnight* (Belfast) 335:23–25.

Welsh, D. 1993. Domestic politics and ethnic conflict. *Survival* 31:63–80.

Wilson, R. 1996. Asking the right questions. *Reconstituting politics, Democratic dialogue* (Belfast) 3:41–59.

Recontextualizing the Conflict
Northern Ireland, Television Drama, and the Politics of Validation

Speaking on *The Late Show* special, "Telling The Troubles" (BBC, 1995), author Ronan Bennett described the two assumptions that until recently have defined most television drama about the Troubles in Northern Ireland: first, that the violence is symptomatic of an intractable tribal conflict whose participants are uniformly brutish and deranged, and, second, that "ordinary decent people" inevitably if not automatically reject the IRA.

This depiction of republicans as either criminal, psychopathic, or politically naive has defined the wider nationalist community with which republicanism is frequently equated in these narratives, as well as others who explicitly identify themselves as Irish. In keeping with Bennett's observations, the political allegiances and aspirations of characters in television dramas are often explained in terms of emotional vulnerability or psychological imbalance.[1] Anne Devlin's heroine in *Naming the Names* (BBC, 1984), for example, turns to the IRA after the death of her only relation and the destruction of their home by a loyalist mob. In *The Long March*, also by Devlin and broadcast by the BBC the same year, the heroine is a weak, unhappy individual seeking community and purpose through her identification with the republican movement.

Media scholars traditionally have assumed that television drama provides an opportunity for the airing of interpretations of social reality generally prohibited in nonfiction programming. In practice, however, drama has rarely proven more open to "alternative" readings of events and issues, and on the subject of Northern Ireland it has maintained an antagonism toward "oppositional" views.[2] This is hardly surprising, given the influence of government policies and political agenda on the conduct of journalists, the content of their coverage, and the commission and production of material about the North.[3] Indeed, despite apparent changes in the nature of recent programming, since at

least 1980 television dramas that take Northern Ireland as their subject
have offered a largely unbroken reflection of official British policy.[4]
What has changed is not the character of the representations portrayed,
but the sociopolitical agenda which they reflect.

While this agenda continues to evolve as a consequence of the fitful
progress of the peace process, it is currently defined by the Joint Declaration signed by John Major and Albert Reynolds in 1993. Like the
Anglo-Irish Agreement before it, the Declaration redefined relations
between Ireland and Britain — and, by implication, between Britain and
the North. Most significantly, the Declaration signaled a new willingness, particularly on the part of the British government, to acknowledge the grievances of the nationalist community, and to accept responsibility for prolonging the conflict.[5]

With few exceptions, the teleplays of the 1990s reflect this transformation. For example, Allan Cubilt's *The Hanging Gale* (BBC, 1995) depicts the physical, psychological, and socioeconomic degradations of
the Famine, Charles Woods's *A Breed of Heroes* (BBC, 1995) acknowledges not only the use of excessive force by the British army but official
attempts to conceal it, and Tom McGurk's *Dear Sarah* (ITV, 1990), a
dramatization of Sarah Conlon's efforts on behalf of her husband and
son wrongly convicted of terrorist crimes, all affirm aspects of nation-
alist-republican historical analysis previously dismissed by the British
government. They serve to recontextualize a conflict whose sociopolitical roots for over two decades were systematically obscured or denied.

One consequence of this process has been the validation of the republican self-image, including the claim of the movement to represent a
politically informed, well-organized, culturally rich and cohesive community. Ronan Bennett's *Love Lies Bleeding* (BBC, 1993) was one of
the first teleplays to challenge the prevailing imagery, offering a portrait
of the republican community in all its diversity. Before discussing Bennett's drama, however, I shall examine two earlier teleplays that recast
the representation of Irish nationalists in the North.

The Drowning of Innocence:
Owen O'Neill's *Arise and Go Now*

Introduced to viewers as "an off-beat tragi-comedy," Owen O'Neill's
Arise and Go Now, which aired on the BBC in 1991, has two main

plotlines. The first involves Kevin, a youth with a talent for poetry who has doubts about his support for the IRA even before his botched ambush of an army convoy nearly kills the Art Og Quartet, a group of traveling Irish poets. His grandfather, Matty, with whom Kevin lives, is a vocal opponent of the IRA, and under his influence, Kevin decides to abandon the Cause. But the local provo chief (who is also the mayor), backed by his dangerously dim-witted henchman, Wolfie, refuses to allow him to leave. When Matty dies of a heart attack induced by a threatening visit from Wolfie, Kevin, no longer intimidated, vows to punish the organization whatever the cost.

Meanwhile, the parish priest, Father Tom Dade, suffering a crisis of faith brought on in part by his observations of violence, racketeering, and self-serving support for the IRA amongst his flock, finally snaps when his bishop commands him to officiate at a republican funeral. Dade resolves to steal the corpse and to unmask the town's numerous sinners by presenting them with tapes of their confessions, which he has been recording secretly for years. Eventually Kevin and Dade join forces and end up with the corpse on a lake in Fermanagh, where they give it a sort of burial at sea. Kevin recites the first six lines of "The Second Coming" before hurling his gun into the waves, while the dead man's funeral carries on as planned, the corpse's absence undetected, paramilitary trappings and all. The teleplay ends with a long shot of Dade and Kevin, marked men seated at opposite ends of a fragile dinghy, their gesture unwitnessed and largely ignored.

There is much to discuss in a text this rich in detail and reference; my purpose here, however, is simply to comment on its representation of republicans and the movement they support. Despite the narrative's obvious condemnation of violence, O'Neill's teleplay validates the *ideals* of republicanism through Kevin's struggle to define himself and his beliefs. "What am I *doing* here?" he asks himself in the opening scene as he lies on a hill with a detonator in his hand. Unlike Wolfie, an obvious sociopath and virtual illiterate whose incompetence is the reason the ambush goes wrong, or the chief, who fails to disguise his brutal nature despite his large private library and support for the arts, Kevin is a genuine son of the republican tradition. Young, handsome, passionate, and artistic, he embodies the spirit of 1916. His poem "about the two kids who were shot by the Paras last week" which he reads aloud for Matty — with whom he has a close and loving relationship despite their differences — demonstrates considerably more depth and far less pretension than the efforts of the Art Og Quartet he so admires. Indeed, it is Kevin's earnest concern for his country and its people that gives such weight to his eventual repudiation of the IRA. "I believe in freedom, Matty, I really do," he cries, trying to explain his paramilitary involvement. "We're not free in this country." But Matty rejects this argument. "Then free yourself!" he urges his grandson. "Free yourself and everything else will fly!"

Through Matty, freedom is transformed from a political catchphrase into a personal ethic, a way to live both wisely and well. "What [the IRA]'re fighting for doesn't stem from love of their country," he tells Kevin. "It's based totally on a hatred for another country. It can never work [because] they don't understand the real meaning of freedom." For Matty, a bird fancier, "the real meaning of freedom" is revealed by his carrier pigeons. One of them flies a thousand miles to Russia and returns with a message from an anonymous but clearly kindred spirit — "God fly with you, brave bird" — only to be shot dead by a volley released at a republican funeral. Significantly, when Kevin and Dade abduct the corpse, they leave the murdered pigeon and a portrait of the Sacred Heart in its place, symbols of (and martyrs to) the values that the contemporary IRA has betrayed.

That substitution is not the only suggestion that the dead man, too, is a victim. "Oh mother of Jesus," Dade laments when he first sees the corpse's face, "he's only a child!" Also suggestive are the circumstances of his death. "He was fishing," Kevin tells Dade. "The Brits used him as target practice." And now, readied for his part in a ceremony commandeered in service to a debased political agenda, "he's going to be used again." Indeed, that his body's absence at its own funeral goes unnoticed is especially telling, as is the reduction of his grieving family to background imagery as his republican comrades drape his coffin with paramilitary insignia and the Irish flag.

"Jesus Christ, whatever happened to the sons of Ireland?" someone asks rhetorically early on in the drama. O'Neill's answer appears to be that the real heroes are dead, disillusioned, or on the run from those who, no longer committed to self-sacrifice, prefer to line their pockets at the people's expense and protect themselves by persuading children to give up their lives.

Anarchy Released: Graham Reid's *You, Me, and Marley*

The representation of the contemporary IRA as a false heir to a once noble tradition reappears with less subtlety in Graham Reid's *You, Me, and Marley* (BBC, 1992). Though the subject of less discussion than *Love Lies Bleeding,* it too was widely praised at the time of its release.[6] In it, Reid tells the story of sixteen-year-old Sean, who lives on an estate in republican West Belfast, where alcoholism, drug abuse, and promiscuity are rampant, the prospects for people his age are few, and unemployment among adults can top 80 percent. In this environment Sean and his chums amuse themselves by stealing cars, which they drive about recklessly before stripping the vehicles of whatever parts they can sell. This practice provokes the wrath of neighborhood car owners, who, suspicious of the RUC (the "Reluctant, Unwilling, and Contrary" police force, as one frustrated observer describes them), enlist the IRA to warn offenders and to punish those who do not take heed. Sean, protected by his wits, his mother, and the reputation of his absent father, a former member of the IRA, barely manages to escape injury; his friend Marley, however, a lovable half-wit, is apprehended and brutally beaten. Later, when Sean fails to stop at an army roadblock, the startled soldiers fire on the stolen car, which careens off the road and overturns. Once again Sean escapes uninjured, but his three passengers, including Marley, are killed in the wreck.

Like much of Reid's work, the dialogue in *You, Me, and Marley* is often self-conscious, its humor strained, and tragedy visible from a considerable distance. Still more disappointing are the characterizations, many of which conform to the absurd conventions that Bennett has described. IRA godfather Reggie Devine, for example, though initially repulsed by the punishment beatings and knee-cappings he allows to continue, participates readily in the violence when his own car is destroyed. Reid's female characters exist only to suffer: Sean's mother Sarah has lost two of her sons to paramilitary violence despite her efforts to protect them, and lives in fear of losing Sean; his sister Rosaleen is a compulsive eater used like a whore by a series of men. Even Sean's girlfriend, Frances, a promising student, clings to the North because of him, only to be left alone and grieving at the end of the drama, her closest friends dead, and Sean himself headed for life as an exile in England.

In fact, Reid's drama is faithful to convention in many ways, not least in his deferential depiction of the army. His scrupulous re-creation of army procedure, for example, serves to absolve the soldiers involved in the crash in which Sean's friends are killed: they shout a warning before they open fire, their bullets are shown striking tail lights and wheels, and it is clear they're not shooting to injure or kill. Afterwards, one of those who fired his weapon is shocked and sickened by the carnage ("They're all dead!" he cries, "They're all fucking dead!"). Given the extent of nationalist protest throughout Northern Ireland following the release of Private Lee Clegg in 1996, Reid's depiction of this incident, similar to the one in which Clegg was involved, is hardly "alternative," however well it may reflect circumstances in which such a tragedy could occur.[7]

Less controversial but equally familiar is Reid's depiction of the conflict as tending to corrupt those employed to defuse it. "Four hours in Castlereagh and he walks away grinning all over his gob," an RUC officer complains of one known offender, supplying a context for police brutality if not an excuse. Back on the estate, as the locals take to the streets to punish Sean and his gang, one priest asks another, "If those thugs in here beat the tripe out of those thugs out there, and if the RUC thugs beat the tripe out of both of them, will you lose any sleep?" Charged with a flock determined to indulge a lynch-mob mentality, it is small wonder even the men of God despair.

Nevertheless, although the portrait is unattractive, Reid's drama does depict a community that is supportive of the IRA. Only the local clergy accuse the republican leadership of creating the culture of despair and destruction of which Sean and his contemporaries are part. One priest tells Reggie, "It's the likes of you . . . that brought them onto the streets in the first place. It's you and your like that taught them how to steal cars and to riot and destroy. They're your monsters!" By contrast, the locals themselves echo Reggie's retort that, if that's the case, then the provos should be allowed to "deal with them in our own way." Reid also shows that for many locals to involve the police or seek help from the army would betray their community. "You ought to be ashamed of yourself, trying to hand one of your own over to the Brits," a woman berates the angry citizen who apprehends Sean near the start of the drama. "What kind of an Irishman are you, anyway?"

Moreover, like *Arise and Go Now,* Reid's drama invokes a tradition that, while now corrupt, at one time stood on firm moral ground. Sean's mother, for example, though no friend of the IRA, acknowledges the abuses that contributed to its rise. When Reggie comes to the house looking for Sean, Sarah reminds him of "the old days" of army raids and internment, "when we were all in this together." Specifically, she recalls a night when Reggie was dragged out of bed by his hair and taken away, "[his] bare feet torn by all that broken glass," leaving Sarah to comfort his terrified wife. Brutal as the British soldiers were, however, she tells him, "they never left anybody in as bad a mess as you left young Marley."

In short, what *You, Me, and Marley* condemns is not so much republican politics as what the IRA became: an organization of sadists and mobsters who exploit the disaffected, directionless, and disadvantaged for their own selfish gain. Described repeatedly as "small" by observers and excused by those who know him best ("Sean's not to blame. He's not a bad kid"), Sean is as much a victim of this menace as was Joseph Devlin, the murdered gunman in *Arise and Go Now*. Knowing he has been encouraged to steal by those to whom he sells the goods, Frances entreats him to "stop hooding": "Let's get away from that crowd," she urges. "Those people that buy the stuff are just using you, Sean." Moreover, although by their actions they do destroy property and put others' lives at risk, unlike almost everyone else around them, Sean and his friends are not malicious, nor do they intend to cause lethal harm. Attacked by vigilantes armed with hurley bats and incited to violence by the IRA, they respond only by throwing turnips at the perpetrators' homes; even after Marley is hospitalized all they do is destroy Reggie's car (restitution for which, unlike Marley, Reggie can freely submit a claim). In retaliation, Reggie attempts to force Sean out of Belfast and has two of Sean's companions knee-capped, while girls dressed in balaclavas and leather bind his friend Mary to a lamppost, drench her with tar, and hang a sign from her neck declaring, "I am a hood."

"What have we been doing?" Reggie asks an associate while Marley is beaten, "What in the name of God has gone wrong?" Reid's answer is even darker than Yeats's poem or O'Neill's teleplay: idealism has been replaced on all fronts with a cynical, self-serving malaise that no one seems able or eager to avoid. Under its influence, the police and other security forces vent their frustrations on those in their custody, the paramilitaries indulge in despotic rule, and young people, exploited by adults eager to profit from their intemperance but quick to turn on them if they can't be controlled, drink, drug, and drive themselves to death. "Your brothers were used, Sean," a police detective tells him. "And the people who used them, where are they today? Sitting back in their comfortable houses, driving good cars, wearing good clothes. And they can afford to do that while people like you and your brothers are prepared to take the risks."[8] Of course, in urging Sean to turn informer, the detective is guilty of using him, too.

Slouching towards Bethlehem: Ronan Bennett's *Love Lies Bleeding*

It is not surprising, given such damning representations, that when Ronan Bennett's *Love Lies Bleeding* was broadcast by the BBC in 1993, it was lauded for its unconventional depiction of the IRA, and hailed as a breakthrough in the representation of the North.[9] In Bennett's thriller, Conn Ellis, serving a life sentence for murder, is released from prison for twenty-four hours and returns to his family home in Belfast after fifteen years inside. There he learns of the murder of his former girlfriend, Leyla, and resolves to use the opportunity of his brief freedom to track down her killers and avenge her death. The plot twists around Conn's ignorance of current republican policy before it reaches its dark denouement, in which it is revealed that Leyla was killed not by loyalist thugs, as Conn had assumed, but at the command of his own friend and comrade, Tomas Macken, as part of a internecine struggle over the political future of the republican movement.

Though his companions discourage him, telling him "there is nothing heroic about revenge," Conn's stubborn desire for vengeance is a familiar motif in dramas about the North. For example, in Neil Jordan's 1984 film *Angel* (released in the United States as *Danny Boy*), the protagonist, having witnessed two murders, spends the rest of the film searching for and dispatching the killers. Sean Miller, the obsessive Irishman who pursues the Harrison Ford character in *Patriot Games* (Phillip Noyce, 1992), and the Tommy Lee Jones character in *Blown Away* (Stephen Hopkins, 1994), are similarly apolitical, the reasons for each man's violence presented largely free of the sociopolitical context out of which, presumably, they evolved.[10]

Yet despite the motivation it assigns to its hero, *Love Lies Bleeding* differs significantly from earlier films and TV dramas by depicting in detail and without condemnation the wider republican community from which the IRA and Sinn Fein draw their support. Upon his release, for example, Conn is welcomed back into that community not as a political prisoner or a military hero but as a beloved son, friend, and neighbor by men and women of all ages and by the happy, healthy children who enliven the party his father has prepared in his honor. In a lengthy sequence shortly thereafter, shot in what appears to be the Conway Mill (a vibrant community center off the Falls Road in Belfast, well known as a venue for left-wing politics and education), the camera follows Conn in conversation with Tomas, who heads the faction within the IRA that favors a cease-fire and all-party talks. Shot in continuous, fluid motion reminiscent of the opening sequence in *A Touch of Evil* (Orson Welles, 1957), their conversation begins on a staircase whose walls are papered with posters documenting a long and distinguished tradition of republican protest. Black-and-white images commemorate the civil rights movement of the 1960s, colorful fliers condemn the use of plastic bullets, while other signs link the conflict in Northern Ireland to struggles for freedom by oppressed peoples elsewhere. The sequence lasts several minutes and occurs in the context of a narrative rich, as Luke Gibbons (1997, 16) has observed, in "allegorical references to the tragedy of the Treaty period," and by extension to previous, more acceptably heroic incarnations of the IRA.[11] Moreover, as they converse the two men are repeatedly interrupted by friends and colleagues, republican activists of all ages and both genders, who welcome Conn fondly and approach or hail Tomas.

This is a far cry from previous depictions in which the IRA and its apologists appeared as shadowy, malignant figures embraced only by those they have terrified into submission or by others as leprous as themselves. The IRA man in *In The Name of the Father* (Jim Sheridan, 1993) who calmly sets fire to a prison guard is an example of the traditional type, as is the earlier figure of IRA godfather Skeffington in *Cal* (Pat O'Connor, 1984); in television drama, less familiar types abound. Even the North fares well in Bennett's teleplay. In contrast to depictions of gray skies, damp streets, and grim urban wasteland so overused by writers like Reid, much of the action occurs in bright weather against pleasant scenery, or in homes that are tidy and warm.[12]

Nevertheless, Conn is an outsider whose disillusionment with the republican movement is suggested even before Leyla's true fate is revealed.[13] Having dismissed the potential effects of a cease-fire, should there be one ("For all the good it'll do!"), he admits that he no longer cares much for the Cause. Given that he was once committed enough to join a hunger strike, in the absence of any other explanation one assumes that his disaffection stems from his grief over Leyla, whom he still imagines dressed like a schoolgirl and not in the suit and Gestapo haircut that she wears in the opening scene.[14] Even Conn's mistaken assumptions about her death reveal how out of touch he is with the movement: while his mission is fueled by a hatred for loyalists, his comrades on both sides of the cease-fire debate are motivated by pure, unemotional, political expediency. The mass execution of his opponents, which Tomas choreographs toward the end of the drama, for example, is the consequence not of animosity, psychosis, or selfish ambition but of conflicting visions for the future of Northern Ireland and the role republicanism ought to play. Ironically, those in favor of negotiation win by virtue of superior firepower. "There was no other way," Tomas tells Conn when it's over. "It [was] for everything in front of us and everything behind. . . . [They were] good comrade[s], but [they were] rigid. [They were] blocking out the future for us. . . . It was [them] or the future."

Conn is not soothed by this argument, however, and remains disgusted by what he has seen. Equally horrified is Frenchwoman Sophie Allen, Leyla's former professor at Queen's. For reasons that seem to imply a liaison between Leyla and Sophie's dead husband Peter, himself a victim of paramilitary violence, Sophie agrees to chauffeur Conn around the city in his quest to determine how Leyla died. In earlier dramas the role of the baffled outsider typically fell to an English character, whose function was to comment upon the nonsensical divisions that drive the conflict in the North.[15] By convention, such characters served to illustrate the dichotomy between Northern Ireland and the rational world (epitomized, predictably, by England). Thus in *We'll Support You Evermore* (BBC, 1985) Geoff Hollins, who comes to Northern Ireland to investigate the circumstances surrounding the death of his son, a British soldier, returns to England no closer to the truth. His son's murder, it is implied, was due not so much to a dangerous covert assignment or an incautious romance as to simply being

English — and therefore rational, sensitive, and self-reflective — in a place where reason, sensitivity, and introspection are virtually unknown. Although Conn, like Hollins, cannot "get anyone to answer a single question" about the murder, in Bennett's thriller it is the IRA that is inscrutable, not the Northern Irish as a whole. Moreover, Conn's confusion is temporary, a product of a historic moment typical, the text implies, of any political movement at a crossroads. Comprehension is possible, at the right time.

After the massacre, which they both witness, Sophie asks Conn, "Are you like that? Like Tomas, those men?" As a confessed and convicted killer himself, Conn's moral position is ambiguous, which complicates his distaste for Tomas's actions. "The thing is with this," he tells her, "once you start, it's difficult. It kind of beats its own path, it's difficult to do anything but follow it." Like Conn's own response to Tomas's arguments, Sophie's reception of this plea is chilly. "Don't you ever stop to think?" she asks rhetorically, before leaning across him to open the passenger door. Though he thanks her and bids her farewell, she drives off without speaking to him again.

Conn and Tomas return to the prison at the end of the drama, where the radio announces "further developments following the recent IRA cease-fire," including "a preliminary meeting between government ministers and leaders of Sinn Fein."[16] Tomas raises his fist in victory and all around him his cohorts cheer. Yet the violence of the massacre that caused this development, Sophie's symbolic expulsion of Conn from her car, Conn's own bitter denunciation of Tomas's methods, and the final sequence of the drama, filmed in the grainy style of a home movie, in which an innocent, laughing, much younger Leyla plays up to the camera and cavorts on a beach, all suggest an affirmation of Marx's assertion that an end which requires such unjust means can never be truly just at all.

Defanging the Beast:
Disarming Republicanism and the Assignation of Blame

Viewed as part of the British government's invitation to militant nationalists (provided they lay down their arms) to participate in the political processes that will shape the future of Northern Ireland, even the rejection of violence upon which these narratives insist could be

called progressive. Although republican ideology asserts the right to
armed struggle — a stance that at least partly explains the traditional
unionist presumption that a vote for Sinn Fein means active support for
the IRA — many self-described republicans take a more ambivalent
view of the use of violence. Indeed, that support for the ideals of a
paramilitary movement can coexist with a rejection of its methods is a
source of frustration for security forces worldwide, whose efforts to
defeat organizations defined as "terrorist" have often been hindered by
those who would not fire a gun themselves yet remain willing to shelter
those who do. By recognizing the complex and often ambivalent relationship between Irish Catholics and republican violence, not only in
the North but throughout Ireland and the diaspora, narratives such as
O'Neill's, Reid's, and Bennett's reach out to a constituency too alienated, perhaps, by its experience of the state to feel adequately represented by the Social Democratic and Labour Party (SDLP).

In making this overture, such dramatic narratives complement a
political process that seeks to retrieve republicans from the margins of
Northern Irish society and reintegrate them into the political mainstream.[17] The importance of this endeavor cannot be underestimated.
As BBC (NI) drama producer Robert Cooper has argued, "it's at least
important to know the enemy": "It's important to see where [republi-
cans] come from, their motivation, even if we judge them to be completely wrong" (Cooper 1995). No doubt this philosophy informs the
demand for inclusive talks, this, and the sense that such a process is
essential if one's goal is a settlement acceptable to all.

But if television is being harnassed as an agent of change, it is worri-
some that such necessary improvements appear so one-sided. While
writers like Bennett contest the stereotypes of the Catholic community
in Northern Ireland that have contributed to anti-Irish racism in Britain
and a general ignorance about the North, Northern Irish Protestants
have been and remain largely absent from television drama.[18] The discrepancy is sadly ironic. One of the mainstays of Protestant unionist
grievance is a sense of underrecognition: while the cause of Catholic
nationalism has been celebrated by the world's media for years, they
argue, the sacrifices and suffering of the Protestant community have
been ignored or downplayed in the political debate both at home and
abroad. As evidence they cite the massacres of Protestants by Catholics
in the seventeenth, eighteenth, and nineteenth centuries, the aggressive

intolerance of the Catholic Church, and the disparity between condemnatory words and political inaction following more recent atrocities involving Protestant victims, such as those at Enniskillen in 1987 and on the Shankill Road in 1993. But it is the deaths of RUC and UDR servicemen, whether on or off duty, retired or volunteer—deaths that many Protestants feel have gone unrecognized and unmourned outside their family circle and the community from which they are largely drawn—that are cited most frequently in the context of grievance. Whether described as a virtue (loyalism) or a vice (siege mentality), the unionist tradition is one of defense, and of service in defense, stretching from 1690 through two world wars to the present day. Recalling those individuals who, in the unionist vision of history, selflessly gave their lives for their country, many Protestants grow bitter: if not for their services as policemen and soldiers, they argue, the Troubles would long ago have erupted into outright civil war.

According to Bill Rolston, film and television drama is, "like it or not, the way most people [outside Northern Ireland] hear about the North" (Rolston 1995). Given the persistence of segregation in the North, TV and film may also be the means by which many within its borders learn about each other. Thus the representation of Protestants on the small and large screens could have a significant effect on the peace process, and it is for this reason that the nature of that representation is of such concern. In Bennett's teleplay, for example, Protestants are equated with loyalists, who appear as the bellicose rivals of the republicans inside the prison, the immediate suspects when Leyla is killed, and the overweight, foul-mouthed, blood-lusty thugs who force Conn and Sophie to their knees, readying them for execution. "Are you fucking Taigs?" one pop-eyed gunman screams at Conn. "Do you think we couldn't smell youse, you dirty fucking Fenian bastards?" Their lives are spared by the intervention of a loyalist chief who recognizes Conn from the prison they share, but he's no more conciliatory than his comrades. "There's people, so-called well-meaning people, who say we have more in common than you think," he tells Conn ominously. "My opinion is, that's a load of bollocks." Conn himself certainly agrees. "That's what they do," he tells Sophie, "that's what they're about. They kill Catholics." Unlike Tomas Macken's republicans, whose motives are clearly political and who select their targets with precision, loyalists kill because killing defines them. They are driven by an irrational hatred, and any Catholic victim will do. "They wouldn't have known anything about [Leyla]," Conn tells Sophie, still certain that loyalists are responsible for her death. "They wouldn't have known who she was, nothing." That they did not, in fact, kill her is not so important as the fact that they would have, eagerly, given the chance.

Any discussion of the potential consequences of televisual representation raises the question of the socioethical mission not only of television drama, but of any fiction, in any medium. Indeed, one could argue that all critical analysis implies a code of evaluation, an often personal standard of excellence against which material is implicitly compared. John Hill's (1988) critique of images of violence in films about the North, for example, implies that the success of any visual fiction concerned with the place or its people should be judged in terms of the level of direct engagement by the text with the political situation there. Hill's analysis is echoed by O'Neill in *Arise and Go Now,* which condemns not only violence, but inaction and indifference in the face of it, which O'Neill depicts as no less irresponsible or morally wrong. Thus the command of the title, borrowed from Yeats, becomes an exhortation not only to reject the IRA, but to actively oppose violence in all its forms. Even those artists who fail to engage with the sociopolitical evils around them are, it is implied, at least partly to blame for their perpetuation.

The need for a theory of responsible practice among writers of fiction is not a new concept. In his 1937 essay, "Blueprint for Negro Writing," for example, Richard Wright (1994, 102) demanded of writers of all races that their work "express a deep, informed, and complex" social consciousness, born of a "tense and obdurate will to change the world" and an awareness of the writer's role as a creator of values. For those in the business of creating values in a society deeply divided by competing interpretations of history and aspirations for the future, this responsibility is especially keen.[19]

I believe creative artists in Northern Ireland share with the British and Irish governments their stated charge to help "remove the causes of the conflict, to overcome the legacy of history" (Framework Document, 1995, paragraph 1; Hume 1996, 170), and to "heal divisions among the peoples of Ireland" ("Message from the Government"; preface to the Joint Declaration, 1993; Hume 1996, 164). Those artists outside the North who (re)turn to it for inspiration or employ its motifs in their work are similarly obliged. Among the makers of recent television drama, three approaches to this endeavor have tended to predominate. The first of these, *retribution*, seeks to right historic wrongs by redressing imbalances and redistributing attention and resources to those who traditionally have been denied them; teleplays like Tom McGurk's *Dear Sarah* and Allan Cubilt's *The Hanging Gale* best illustrate this approach. *[Re]construction*, by contrast, seeks to remove the causes of conflict by manufacturing a national sense of self, achieved in large part by deemphasizing (if not denying) the existence of difference, or else by suggesting that some cultures are less essential than others, and therefore may be modified or erased without ill effect. Marie Jones's 1995 stage play, *A Night in November*, is the most egregious example of this approach.[20]

An alternative method, described by Norman Vance (1996) as a "rich, ample" artistic vision, "incorporates rather than denies or glosses over communal and sectarian difference." This third model, *reflection*, seeks to harmonize the diverse political and cultural elements that compose Northern Irish society by reflecting the felt identities of its inhabitants, however offensive they may be to others, and however apparently irrational, illogical, or poorly explained by prevailing theories of academic analysis. In this model, the potential for offense is offset by a scrupulous pursuit of "balance" in terms of access to the means of expression and dissemination, and the active recruitment of underrepresented groups.

Eamonn McCann has argued that to tell the story of Northern Ireland within such traditionally liberal notions of balance means "you're telling it from a place where nobody lives, from an experience no one actually has" (McCann 1995); given the ever-increasing popular support for integrated education and other such initiatives throughout the North, however, this kind of experience may become more common. Nevertheless, all three approaches do have weaknesses. As a kind of cultural affirmative action policy, like its analog in employment and education, retribution can be perceived as reverse discrimination, especially when the realities of advantage and disprivilege are more complex than its theory allows.[21] Similarly, because it effectively imposes on others the will of those empowered to shape the agenda, reconstruction can be experienced as an exercise in propaganda, or worse, as cultural genocide, by those whose identity is slated for modification.[22] And even a policy of genuine reflection cannot guarantee that all communities will be equally interested in telling their stories or will put opportunities for self-expression to equal use, nor that even when resources are used to their fullest, mutual understanding will result.[23]

A recent study by Mícheál Roe et. al. (1997) of adolescents in Belfast suggests that forgiveness is prerequisite for healing at both the individual and the national level. Yet forgiveness, which "entails a willingness to give up one's right to resentment . . . while fostering the undeserved qualities of compassion, generosity, and even love toward [one's] victimizers" (3), is difficult, especially for the young, for whom bitterness is often contingent on their relationship to the victim and the proximity and severity of the injury sustained. Many of the youths who participated in the study expressed an ambivalent respect for forgiveness but little understanding of what it involves, while others admitted they were unable to shed resentment or desired revenge even while recognizing that it would lead only to "more problems" if those who had hurt them were punished in kind (13).

Interviews with adult leaders of cross-community programs in Belfast, by contrast, reveal a process of which creative artists would be wise to take note. Almost all who gave testimony had experienced a transformation of vision through which the Other became human, like themselves, and therefore redeemable: "I didn't see them as enemies anymore. I saw them as friends to be won" (Roe et al. 1997, 17). This process, through which an inclination toward empathy enables forgiveness which itself motivates an effort to inspire forgiveness in others, with reconciliation as the ultimate goal, belies the assumption that respect, forgiveness, and even affection can be achieved by an act of will. It is an uncomfortable truth that peace, like faith or love, cannot be "willed," for all that a person or a people may truly long to shed doubt or bitterness, or turn away from violence. What factors produce the inclination toward a literal revision of one's self and one's relationship to others will always be a mystery that no political or artistic agenda can ever guarantee.

Mindful of these difficulties, I would like to propose a fourth model of practice for writers in divided societies, a model which seeks not to make peace or induce reconciliation, but rather to encourage the conditions necessary for their spontaneous generation. Peace, once rooted,

can be nurtured, and artists, writers, and other teachers must be prepared to assist in its preservation. In practice, this means not only
applauding those who are able to forgive and encouraging others who
are trying to do so, but refusing to condemn or ignore those who cannot. It also means staunchly declining to be among those who do not
seek a settlement, or who propose solutions that are certain to fail,
or who by their words or actions (or by their silence or their failure to
act) worsen the conflict in any way. In William Trevor's film adaptation
of his short story, *Attracta* (1983), the title character, a Protestant
schoolteacher, chastises herself for failing to tell her students a story of
redemption, and for telling instead a story of despair. A lifelong resident of a small town near Cork, Attracta is "happy just teaching [her]
handful of Protestant children" — happy, that is, until she reads about
Penelope Vade, age twenty-three, and her husband Roderick, a soldier
murdered in Belfast by the IRA, which sends his severed head to her
through the post. Having traveled to Belfast to declare her intention to
work with cross-community groups, Vade is gang-raped by her husband's murderers and subsequently kills herself, "because she had lost
all faith in human life." For telling her students this story (to which,
ironically, they are inured), Attracta loses her job and ends her days in
an institution, where she laments her failure to tell her students her own
"horror story," with its very "different ending": orphaned as a child
when her parents were killed by mistake in an ambush, Attracta became friends with the couple responsible for their deaths, a Protestant
man and his married Catholic lover, whose politics and personal lives
forever put them at odds with the town. "Every day of my life I should
have honored in my classroom the small, remarkable thing that happened in this town," Attracta tells a companion at the home for the
insane. "Two violent people [were] calmed by time and circumstance.
. . . Monsters don't remain monsters forever."

Of course all drama need not convey this message, but no drama,
nor indeed any work of art, should obscure the fact that redemption is
possible, nor should drama aggravate wounds that have yet to heal. To
do so is irresponsible when lives have been lost and while others remain
at risk.[24] While the work of Bennett, Reid, and O'Neill especially have
enriched the representation of the people and passions that inhabit the
North, writers can and must do more to confront the factors that keep
conflict alive. What is needed in Northern Ireland, as it is in any divided

community from Sarajevo to Jerusalem to South Central Los Angeles, is "an imaginative solution, a view of living in this place which transcends the sectarian division. Surely it is one of the functions of the artist to do that — who other than the creative artist can envision that?" (McCann 1995).

Notes

1. Hughes (1996) notes that "Belfast as a 'Troubles' city" has acquired a similar reputation for insanity and violence.

2. One influential text that makes this assumption is *Televising Terrorism: Political Violence and Popular Culture* (Schlesinger et al., 1983). For evidence to the contrary, see Pettit (1992).

3. The manipulation of the news media — and of television in particular — to influence public opinion both within and outside Northern Ireland has been extensively documented. See, for example, Curtis (1984), Schlesinger (1987), and Curtis and Jempson (1993). Other important texts include Rolston (1991) and Miller (1994), who argue that the media have been used to solicit consent not only for official policy, but for the British government's interpretation of past events and its agenda for the future.

4. My research has relied primarily on materials available through the University of Ulster's Film and Sound Resource Unit in Coleraine, Northern Ireland, whose archives of television drama effectively begin with 1980.

5. The subsequent release of the Framework Document in 1995 affirmed the principles of the Declaration while outlining a program for discussion and negotiation. Both documents are reprinted in full, together with the 1985 Anglo-Irish Agreement, in Hume (1996).

6. Though intended chiefly for television, *You, Me, and Marley* won the Michael Power Award for Best British Film at the Edinburgh International Film Festival in 1992.

7. Private Lee Clegg was convicted of the murder of teenage joyrider Karen Reilly and Martin Peake in West Belfast in 1990. His release in 1995 after only four years in custody led to widespread rioting in nationalist areas of the North (Bew and Gillespie, 1996).

8. O'Neill levels the same accusation in *Arise and Go Now* through the chief's defense of IRA extortion and the luxuries it affords: "So you have a BMW, you've had a couple of Caribbean holidays this year . . . if you're a member of a club you might as well use the facilities."

9. The *Radio Times* and other BBC promotional materials, for example, made much of the drama's challenge to conventions of characterization and plot.

10. Decontextualization is, of course, a method of delegitimization, an approach shared with the British government by successive American administra-

tions until President Clinton's decision to grant Gerry Adams a visa in 1995. It is not insignificant that the more recent big-budget depiction of the IRA, *The Devil's Own* (Alan Pakula, 1997), provides its hero, played by Brad Pitt, not only with a conscience and boyish good looks, but with clearly political motives for his paramilitary involvement.

11. Gibbons also notes that Brendan Gleeson, who played Michael Collins in the RTE/BBC drama *The Treaty* not long before, plays Tomas Macken in Bennett's thriller.

12. The more dreary imagery is popular with publishers in the United States. See, for example, Eoin MacNamee's overrated novel *Resurrection Man* (1996) and Adrian McKinty's article in *Harper's Magazine,* which includes this description of Carrickfergus: "The sky is cemetery gray, and the slate rain is coming down in sheets. The cold wind whips at us straight from some frozen wasteland in the Arctic Circle, and the haar fog and damp air have slunk beneath our coats, dissolving a caustic chill deep into our scunnered bones. A dead seal lies on the beach, and the gale from off the lough brings up the smell of decaying seaweed and effluent. Oil floats on the water, and behind us the massive coal-fired power station pumps out a snarl of black smoke and toxins" (1997, 61).

13. In this depiction Conn is much like O'Neill's hero, Kevin, whose capacity for love and talent for poetry separates him from others in the IRA. In *You, Me, and Marley,* Sean is also distinctive: of all his friends he alone has a job, even if only through a Youth Training Programme (YTP) scheme, and he and Frances have no use for condoms since, unlike other couples their age, they are not sexually active.

14. This style was made famous by the character of Jude in Neil Jordan's *The Crying Game* (1993). For a discussion of the representation of republican women in British television drama, see Cornell (1998).

15. In Stewart Parker's six-part dramatic series *Lost Belongings* (ITV, 1986) this role is assigned most visibly to a Belgian, whose bewilderment is compounded by her own nation's successful management of its diverse population. Parker's overpopulated drama does feature a likable Englishman, however, and an American woman, both of whom eventually shed their affinity for Ireland, the Irish, and, in the American's case, the armed struggle, to condemn the nonsensicality of the conflict and the hatreds it fuels.

16. Broadcast nearly twelve months before the IRA cease-fire in 1994, Bennett's drama was curiously prescient.

17. Tony Blair's prompt embrace of the Mitchell Principles, spurring the IRA to resume its cease-fire and so enabling the start of inclusive talks, provides a parallel political example of this approach.

18. James Hawthorne, who served as BBC(NI) controller from 1978 to 1987, has explained the discrepancy in terms of the aesthetic shortcomings of the Protestant ethos: "The Catholic case is sometimes more lyrical because it's about change, whereas the conservatism of the Protestant ethos, not well artic-

ulated, is of less interest to the ardent journalist and dramatist" (*The Late Show* special, "Telling The Troubles," BBC, 1995). Needless to say, this view is not one to which I subscribe.

19. Brett (1996) has observed that even interpretive centers, a mainstay of the modern tourist industry in Ireland, are imprinted with the cultural ideology of their designers.

20. For a more detailed discussion of Jones's play, see Cornell (1997).

21. Rooney and Woods (1996), for example, have shown that both Protestant and Catholic working-class neighborhoods suffer from appalling levels of unemployment, poverty, and unwed pregnancy.

22. Moreover, reconstruction matches the description of other ill-conceived efforts to promote reconciliation by foregrounding culture "as a displacement of political deadlocks we just can't currently solve" (Eagleton 1997, 12).

23. Indeed, such an approach could perpetuate a hostile segregation, as a consequence of which virtually all contact between opposing factions becomes volatile and conflict remains effectively uncontained. This kind of blinkered multiculturalism seems to characterize interracial relations in much of the United States.

24. It should be noted too that to follow this rule does not limit the forms of expression available. Satire, comedy, and romance, for example, are as able as drama to explore serious themes; moreover, artistic devaluation is not inevitable when writers find inspiration in a sociopolitical cause.

Works Cited

Bew, P., and G. Gillespie. 1996. *The Northern Ireland peace process, 1993–1996: A chronology.* London: Serif.

Brett, D. 1996. *The construction of heritage.* Cork: Cork University Press.

Cooper, R. 1995. Interview with Sarah Dunant for "Telling the Troubles." *The Late Show.* British Broadcasting Company. 21 September.

Cornell, J. 1997. "The Other Community": Northern Ireland in British television, 1995. *New Hibernia Review* 1:2.

———. 1998. Evolving representations of Republican women: Northern Ireland and the socio-politics of British television drama. *Writing Ulster 5.*

Curtis, L. 1984. *Ireland: The propaganda war.* London: Pluto.

Curtis, L., and M. Jempson. 1993. *Interference on the airwaves: Ireland, the media, and the broadcasting ban.* London: Information on Ireland.

Eagleton, T. 1997. The ideology of Irish studies. *Bullán* 13:1.

Gibbons, L. 1997. Demisting the screen: Neil Jordan's *Michael Collins. Irish Literary Supplement* (Spring).

Hill, J. 1988. Images of violence. In *Cinema and Ireland,* edited by K. Rockett, L. Gibbons, and J. Hill. London: Routledge.

Hughes, E. 1996. "Town of shadows": Representations of Belfast in recent fiction. *Religion and Literature* 28:2–3.

Hume, J. 1996. *Personal views: Politics, peace and reconciliation in Ireland.* Dublin: Town House.

Jones, M. 1995. *A night in November.* Dublin: New Island Books.

McCann, E. 1995. Interview with Sarah Dunant for "Telling the Troubles." *The Late Show.* British Broadcasting Company. 21 September.

McNamee, E. 1994. *Resurrection man.* London: Picador.

McKinty, A. 1997. Mean season. *Harper's Magazine.* September.

Miller, D. 1994. *Don't mention the war: Northern Ireland, propaganda, and the media.* London: Pluto.

Pettit, L. 1992. Situation tragedy? The "Troubles" in British television drama. *Irish Studies Review,* no. 1.

Roe, M. D., W. Pegg, K. Hodges, and R. Trim. 1997. Social identity, ethnic memories and forgiving the other side in Northern Ireland. Paper read at annual meeting of the American Conference for Irish Studies, Albany, New York.

Rolston, B., ed. 1991. *The Media and Northern Ireland: Covering the Troubles.* Milton Keynes: Open University Press.

——. 1995. Interview with Sarah Dunant for "Telling the Troubles." *The Late Show.* British Broadcasting Company. 21 September.

Rooney, E., and M. Woods. 1996. *Women, community and politics in northern Ireland: A Belfast study.* Belfast: University of Ulster Press.

Schlesinger, P. 1987. *Putting "reality" together: BBC News.* 2d ed. London: Methuen.

Schlesinger, P., G. Murdock, and P. Elliot. 1983. *Televising "terrorism": political violence in popular culture.* London: Comedia.

Vance, N. 1996. Catholic and Protestant literary visions of "Ulster": Now you see it, now you don't. *Religion and Literature* 28:2–3.

Wright, R. 1994. In *Within the circle: An anthology of African American literary criticism from the Harlem Renaissance to the present,* edited by A. Mitchell. Durham: Duke University Press.

Notes on Contributors

JENNIFER C CORNELL is an assistant professor of English at Oregon State University in Corvallis. She won the 1994 Drue Heinz Prize for her collection of short fiction *Departures* (University of Pittsburgh Press, 1995), which was published in Britain and Ireland as *All There Is* (Brandon Press, 1995). She is the author of several articles on the representation of Northern Ireland in British television drama, and a recipient of a 1998 Creative Writing Fellowship from the National Endowment for the Arts.

JOHN P. HARRINGTON is dean of the Faculty of Humanities and Social Sciences at The Cooper Union in New York City. He is the author of *The Irish Beckett* and *The Irish Play on the New York Stage* and editor of the Norton *Modern Irish Drama* anthology.

MAUREEN S. G. HAWKINS is an assistant professor of English at the University of Lethbridge (Alberta, Canada). She has also taught at the University of Toronto and at York and Trent universities in Canada, at the University of Montevallo and at Loyola (New Orleans) and Indiana universities in the United States, and at the University of Sierra Leone in West Africa. She coedited *Global Perspectives on Teaching Literature* (NCTE, 1993), and has written articles on eighteenth- through twentieth-century Irish, British, and American historical drama, on intertextuality and cultural identity, and on dramatic works by Amiri Baraka, Brendan Behan, Dion Boucicault, Brian Friel, Lady Gregory, Neil Jordan, Louis MacNeice, and Wole Soyinka. She is currently working on books on the treatment of the Irish hero in historical drama, on the treatment of the Irish heroine in historical drama, and on Irish dramatic adaptation.

WILLIAM A. HAZLETON is professor of political science at Miami University in Oxford, Ohio. His research and writing have focused on the role of elected officials and bodies in Northern Ireland. He is currently working on the broader questions of devolution and accountability and their possible consequences for the peace process.

KIM HODGES was a research assistant in psychology at Seattle Pacific University and the Centre for the Study of Conflict, University of Ulster, at the time of these studies. Currently she is an adoption social worker at Medina Children's Services in Seattle, working with hard-to-place children and youth.

HELEN LOJEK is professor of English at Boise State University in Idaho. She has published several articles on contemporary Irish drama and is working on a book about Frank McGuinness.

ROGER MAC GINTY is research development officer at INCORE (Initiative on Conflict Resolution and Ethnicity) at the University of Ulster (Magee College) where he is the coordinator of the Coming Out of Violence research project that compares peace processes in Northern Ireland, Israel/Palestine, Sri Lanka, South Africa, and the Basque Country. He has authored several articles on Northern Ireland and also edits the *Ethnic Conflict Research Digest,* which publishes reviews of recent publications on the dynamics and management of ethnic conflict.

JAMES WHITE McAULEY is a reader in sociology in the School of Human and Health Sciences at the University of Huddersfield, England. Born in Belfast, he was educated at the University of Ulster and the University of Leeds. He has written widely on political sociology and the conflict in Northern Ireland. In 1994 he published *The Politics of Identity: A Loyalist Community in Belfast.* Since then, he has written several articles on unionist reactions to the peace process in Ireland. He continues to research the unionist community in Northern Ireland and is also engaged in a research project on the Irish diaspora and the experiences of the Irish in Huddersfield.

ELIZABETH J. MITCHELL grew up in Northern Ireland and gained an undergraduate degree in geography and geology from Queen's University, Belfast. She attended Rutgers University as a nontraditional student and was awarded the American Sociological Association's Best Dissertation of the Year Award for her doctoral dissertation, *Class and Ethnicity in the Perpetuation of Conflict in Northern Ireland.* She has taught sociology at Rutgers University and Bucknell University. Her current research compares conflict and peacemaking in ethnically divided societies.

WILLIAM PEGG was a youth in the midst of the early years of the Troubles in Belfast. A graduate of the Peace Studies program at Magee College in Derry, he currently is on the staff of the Northern Ireland Children's Holiday Scheme, directing cross-community and cross-border reconciliation programs with adolescents at risk for participating in political violence.

MARILYNN RICHTARIK is assistant professor of English at Georgia State University in Atlanta. She is the author of *Acting Between the Lines: The Field Day Theatre Company and Irish Cultural Politics, 1980–1984* and is currently researching a critical biography of Stewart Parker.

MÍCHEÁL D. ROE is professor and chair of psychology at Seattle Pacific University and research associate at the Centre for the Study of Conflict, University of Ulster at Coleraine. Currently he is coordinating research teams in Northern Ireland, the Republic of Ireland, Australia, and the United States who are carrying out a multinational study on the reproduction of ethnic memories across generations and across emigrations.

BILL ROLSTON is a senior lecturer at the University of Ulster at Jordanstown. His published works include *Drawing Support: Murals in the North of Ireland* (1992); *Drawing Support 2: Murals of War and Peace* (1996); and *The Media and Northern Ireland: Covering the Troubles* (1991). Other research interests have included novels of the Northern Ireland conflict, community politics, the issue of truth in relation to past human rights abuses, and most recently, songs of the Troubles. He lives in Belfast with his partner Anna and children, Nalina and Kevin.

REBECCA A. TRIMM worked as research assistant in psychology at Seattle Pacific University on the qualitative study of forgiveness. Currently she is on the staff of the Urban Promise Ministries, performing community development work in inner-city Camden, New Jersey.

Index

POLITICS AND PERFORMANCE
IN CONTEMPORARY
NORTHERN IRELAND